The Indoctrination of the Wehrmacht

The Indoctrination of the Wehrmacht

Nazi Ideology and the War Crimes of the German Military

Bryce Sait

berghahn
NEW YORK • OXFORD
www.berghahnbooks.com

First published in 2019 by
Berghahn Books
www.berghahnbooks.com

© 2019, 2021 Bryce Sait
First paperback edition published in 2021

All rights reserved. Except for the quotation of short passages for the purposes of criticism and review, no part of this book may be reproduced in any form or by any means, electronic or mechanical, including photocopying, recording, or any information storage and retrieval system now known or to be invented, without written permission of the publisher.

Library of Congress Cataloging-in-Publication Data

Names: Sait, Bryce, author.
Title: The Indoctrination of the Wehrmacht : Nazi Ideology and the War Crimes of the German Military / By Bryce Sait.
Description: First edition. | New York : Berghahn Books, 2019. | Includes bibliographical references and index.
Identifiers: LCCN 2018054904 (print) | LCCN 2018055409 (ebook) | ISBN 9781789201505 (ebook) | ISBN 9781789201499 (hardback : alk. paper)
Subjects: LCSH: Germany. Wehrmacht--History. | National socialism and education. | World War, 1939-1945--Atrocities--Germany.
Classification: LCC D757 (ebook) | LCC D757 .S245 2019 (print) | DDC 940.54/1343--dc23
LC record available at https://lccn.loc.gov/2018054904

British Library Cataloguing in Publication Data
A catalogue record for this book is available from the British Library

ISBN 978-1-78920-149-9 hardback
ISBN 978-1-80073-200-1 paperback
ISBN 978-1-78920-150-5 ebook

Contents

Introduction	1
Chapter 1. A Political Military?	15
Chapter 2. The Goals and Effects of Indoctrination	30
Chapter 3. The Beginnings of Nazi Ideological Education in the Wehrmacht	41
Chapter 4. The Lead-Up to War and the Poland Campaign	59
Chapter 5. The Hitler Youth and the Reich Labour Service	97
Chapter 6. Christianity and the Military Chaplaincy: A Competing Influence in the Wehrmacht?	117
Chapter 7. The Serbian Campaign and the Eastern Front	142
Conclusion	179
Bibliography	185
Index	197

Introduction

～

According to 'The Bolshevist World Threat', a piece of educational material distributed to soldiers and officers of the German military, Nazism was 'the sworn enemy of Jewish Bolshevism'. As the goal of the 'Jewish Bolshevists' was to 'exterminate entire peoples', National Socialism sought to safeguard Germany from this menace from the East. It also wanted to prevent Germany from becoming a state like Russia, in which 'almost 98% of all leading positions [were] held by racially foreign Jews'.[1]

The kind of language expressed in this document would have been unremarkable in June 1941, when the Nazi regime launched a war of extermination against the Soviet Union. In a campaign based upon eliminating an enemy defined in racial and ideological terms, the Nazi leadership, with the approval of military generals, sought to annihilate the 'Jewish Bolshevist' system and to 'rid Europe of Jews'.[2] In notable contrast, however, this document, used by the Wehrmacht in the education of its soldiers in 'everyday political questions', was issued in 1936. Three years before the start of the Second World War, and almost five years before the beginning of the war against the Soviet Union, the German military was training its soldiers to view their enemy in racial and ideological terms.

For many years after the Second World War, historians of Nazism, and the public at large, assumed that although the Nazi regime made use of organisations like the SS to carry out its ethnic policies, the Wehrmacht was not involved in these actions.[3] In this version of history, the German military either resisted these policies or attempted to keep its distance from the Nazi regime. In turn, there existed a distinction in approaches between the ideologically motivated men of the SS and the supposedly 'clean', apolitical

Wehrmacht.[4] More recent scholarship, however, has shown this interpretation to be false. Based mainly on postwar accounts from Wehrmacht veterans, it was accepted and propagated by many German historians, as well as non-German historians in the West who were largely ignorant of the realities of the war on the Eastern Front.[5]

A number of historians such as Jürgen Förster, Manfred Messerschmidt, Dieter Pohl, Hannes Heer, Walter Manoschek, Hans Safrian, Wolfram Wette, Omer Bartov and Ben Shepherd have since demonstrated that the Wehrmacht played a significant role in National Socialist racial policy.[6] Among the groundbreaking developments in Wehrmacht scholarship was Bartov's work on the German army, beginning with *The Eastern Front, 1941–45: German Troops and the Barbarisation of Warfare*,[7] along with an exhibition by the Hamburg-based Institute for Social Research, titled 'War of Extermination: Crimes of the Wehrmacht'. This display was first presented to the German and Austrian public from 1995 to 1999, and outlined the crimes of the German armed forces during the war against the Soviet Union. The controversy and public reaction it aroused demonstrated the extent to which the association of the Wehrmacht with such activities was relatively unknown or suppressed within postwar German and Austrian society. While numerous errors were found in the original exhibition, resulting in its withdrawal and revision, when it was reopened in 2001 as 'Crimes of the Wehrmacht: Dimensions of a War of Annihilation 1941–1944' it maintained that it was nonetheless correct in its original, overarching argument: that the German army was heavily involved in atrocities against Soviet civilians and prisoners of war.[8]

The so-called 'war of extermination' that Germany carried out against the Soviet Union has dominated scholarship on the crimes of the German army.[9] This campaign was the largest in which the Wehrmacht took part. It had a strong racial and ideological basis, and it was the main stage for the military's criminal activity.[10] The army's involvement in war crimes on the Eastern Front is often explained within the framework of a number of notorious orders that the military leadership issued before and during the campaign, including the 'Commissar Decree' and the 'Guidelines for the Conduct of German Troops in the East'. When coupled with the horrific conditions of the campaign, these 'criminal orders' resulted in the occurrence of atrocities on a vast scale.[11]

Within this context, scholars have offered more specific explanations for perpetrator motivation. These have included the picture of soldiers who engaged in wanton violence and destruction due to a vicious 'German' antisemitism. However, the chief proponent of this argument, Daniel Goldhagen, could not offer a very convincing explanation of the origins of such attitudes other than the factor of German nationality.[12] While relating specifically to a reserve police battalion, Christopher Browning's contrasting picture of dutiful men who, becoming conditioned to extreme violence and concerned with group pressure and the prospect of career advancement, dispassionately obeyed orders, has also been cited as a theoretical framework within which to account for the behaviour of members of the military.[13] Omer Bartov has noted that Browning's contention that obedience and peer pressure played a greater role than ideology and racism has represented the consensus within German scholarship on the Wehrmacht.[14]

Since the revelation of the military's participation in atrocities in the Soviet Union, researchers have looked beyond the Soviet campaign to reveal involvement in war crimes on other fronts. Walter Manoschek, Hans Safrian and Ben Shepherd have documented the extensive involvement of army units in atrocities during the campaign in the Balkans.[15] The studies carried out by Jochen Böhler and Alexander B. Rossino uncovered the widespread participation of German soldiers in the murder of civilians, including Jews, in Poland in 1939.[16] While there were a number of racially driven directives handed down before the invasion of Poland, these transgressions took place well before the notorious 'criminal orders' associated with the invasion of the Soviet Union. They also occurred before the supposed 'brutalisation' of soldiers who fought in the Soviet Union. Bartov has argued that this brutalisation came about due to the Eastern Front's particularly horrific fighting and conditions,[17] and led to a 'perversion of discipline'[18] and 'distortion of reality', with soldiers becoming increasingly reliant on Nazi visions of the war and the enemy.[19] This raises a number of questions about the impetus behind these occurrences. In their attempts to account for Wehrmacht atrocities in Poland, Böhler and Rossino have questioned the notion of dispassionate obedience, arguing that there existed a lack of explicit orders from above, and instead the presence of vague, yet ideologically tainted instructions to act ruthlessly against civilians. Importantly, Rossino and Böhler have revealed the widespread presence of vehement antisemitism among German troops.[20]

Böhler and Rossino's works display parallels with earlier research carried out by Omer Bartov, Stephen G. Fritz, Walter Manoschek, Hans Safrian and Wolfram Wette. These studies emphasise the influence of racism and ideology on the behaviour of troops,[21] staking out a third position between Browning's circumstantial interpretation of war crimes and Goldhagen's view of a natural, 'German' antisemitism.[22] In attempting to account for the origins of Nazi ideology among troops, Bartov looks for accountability in other Nazi organisations such as the Hitler Youth and Reich Labour Service, and focuses on the period during and after the Barbarossa campaign in assessing the role of military propaganda.[23]

This leads to questions about the involvement of German soldiers in atrocities during the Polish and Serbian campaigns of 1939 and early 1941, which were, as Böhler and Rossino have established, carried out with clear evidence of fervent antisemitic and anti-Slavic sentiments among troops.[24] However, both Böhler and Rossino point out the limits to our knowledge of the possible origins of such attitudes and behaviour. Böhler writes that it is an area 'that has not yet been well researched',[25] while Rossino argues that looking solely to organisations like the Hitler Youth or Reich Labour Service is unconvincing. Regimental personnel surveys of those who took part in the Poland campaign show that, at least during the Poland campaign in 1939, 'most soldiers were too old to have belonged to the Hitler Youth'.[26] This demonstrates the need for further investigation into the potential origins of ideological motivation among troops at the lower levels, particularly the role that their experience in the armed forces may have played.

The literature that has dealt with the influence of Nazi ideology within the Wehrmacht has been a factor in this lack of understanding. It has commonly followed two paths. That which I have described above is concerned with military atrocities during the Second World War. However, studies of German atrocities rarely pay close attention to the period before 1939,[27] with Wolfram Wette's *The Wehrmacht: History, Myth, Reality* and Ben Shepherd's *Hitler's Soldiers: The German Army in the Third Reich*[28] notable exceptions, in that they investigate the well-established antisemitism, anti-Slavism and anti-Bolshevism that existed in the German military during, and indeed well before, the Nazi era. As Bartov has pointed out, the other path, which documents the prewar politicisation of the military, seems to deal with a separate subject matter to the work of historians who tackle the involvement of the military in atrocities.[29] While these works thoroughly investigate and document the process in question, they concentrate on developments at the highest levels, with less focus upon how it may have influenced the experience of the rank and file. More significantly, they make little effort to question the possible relationship between the military's prewar politicisation and its later involvement in war crimes. It is important to note, however, that many of these works were published well before the majority of studies that documented such involvement had emerged. Daniel Uziel's *Propaganda Warriors* is an example of scholarship that documents the politicisation of the Wehrmacht and its production of Nazi propaganda, but the main focus of this work is upon the military's production of propaganda for the public, rather than for the indoctrination of its own men.[30]

The approach taken by these scholars, however, points to a common thread that runs through these works: the absence of a detailed study of training within the Wehrmacht as a possible influence on troops' wartime behaviour and attitudes. If concerned with the lower ranks, scholars have often looked to indoctrination in the Hitler Youth and Labour Service as explanations for racism, ideological conviction and violence towards the Reich's ideological and racial enemies, with less emphasis on the military's role in fostering Nazi ideology.[31]

While these works have made important contributions to the historiography, documentary evidence illustrates that it is problematic to appraise the wartime conduct of soldiers, particularly when questioning the extent of the ideological impetus behind it, without a detailed examination of and reference to the way in which the army itself trained them. The indoctrination that young men experienced in schools, the Hitler Youth and the Reich Labour Service is important, and this study does not discount them as important factors.[32] However, one needs to look at indoctrination as a long-term process that began, but did not finish, in these organisations.

In fact, indoctrination intensified once young men reached military age in order to build upon the foundations laid by the Hitler Youth and Reich Labour Service. The military leadership recognised the role that it would play in this process. Many young conscripts had indeed received ideological schooling before joining the army, and the Wehrmacht went about customising political instruction in the military to build upon it. Moreover, early on in the course of the Third Reich, the military came to view its role in indoctrinating young recruits and longer-serving officers alike as being the most important in forming the attitudes, or at least influencing the martial conduct, of millions of men. Internal correspondence reveals that, particularly early on, the military was dealing with a diverse group. While many who willingly joined the military before conscription had a history of involvement in Nazi organisations, many entrants to the armed forces, once conscription came into force, confounded the military's expectations and displayed a disappointing lack of ideological conviction, or even basic knowledge of the tenets of Nazism.[33] Senior officials within the military were also concerned that career soldiers and officers had not served in the Hitler Youth and Labour Service, thus missing out on years of ideological schooling.[34]

This indicates that while many who were to serve in the Second World War did receive prior political indoctrination, it is not enough to look to these other bodies in accounting for the influence of Nazism upon troops, since many, particularly in the early years of the Nazi regime, did not encounter formal ideological education until they became members of the military. A detailed examination of the military's programme of ideological education, set within the context of the wider experience of recruits, can help to fill a gap in our knowledge. This approach builds upon existing scholarship by looking beyond the temporal margins of the Second World

War, and by shifting the focus towards the Wehrmacht itself as a factor in the indoctrination of soldiers and officers. This places military service in the Nazi era within the broader framework of the socialisation of young men that 'began in school and in the Hitler Youth, continued in the Reich Labour Service, and culminated in the Wehrmacht'.[35]

It also expands upon the work of historians who have previously looked at the prewar Nazification of the military.[36] It will examine how this process filtered down through the ranks and translated into the education of the regular members of the armed forces. In doing so, this analysis will approach the fields of the military's prewar politicisation, and the involvement of officers and soldiers in war crimes, as parts of the same area of historical enquiry. By focusing specifically upon indoctrination in the military, it will also expand upon other works concerned with Nazi ideology and indoctrination, such as Koonz's *The Nazi Conscience*, Herf's *The Jewish Enemy* and Matthäus, Kwiet, Förster and Breitman's *Ausbildungsziel Judenmord?*.[37]

This book will also stand as a counterpoint to one relevant work carried out on the Wehrmacht, which deals directly with the influence of ideology on the attitudes and behaviour of German soldiers. Sönke Neitzel and Harald Welzer's *Soldaten: On Fighting, Killing and Dying* uses secretly recorded conversations of German prisoners of war, gathered by Allied intelligence services, to assess the attitudes of German soldiers towards the war and the Nazi regime.[38] As will be demonstrated and discussed in further detail, the authors argue that the majority of soldiers were 'apolitical', and that historians should 'stop overestimating the effects of ideology'.[39] Yet much of the evidence that Neitzel and Welzer present indicates that many soldiers were anything but 'apolitical', with numerous examples of men whose attitudes and frames of reference clearly were influenced by Nazism. The authors, however, seem to dismiss such indicators of ideology, and the subsequent importance of ideology, because as they rightly point out, very few soldiers were uncritical, fanatical 'ideological warriors'.

This approach is, however, not sufficiently subtle or complex. It is not realistic or useful to group soldiers within such separate and contrasting categories. As will become clear, many members of the Wehrmacht were critical of numerous aspects of the Nazi regime and its ideology. Yet this does not mean that they were not influenced by Nazi ideology at all. Many who voiced criticisms of Nazism still agreed with, or were clearly influenced by, many of its tenets, particularly in the way in which they viewed the war and the enemy they faced. Herein lies the danger in categorising people in such a distinct manner. As this study will demonstrate, there were many differing degrees of ideological accord, for many differing reasons, which need to be closely investigated in order to allow a more complex picture of the attitudes of members of the Wehrmacht.

***

This book examines documents that historians have largely overlooked in accounting for the involvement of the German military in war crimes. The unpublished documents it uses are drawn from various German archives. They are examples of the educational material that German soldiers, from 1933 onwards, encountered during their training and while deployed in the field, as well as correspondence within the military concerning ideological education. These documents include examples of compulsory lessons and training material undertaken during the basic training of conscripts and officers, as well as the ideologically tainted lessons and newsletters they received on a regular basis both in training camps and later in the field. The documents will illustrate how soldiers were trained to see their role, particularly in the campaigns that took place in the East, against people portrayed as ethnically and ideologically alien, and as occupiers of lands that rightfully belonged to Germany. Importantly, this book also examines indoctrination material issued within the Hitler Youth and the Reich Labour Service in order to investigate the political schooling that took place within these organisations, along with the relationship they bore to later political training in the armed forces. This is critical, since I am not trying to argue that indoctrination in the military is the sole explanation for ideological conviction and subsequent military atrocities, nor can any of this be understood in isolation from other potential causal factors.

This work will also include an examination of theoretical and empirical studies on military training and indoctrination. This will provide a framework within which to place this specific study. It will set out the theories, processes and goals of indoctrination and military training, and, in turn, question the influence that this programme may have had upon soldiers and their conduct at war. The case studies examined will be drawn from the fields of history, sociology, political science and psychology.[40] To further investigate the link between training and attitudes, it will also examine internal correspondence within the military, along with *Feldpostbriefe*, letters that soldiers sent home from the front while deployed, which can reveal the attitudes of individual soldiers and officers of varying ranks.

The first chapter of this work will attempt to explain how and why the military aligned itself with the Nazis and began implementing political schooling within its ranks. It will do so by analysing the position in which the military found itself in the aftermath of the First World War and during the Weimar Republic, as well as by evaluating the political persuasions that existed within the armed forces during and before this period.

Chapter two will set out a theoretical framework that will examine how indoctrination is carried out in military organisations, as well as investigating the extent to which it can influence behaviour. Chapter three will address the onset of ideological schooling in the German military, providing examples of indoctrination material and demonstrating how it sought to shape the attitudes and conduct of soldiers and officers. It also cites examples of disagreement with the encroachment of Nazi ideology, or certain aspects of it, to show that Nazism did not have a stranglehold over the military, with some viewing the Nazis with outright disdain.[41] Chapter four looks at indoctrination during the crucial lead-up to the Second World War, before looking at how the analysis of prewar political schooling can add further depth to our understanding of German war crimes during the invasion of Poland.

Chapter five addresses the wider context within which military indoctrination took place by examining political schooling in the Hitler Youth and Reich Labour Service – what it involved, how it was carried out, and how its level of success often varied according to the background of the recruits and the areas in which it attempted to school them. It will also demonstrate how it related to indoctrination within the armed forces.

Chapter six examines the ongoing influence of a competing ideology within the German military: Christianity. Throughout earlier chapters it will become clear that some aspects of ideological schooling were more successful than others. One that was relatively unsuccessful, and a common cause for dissent among soldiers and officers, was Nazism's incompatibility with Christianity. Numerous members voiced their dissent on the grounds of religious belief.[42] Christianity had, after all, long held an important place within the German armed forces, as it had done in German society generally.[43] This chapter will seek to address the tension that existed between Nazism and Christianity, and how the military dealt with it, with a particular focus on the ongoing presence of the military chaplaincy.

Chapter seven will look at the military's war crimes in the Balkans and in the Soviet Union, looking at how an analysis of ideological training of soldiers and officers can add to our existing knowledge. It will also further address the reception of Nazi ideology within the ranks by looking at *Feldpostbriefe*, letters that soldiers sent home from the front.

Throughout this study, there will be a focus upon the relationship between orders and ideology, and how this relationship influenced the activities of soldiers. Within the context of the debate over the relative importance of ideology and orders, which is perhaps most clearly visible in the respective theses of Bartov and Browning, this study will emphasise the importance of ideology. This is not to say that it will regard orders and obedience to them as unimportant, as this clearly was not the case. It is, however, crucial to understand the way in which orders were often issued and carried out. The system under which the German army operated relied upon commanders being able to issue relatively unspecific orders that often did not explicitly order men to carry out specific actions, but instead gave them a broader overall goal or task to achieve. It was left up to the lower-ranking men to decide how they would achieve it. This allowed, and indeed encouraged, a high level of initiative and independence.

In this sense, 'obedience' or following directives was a factor, but not in the strict sense of blindly following orders and doing exactly what one was told. Military actions did not always work that way. Looking at the way in which soldiers were trained thus fills an important gap in understanding the process of how imprecise orders were often enacted in such brutal ways. An analysis of the Wehrmacht's ideological education programme can help us to better comprehend soldiers who carried out atrocities against Nazism's ideologically defined enemies without specific orders to do so, or at the very least, how the directives handed down from commanders were often interpreted in the most radical sense, with the principles of Nazism foremost in acting against enemies.

This analysis also suggests that the presence of political indoctrination may even have convinced those unmoved by Nazi ideology that committing atrocities was part of their duty, due to a number of factors, least of all the status it gained as being 'as binding as any order'.[44] The military's programme of ideological instruction sought to foster an attitude that saw violence against non-military targets, particularly those in the East, who were deemed racially and ideologically alien,[45] as necessary, encouraged and, importantly, well within the perceived bounds of duty for a German soldier. This means that while not all soldiers became ideologues, at the very least the weight of expectation was placed upon the shoulders of such men. In this sense, the German army's programme of indoctrination allows us to view orders within the military, and the command principle that underpinned them, within the wider context of years of rigorous ideological schooling.

Notes

1. 'Die Bolschewistische Weltgefahr', in Reichskriegsministerium (ed.), *Richtlinien für den Unterricht über politische Tagesfragen*, 15 October 1936 edition, 3–6. Archival documents from the archives of the Institute for Contemporary History in Munich (Institut für Zeitgeschichte, Munich; hereafter IfZ), Da 33.60.
2. Wolfram Wette, *The Wehrmacht: History, Myth, Reality* (Cambridge, MA, 2006), 98.
3. Omer Bartov, 'Savage War: German Warfare and Moral Choices in World War II', in Berel Lang and Simon Gigliotti (eds), *The Holocaust: A Reader* (Carlton, VIC, 2005), 224; Ute Frevert, *A Nation in Barracks: Modern Germany, Military Conscription and*

Civil Society (New York, 2004), 259–60; Jürgen Förster, 'Complicity of Entanglement? Wehrmacht, War and Holocaust', in Michael Berenbaum and Abraham Peck (eds), *The Holocaust and History: The Known, the Unknown, the Disputed and the Reexamined* (Bloomington, IN, 1998), 266.
4. Omer Bartov, *Germany's War and the Holocaust: Disputed Histories* (London, 2003), 7–8.
5. Ibid. See also Omer Bartov, *Hitler's Army: Soldiers, Nazis and War in the Third Reich* (Oxford, 1991), 7–10; Wette, *The Wehrmacht*, especially chapter five, 'The Legend of the Wehrmacht's "Clean Hands"', 195–250; Frevert, *A Nation in Barracks*, 259–60; for works that propagated the notion of the 'clean Wehrmacht', see, for example, Erich von Manstein, *Lost Victories* (London, 1958); B.H. Liddell Hart, *The Other Side of the Hill: Germany's Generals: Their Rise and Fall, with Their Own Accounts of Military Events, 1939–1945* (London, 1948).
6. See, for example, Hannes Heer and Klaus Neumann (eds), *War of Extermination: The German Military in World War II 1941–1944* (Oxford, 2000); Dieter Pohl, *Die Herrschaft der Wehrmacht: deutsche Militärbesatzung und einheimische Bevölkerung in der Sowjetunion 1941–1944* (Munich, 2008); Wette, *The Wehrmacht*; Walter Manoschek (ed.), *Die Wehrmacht im Rassenkrieg: Der Vernichtungskrieg hinter der Front* (Vienna, 1996); Jürgen Förster, *Die Wehrmacht im NS-Staat: Eine strukturgeschichtliche Analyse* (Munich, 2007); Mary R. Habeck, 'The Modern and the Primitive: Barbarity and Warfare on the Eastern Front', in George Kassimeris (ed.), *The Barbarisation of Warfare* (London, 2006); see also more general works on the Second World War that document Wehrmacht involvement in war crimes, including Richard Bessel, *Nazism and War* (London, 2004), 103–27; Richard J. Evans, *The Third Reich at War* (London, 2008), 19–27, 175–78, 236–39; Ian Kershaw, *Hitler* (London, 2010).
7. Omer Bartov, *The Eastern Front, 1941–45: German Troops and the Barbarisation of Warfare* (Basingstoke, 1985).
8. 'Report of the committee reviewing the exhibition Vernichtungskrieg: Verbrechen der Wehrmacht 1941 bis 1944, November 2000 (excerpt)', in Hamburg Institute for Social Research (ed.), *Crimes of the Wehrmacht: Dimensions of a War of Annihilation 1941–1944* (Hamburg, 2002).
9. Christian Hartmann, Johannes Hürter and Ulrike Jureit, 'Verbrechen der Wehrmacht: Ergebnisse und Kontroversen der Forschung', in idem (eds), *Verbrechen der Wehrmacht: Bilanz einer Debatte* (Munich, 2005), 21–28; see also Jochen Böhler, *Auftakt zum Vernichtungskrieg: Die Wehrmacht in Polen 1939* (Frankfurt, 2006), 9–11. See, as examples, Bartov, *The Eastern Front*; idem, *Hitler's Army*; idem, 'Operation Barbarossa and the Origins of the Final Solution', in David Cesarani (ed.), *The Final Solution: Origins and Implementation* (London, 1996), 119–36; idem, 'Soldiers, Nazis and War in the Third Reich', *The Journal of Modern History* 63(1) (March 1991), 44–60; Jürgen Förster, 'Operation Barbarossa as a War of Conquest and Annihilation', in Lang and Gigliotti, *The Holocaust: A Reader*, 184–97; idem, 'Der Weltanschauungs- und Vernichtungskrieg im Osten' in *Das deutsche Reich und der Zweite Weltkrieg Band 9/1: Der deutsche Kriegsgesellschaft 1939 bis 1945* (Munich, 2004), 519–538; idem, 'Geistige Kriegführung in der Phase der ersten Siege', in *Das deutsche Reich und der Zweite Weltkrieg Band 9/1*, 506–19; Stephen G. Fritz, '"We Are Trying ... to Change the Face of the World" – Ideology and Motivation in the Wehrmacht on the Eastern Front: The View from Below', *The Journal of Military History* 60(4) (1996), 683–710; Ben Shepherd, *War in the Wild East: The German Army and Partisans* (Cambridge, MA, 2004); Walter Manoschek and Hans Safrian, 'Österreicher in der Wehrmacht', in Ernst Hanisch, Wolfgang Neugebauer and Emmerich Talos (eds), *NS-Herrschaft in Österreich*

(Vienna, 2000), 123–158; Horst Boog et al. (eds), *Der Angriff auf die Sowjetunion* (Frankfurt, 1991); Wette, *The Wehrmacht*.
10. Hartmann, Hürter and Jureit, 'Verbrechen der Wehrmacht: Ergebnisse und Kontroversen der Forschung', in idem, *Verbrechen der Wehrmacht*, 23.
11. See Bartov, *Hitler's Army*; idem, 'Savage War'; Wette, *The Wehrmacht*, 94–131; Bessel, *Nazism and War*, 117–27; Förster, 'Operation Barbarossa as a War of Conquest and Annihilation'; Helmut Krausnick et al. (eds), *Anatomy of the SS State* (London, 1968), 318–19.
12. Daniel Goldhagen, *Hitler's Willing Executioners* (New York, 1996).
13. Christopher R. Browning, *Ordinary Men: Police Battalion 101 and the Final Solution in Poland* (London, 2001).
14. See Bartov's discussion of Browning's thesis in Bartov, *Germany's War and the Holocaust*, 132–57.
15. Walter Manoschek, 'Partisankrieg und Genozid: Die Wehrmacht in Serbien 1941', in *Die Wehrmacht im Rassenkrieg*; idem, 'The Extermination of the Jews in Serbia', in Ulrich Hebert (ed.), *National Socialist Extermination Policies: Contemporary German Perspectives and Controversies* (New York, 2000), 163–85; idem, *'Serbien ist judenfrei': Militärische Besatzungspolitik und Judenvernichtung in Serbien 1941/42* (Munich, 1993); Walter Manoschek and Hans Safrian, 'Österreicher in der Wehrmacht', in Ernst Hanisch, Wolfgang Neugebauer and Emmerich Talos (eds), *NS-Herrschaft in Österreich* (Vienna, 2000), 123–58; Ben Shepherd, *Terror in the Balkans: German Armies and Partisan Warfare* (Cambridge, MA, 2012).
16. Jochen Böhler, *Der Überfall: Deutschlands Krieg gegen Polen* (Frankfurt, 2009); idem, *Auftakt zum Vernichtungskrieg: Die Wehrmacht in Polen 1939* (Frankfurt, 2006); idem, *"Grösste Härte …": Verbrechen der Wehrmacht in Polen, September, Oktober 1939* (Warsaw, 2005); Alexander B. Rossino, *Hitler Strikes Poland: Blitzkrieg, Ideology, and Atrocity* (Lawrence, 2003). See also Evans, *The Third Reich at War*, 102–5 and Kershaw, *Hitler*, 523–25.
17. Bartov, *Hitler's Army*. On the nature of the conditions, see chapter one, 'The Demodernization of the Front', 12–28.
18. Bartov, *Hitler's Army*, 94–96.
19. Ibid., 106–78.
20. Böhler, *Auftakt zum Vernichtungskrieg*; idem, *"Grösste Härte …"*; Rossino, *Hitler Strikes Poland*.
21. Bartov, *Hitler's Army* and idem, *The Eastern Front*; Stephen G. Fritz, *Frontsoldaten: The German Soldier in World War II* (Lexington, 1995); Manoschek, 'Partisankrieg und Genozid: Die Wehrmacht in Serbien 1941', in *Die Wehrmacht im Rassenkrieg*; idem, 'The Extermination of the Jews in Serbia'; idem, *'Serbien ist Judenfrei': militärische Besatzungspolitik und Judenvernichtung in Serbien 1941/42*; Manoschek and Safrian, 'Österreicher in der Wehrmacht'; Wette, *The Wehrmacht*. See also Habeck, 'The Modern and the Primitive', 84–96.
22. Bartov, *Hitler's Army*; idem, *The Eastern Front*; idem, *Germany's War and the Holocaust*, 130–32.
23. Bartov, *Germany's War and the Holocaust*, 106–79. See also Claudia Koonz, *The Nazi Conscience* (Cambridge, MA, 2003), 10–11.
24. See Böhler, *Auftakt zum Vernichtungskrieg*, 20; Rossino, *Hitler Strikes Poland*, 217–21.
25. Böhler, *Auftakt zum Vernichtungskrieg*, 36.
26. Ibid., 220.

27. See Koonz, *The Nazi Conscience*, 10–11. For examples, see Bartov, *Hitler's Army*; Böhler, *Der Überfall*.
28. Wette, *The Wehrmacht*, 1–90; Ben Shepherd, *Hitler's Soldiers: The German Army in the Third Reich* (New Haven, 2016), chapters one and two.
29. See Bartov, *Germany's War and the Holocaust*, 65–72. For examples of such works, see Militärgeschichtliches Forschungsamt (ed.), *Das deutsche Reich und der zweite Weltkrieg* (Munich, 2004). In particular, see Jürgen Förster's essay 'Geistige Kriegführung in Deutschland 1919 bis 1945' in Volume 9, Part 1, 506–19; Förster, *Die Wehrmacht im NS-Staat*; Karl Demeter, *The German Officer Corps in Society and State 1650–1945* (London, 1965); Michael Salewski, 'Wehrmacht und Nationalsozialismus 1933-1939', in Militärgeschichtliches Forschungsamt (ed.), *Handbuch zur Deutschen Militärgeschichte 1648-1939* (Munich, 1978); F.L. Carsten, *The Reichswehr and Politics, 1918–1933* (Oxford, 1966); Manfred Messerschmidt, *Die Wehrmacht im NS-Staat: Zeit der Indoktrination* (Hamburg, 1969); Robert O'Neill, *The German Army and the Nazi Party, 1933–1939* (London, 1966); Klaus Jürgen Müller (ed.), *Armee und Drittes Reich 1933–1939: Darstellung und Dokumentation* (Paderborn, 1989).
30. Daniel Uziel, *Propaganda Warriors: The Wehrmacht and the Consolidation of the German Home Front* (Oxford, 2008).
31. See Bartov, 'Operation Barbarossa', 124; idem, *Hitler's Army*; Böhler, *Auftakt zum Vernichtungskrieg*, 20; Rossino, *Hitler Strikes Poland*, 217–21. See also Felix Römer, *Kameraden: Die Wehrmacht von innen* (Munich, 2012), 60–110.
32. Michael H. Kater, *Hitler Youth* (Cambridge, MA, 2004); Detlev Peukert, 'Youth in the Third Reich', in Richard Bessel (ed.), *Life in the Third Reich* (Oxford, 1987), 25; Michael Burleigh and Wolfgang Wippermann, *The Racial State: Germany 1933–1945* (Cambridge, 1991), 205; Gerhard Rempel, *Hitler's Children: The Hitler Youth and the SS* (Chapel Hill, 1989); David Welch, *The Third Reich: Politics and Propaganda* (London, 1993); Jill Stephenson, 'Inclusion: Building the National Community in Propaganda and Practice', in Jane Caplan (ed.), *Nazi Germany* (Oxford, 2008), 99–121.
33. Bundesarchiv/Militärarchiv, Freiburg (hereafter BA/MA) RW6/161, *Erster nationalpolitischer Lehrgang für Lehrer der Kriegsschulen, Akademien usw vom 17.1.37 bis 23.1.37 in Berlin*, 23.
34. Ibid., 24.
35. Ute Frevert, *Die kasernierte Nation: Militärdienst und Zivilgesellschaft in Deutschland* (Munich, 2001), 315–17.
36. O'Neill, *The German Army and the Nazi Party*; Frevert, *Die Kasinierte Nation*; Carsten, *The Reichswehr and Politics*; Förster, *Die Wehrmacht im NS-Staat*; idem, 'Die politisierung der Reichswehr/Wehrmacht', in *Das deutsche Reich und der Zweite Weltkrieg Band 9/1*, 484–505; idem, '"Aber für die Juden wird auch noch die Stunde schlagen, und dann wehe ihnen!" Reichswehr und Antisemitismus', in Jürgen Matthäus and Klaus-Michael Mallman (eds), *Deutsche, Juden, Völkermord: Der Holocaust als Geschichte und Gegenwart* (Darmstadt, 2006), 21–37; Klaus Jürgen Müller, *The Army, Politics and Society in Germany, 1933–45: Studies in the Army's Relation to Nazism* (Manchester, 1987); Salewski, 'Wehrmacht und Nationalsozialismus'.
37. Koonz, *The Nazi Conscience*; Jeffrey Herf, *The Jewish Enemy: Nazi Propaganda during World War II and the Holocaust* (London, 2006); Jürgen Matthäus et al. (eds), *Ausbildungsziel Judenmord?: Weltanschauliche Erziehung von SS, Polizei und Waffen SS in Rahmen der Endlösung* (Frankfurt, 2003).
38. Sönke Neitzel and Harald Welzer, *Soldaten: On Fighting, Killing and Dying* (London, 2012).

39. Ibid., 319.
40. For example, Joanna Bourke, *An Intimate History of Killing: Face to Face Killing in Twentieth Century Warfare* (London, 1999); Gregory G. Dimjian, 'Warfare, Genocide, and Ethnic Conflict: A Darwinian Approach', *Baylor University Medical Center Proceedings* 23(3) (July 2010), 292–300; Eyal Ben-Ari, *Mastering Soldiers: Conflicts, Emotions and the Enemy in an Israeli Military Unit* (London, 1998); Adam Lankford, *Human Killing Machines* (Plymouth, 2009); Robert Jay Lifton, *Thought Reform and the Psychology of Totalism: A Study of Brainwashing in China* (London, 1961); Ben Shalit, *The Psychology of Conflict and Combat* (New York, 1988); Hugo Slim, *Killing Civilians: Method, Madness and Morality in War* (London, 2007); Denise Winn, *The Manipulated Mind: Brainwashing, Conditioning and Indoctrination* (London, 1983); E.S. Williams (ed.), *The Soviet Military: Political Education, Training and Morale* (Basingstoke, 1987).
41. O'Neill, *The German Army and the Nazi Party*, 5–8, 139.
42. BA/MA RW 6/V. 166, *Sommer-Lehrgang für Offiziere in Bad Tölz*: 'Vortragsreihe über nationalsozialistische Weltanschauung und Zielsetzung vom 11.-17.6.1939 in Bad Tölz'.
43. Demeter, *The German Officer Corps*, 220; O'Neill, *The German Army and the Nazi Party*, 75; Frevert, *A Nation in Barracks*, 187–88.
44. O'Neill, *The German Army and the Nazi Party*, 71.
45. See Vejas Gabriel Liulevicius, *War Land on the Eastern Front: Culture, National Identity and German Occupation in World War I* (Cambridge, 2000), 247–56; idem, *The German Myth of the East: 1800 to the Present* (Oxford, 2009), 170.

Chapter 1

A POLITICAL MILITARY?

When the National Socialists came to power in 1933, their leader, Adolf Hitler, had ambitious plans to reshape Germany. The new society that he wished to build would be based upon the values of race and militarism, with wars of conquest as the ultimate goal.[1] In fact, Nazism was inseparable from war. Its ideology revolved around it, and once they had gained power, the Nazis steered Germany on a 'remarkably consistent, if irrational and self-destructive, course to war'.[2] Of course, in order to achieve these goals, much would depend upon the German military. Weakened by the First World War and the resulting Treaty of Versailles, it needed rebuilding. Just as importantly, Hitler needed to gain the military's support to cement his domestic authority and to implement his agenda.[3]

During the Weimar Republic, the military, then known as the Reichswehr, had remained officially 'apolitical' and committed to upholding the constitution. Its members had to swear an oath to the Weimar constitution[4] and they were banned from taking part in party politics.[5] However, beneath the surface of apolitical service to the republic, there was much about the situation in which the Reichswehr found itself that caused deep resentment among its soldiers and officers. The nature of the new democratic and, because of the Versailles Treaty, demilitarised German state meant that the military had been drastically downsized. Moreover, it had also lost the influential position within society that it had held during the imperial age. Many within its ranks felt rejected and alienated by the new state.[6] The new constitution had signalled an end to many of the special rights, as well as the social prestige, that had been enjoyed by members of the Imperial German Army, causing deep resentment among both the soldiers themselves and numerous right-wing political parties.[7] The absence of conscription not only reduced the number of personnel available to the military, it also resulted in much less interaction taking place between the military and wider society, adding to the army's sense of estrangement from the Weimar Republic.[8]

The Reichswehr officer corps was led by the right-wing, antisemitic Hans von Seeckt.[9] Seeckt was not a supporter of the Weimar Republic; at best he accepted it only as a temporary state of affairs due to the lack of alternatives.[10] He organised the interwar army as a kind of 'state within a state', never fully integrating it into the political life of the Weimar Republic.[11] Many members of the armed forces, having been socialised in the old army structures, and particularly in the case of the officer corps, drawn from the upper classes, shared Seeckt's sentiments. They viewed the new democratic model of government with disdain, seeing it as alien to the world of the army and the officer corps, and at odds with their own political views, with many having links to anti-republican forces.[12] In turn, the Reichswehr was the institution that stood furthest from democracy and the state during the Weimar Republic.[13]

A directive issued by the Reichswehr ministry shortly before the Nazis came to power gives an idea of the military's position during the Weimar Republic. It contained lines such as 'Unlike in earlier wars of conquests, unlike campaigns of the Kings and other such expeditions and plundering … our voluntary army serves purely for the defence of the nation's borders'.[14] The Reichswehr was to protect the Fatherland, which although

> reduced in size, weakened, indebted and humbled, is still our Fatherland, our home, and in spite of all the hardships that have fallen upon us, our future and the future of our children is tied up with its future. Although our country is war-torn, beneath the ruins there exists the possibility for a new, better life for us all, but this is only achievable through hard work.[15]

This was hardly the sort of rhetoric that would inspire loyalty within the officer corps who had served the Kaiser. Its resigned tone seemed to offer little to soldiers in comparison to what the Nazis promised.

The Nazi regime's formation signalled a substantial change in the situation facing the Reichswehr. For many members of the armed forces, Hitler presented an appealing alternative to the future they saw under the Weimar Republic.[16] According to Robert O'Neill, there existed 'fertile soil awaiting the policies and ideas of Adolf Hitler'.[17] Many within the military viewed the Nazi Party as the promise of an ideal regime. It was authoritarian and nationalistic, and it seemed to guarantee the remilitarisation of German society and the restoration of the military's former standing within the state.[18] The Nazis' seizure of power was also a long-awaited opportunity to discard the democratic Weimar model, and to suppress liberal and left-wing elements within the country.[19] National Socialism found particularly high levels of support among younger officers.[20] According to one officer who was later to become involved in resistance against Hitler, General Hans Oster, many members of the armed forces welcomed the return to 'a vigorous patriotic policy, rearmament, reintroduction of military service', since 'to the officers, this meant a return to older traditions'.[21]

This is not to say, however, that the Nazi regime was greeted with unconditional enthusiasm by all members of the military. Some senior, conservative officers, Generals Werner von Fritsch, Ludwig Beck and Kurt von Hammerstein among the most prominent, were disturbed by the radical nature of the Nazi Party, and were appalled by the Nazis' use of street violence and coercion.[22] The socialist leanings held by some members of the Nazi Party and the SA also alarmed many within the officer corps, not only because of their conservative politics, but also because many of them were drawn from the upper classes.[23] They also saw in the SA, the paramilitary wing of the Nazi Party, a possible competitor for the role as the main military force within Germany.[24]

While these elements did exist, and continued to oppose the onset of Nazism within the military, for many officers the perceived benefits of the new regime won out over any misgivings they may have had about the extremists that had taken power.[25] The military was in a difficult position, both domestically and internationally, and felt itself extremely vulnerable within both spheres. The Treaty of Versailles had resulted in a drastic downsizing of the German armed forces, restricting it to 100,000 men. On an international level, the restrictions placed upon the Reichswehr had rendered it incapable of defending Germany from foreign aggression,[26] with the military making attempts to skirt the regulations of Versailles through secret rearmament and involvement with veteran soldiers' associations that helped to boost its resources.[27] From the perspective of the officer corps in 1933, the highly desirable goals of overthrowing the restrictions of Versailles and of regaining military might could most logically and easily be pursued under Hitler.[28]

The Nazi Party's agenda sought to address the military's issues. On 3 February 1933, shortly after becoming Chancellor, Hitler gave a speech to a number of Reichswehr generals, promising to 'stand at the side of' and 'work for' the army, which he said he regarded as the most important institution of the state. More specifically, he expressed his plans to crush Marxism and democracy, to overturn the Treaty of Versailles, to rebuild the economy and the military, and to militarise German society.[29] The Nazis also seemed to have learned the lessons of the First World War. They would prepare Germany for future conflicts by harnessing the entire resources of a nation and ensure that the military would not suffer another humiliating defeat. Furthermore, it was clear that the new regime would suppress domestic dissent and ignore international protests against their rearmament plans.[30] Hitler had also spoken of the military as acting as one of the two 'pillars' of the state. The Nazi movement would be one pillar, supporting the nation politically, and the armed forces would be the other, supporting it militarily as the nation's 'sole bearer of arms'.[31] Hitler's statements implied that many of his political aims aligned with the military's own interests, however untruthful his proclamations regarding the military's future autonomy within the state might have been.

Perhaps the most enthusiastic of the military elites in his support of the new regime was the minister of defence, General Werner von Blomberg. Appointed in 1933, Blomberg made it clear that the military would abandon its role as a supposedly apolitical organisation,[32] ordering his men to back the new 'national movement' in a directive on 11 April 1933.[33] Blomberg also sought to coordinate the military's ideology with that of the regime. He took the notable step of ordering that the 7 April 1933 'Law for the Restoration of the Professional Civil Service' would apply to the ranks of the military. This law, which legislated the dismissal of 'non-Aryans' from their posts, did not initially apply to the armed forces. Blomberg, however, took the initiative and voluntarily adopted the legislation, dismissing Jews (with exceptions made for veterans of the First World War) and giving Nazi racial ideology official status within the military.[34] (However, as Brian Rigg has pointed out, some Jews and many *Mischlinge* managed to serve in the German army during the Third Reich.)[35] In another unprompted display of political loyalty, Blomberg incorporated the swastika into the military's crest.[36] When Hitler merged the offices of President and Chancellor upon President Hindenburg's death in August 1934, members of the military swore a new oath pledging 'unconditional obedience' to Hitler himself, rather than to the state, indicating a further step towards a Nazified military.[37] The pledge was quite different to the previous one, in which soldiers swore an oath to 'defend the German Reich' and to 'protect the government instated by the people'.[38] In another instance of a senior army officer acting on his own initiative, the new oath was formulated by General Walther von Reichenau.[39]

Not all members of the armed forces agreed with the actions of Blomberg and Reichenau. Blomberg's move to dismiss Jews from the military was seen by some, including Erich von Manstein, as an attack on the officer corps.[40] Manstein wrote that the officer corps should not 'bend to the will of outsiders', and that it should 'have the right to have a say, for the protection of those affected and above all the protection of its own honour'.[41] It should be noted, however, that Manstein was an exception, and moreover he did not call into question Nazi racial thought or the dismissal of Jews from the civil service.[42] He stated that 'we should not look at this question from the point of view of those affected, but much more from that of whether it is reconcilable with the honour of the army to be disloyal to comrades in order to prevent political difficulties',[43] suggesting that the encroachment of the regime's political influence on the military was the real problem for Manstein (who was later to issue some of the most notorious anti-Jewish orders to his men during the Barbarossa campaign),[44] rather than the government's actual ideology. The formulation of the oath to Hitler also drove other officers to despair; General Ludwig Beck wrote that the day on which the oath was sworn was 'the blackest of [his] life'.[45]

A further factor in Blomberg's efforts to conform the military to the new order was the rivalry that existed with the Nazi paramilitary organisation, the SA. Klaus Jürgen Müller has argued that the army sought to secure its position in the new state by demonstrating to Hitler that he could rely upon the military's loyalty, in return for his guarantee that the military would remain the state's primary armed force, a position that many within the officer corps regarded as being threatened by the SA.[46] Indeed, according to Blomberg, in February 1934 Ernst Röhm, the leader of the SA, had demanded that the SA should take over national defence from the army, which would continue to exist only as a trainer of soldiers for the SA; this horrified military leaders.[47] However, viewing the ideological conformity of the military with the Nazi regime within the context of a political power struggle with the SA can be problematic. It takes the focus away from the pre-existence of attitudes within the military that bore similarities to those of the Nazis,[48] along with the fact that the military had willingly begun the process of 'Nazification' from within, rather than at the behest of the Nazi Party.[49]

Indeed, many of the steps taken by the military in the early months of the Nazi era suggest that the values and goals shared by the Nazi Party and the army were more than convenient and superficial, and in truth went beyond the mere merging of interests. They also suggest that for the ideology of a new, radical regime to gain such a strong foothold in an organisation like the German military, elements of that ideology must have existed there in the first place.

The German military was indeed an organisation that, even during the imperial and Weimar eras, had been pervaded by some of the more abstract sentiments that the Nazi Party espoused.[50] The political atmosphere within the armed forces had long been characterised by right-wing views, and did not begin as a reaction to the Weimar Republic. The Prussian officer corps was generally authoritarian, nationalist, anti-liberal, antisemitic and opposed to the Social Democrats.[51] It also saw itself as a bulwark against potentially dangerous social change; it was wary of the bourgeois middle class and it harboured a particular fear of Germany's emerging industrial working class.[52] Abhorrence of the Social Democrats was so strong that during the latter stages of the nineteenth century the army undertook a number of measures to curtail the influence of such views within its ranks. Although they could not be completely eradicated, Social Democratic publications were banned, and the military kept a close eye on any conscripts who were suspected of having Social Democratic sympathies.[53] In 1885, for example, the military weekly newspaper warned its men of forces that 'gnawed at the roots and essence of the state – forces called liberalism, democracy, anarchy and, first and foremost, socialism'. To prevent soldiers from forming such leanings, the military provided its men with political schooling that emphasised loyalty to the king and condemned Social Democrats as being anti-military, anti-monarchy and anti-Christian.[54]

Officers who had been socialised within such an organisation were unlikely to have mourned the passing of a 'socialist republic'.[55] The situation was not helped by the fact that the Weimar Republic was also associated with the shame of defeat and domestic upheaval at the end of the First World War.[56] While there were officers who, having accepted the Weimar Republic as a temporary measure to avert national chaos, concentrated on building the military into the most capable force possible,[57] numerous others refused to defend the republic in times of crisis, and many refused to wear the black, gold and red on their uniforms, or to fly the new national flag above their barracks.[58]

Antisemitism had also long been present within the German officer corps, with Messerschmidt arguing that it was a 'fixed attitude' that was characterised by a willingness by officers to engage in 'social and political demonisation' of Jews.[59] In a sense, the military echoed wider societal prejudices that existed within Germany. Peter Pulzer has argued that 'at no stage in German history between 1871 and 1933 was there a consensus that the Jew was a citizen like any other'.[60] While Jews had experienced social, economic and political emancipation by the 1860s across the German states, and German Jews living in the imperial era did not encounter the virulent and popular antisemitism that the Dreyfus affair had unleashed in France, or the pogroms of Russia,[61] they still faced discrimination in the ensuing decades when competing for careers. The military provided the worst example of intolerance.[62] Although the law did not dictate that Jews were to be excluded from the officer corps, it proved almost impossible for Jews to become officers, particularly in Prussia, where Jews were even excluded from the ranks of the reserve officers from 1885 onwards. It was also more difficult to gain promotion.[63] In 1910 there was not a single Jewish officer in the Prussian army, apart from a few who had converted to Christianity, which contrasted with the presence of thousands of Jewish officers in the Austro-Hungarian army, the hundreds that served in Italy and, in spite of the Dreyfus affair, in France.[64]

There is clear evidence that antisemitism continued to exist, and even became more pronounced, within the German armed forces during the First World War, in spite of the fact that many Jews actually served in the military.[65] This was not initially the case. In the earliest months of the war, the armed forces were marked by indicators of the sense of unity and euphoria that had gripped the nation, a sentiment that extended to German–Jewish relations. However, this soon wore off once it became clear that the war would not end as quickly and successfully as hoped, giving way to disappointment and frustration, with antisemitism flaring up again in both the civilian and military spheres.[66]

Jews were often discriminated against, passed over for promotion and targeted by nationalists as being cowards and war profiteers. One Jewish soldier, Julius Marx, wrote in October 1914 of the prejudice that he faced from his comrades: 'Others look at me suspiciously as a Jew. At the beginning of the war it seemed that every prejudice had disappeared. There were only Germans. Now you hear the old hateful phrases again'. In 1916 he wrote: 'The average German doesn't like Jews. I want nothing other than to be a German soldier. But people make sure that I know differently'.[67]

The most notorious example of the military's antisemitism during the First World War became known as the 'Jewish Head Count'. In October 1916, the Prussian war ministry initiated a survey to gather statistics on the number of Jews who were serving at the front. In spite of its apparently non-discriminatory intentions, its existence was a concession to antisemitic elements, and, having found sympathisers within the military command, indicated that antisemitism was having an effect on official policy. The information gathered in the survey was to be used to capitalise upon suspicions that Jews were shirkers, and subsequently to prevent their access to the public service and officer corps.[68] The survey helped to further differentiate German Jewish soldiers from their non-Jewish comrades; Jewish soldiers were often singled out by their commanding officers for humiliation, or were arbitrarily sent to the front. When the statistics confirmed that Jewish soldiers were actually well represented at the front, confounding the expectations of antisemitic agitators, the results were not published.[69]

The aftermath of the First World War saw a number of further developments in the nature of the prejudices that existed within the German military. These included a further rise in antisemitism, a radicalised attitude towards the lands and people where the German army had fought on the

Eastern Front, growing anti-Bolshevism and, critically, the conviction that Judaism and Bolshevism were somehow linked.[70]

The shift towards a racial antisemitism in military circles was due to a number of factors. Firstly, it reflected broader developments in antisemitism that took place in the late nineteenth century, in which earlier prejudice, based upon religion,[71] had evolved into a prejudice based upon the supposedly biologically 'otherness' of Jews, which made assimilation and conversion to Christianity irrelevant, and indeed undesired, by antisemites in order to avoid inter-racial mingling.[72] More specifically within the German military, the notion of racial differentiation was reinforced during the First World War when many German soldiers encountered *Ostjuden*, 'Eastern Jews', while serving on the Eastern Front. While relationships with the Jews under the German occupation of parts of Eastern Europe were generally good, many viewed them with suspicion.[73] According to Noah Isenberg, German soldiers were 'generally shocked by the abject conditions in which they found Eastern Jews: squalor, filth and horror. Many felt … as if they had "entered a totally different world, the world of the Orient"'.[74] The experience helped to give credence to pre-existing stereotypes of Eastern Jews, and to confirm beliefs in German superiority.[75]

The German army's experience on the Eastern Front also helped to influence views on Eastern Europe and its peoples, and its conduct there contained elements that were radicalised by the Nazi Party in its approach to the East.[76] While the German image of Eastern Europe had long been marked by negative visions of a wild, chaotic and underdeveloped region populated by primitive peoples,[77] the military's occupation helped to reinforce such attitudes. German soldiers encountered wretched and displaced people, as well as filth, disorder and chaos in the streets of Eastern European towns and cities. The army's occupation of the territory also contained an imperialistic impulse that saw a mission to civilise and order the lands and peoples that came under German military rule. The occupation was marked by 'colonial-style condescension and casual brutality', with German military authorities showing little concern for local, non-German populations.[78] This did not necessarily mean that the military's future participation in genocidal actions in Eastern Europe was inevitable. The German army's occupation during the First World War was much more restrained and had quite different outcomes in mind.[79] However, the military's experience of the region resulted in it coming to see the East in terms of 'spaces and races', both of which were backward and threatening, and in need of ordering by German mastery, forming a mentality that had the potential to be exploited and radicalised by the Nazis.[80]

Many of the prejudices that existed within the military were manifested in the 'Stab in the Back' myth, a phrase invoked most prominently by

General Erich Ludendorff, which sought to shift the blame away from the military, which was supposedly 'undefeated on the field of battle', and onto other elements within German society.[81] The myth asserted that the soldiers who stayed on and fought at the front were betrayed by agitators on the home front: pacifists, democrats, socialists and Jews.[82]

The atmosphere of upheaval and revolution, the harsh peace terms imposed by the Treaty of Versailles, along with the establishment of the Weimar Republic, further contributed to antisemitic, anti-socialist leanings among officers, with Germany's plight being blamed upon an enemy that was 'Jewish inspired'.[83] Within anti-republican circles, the Weimar Republic itself came to be referred to as the 'Judenrepublik',[84] and in 1919, General Ludendorff propagated the myth of Jewish responsibility, railing against the 'international, pacifist, defeatist Jews ... who systematically destroyed our racial inheritance and national character'.[85] Jews also came to be associated with revolutionary agitation at home and abroad.[86] The then Lieutenant Colonel Werner von Fritsch, who later served as commander-in-chief of the army under the Nazis, wrote that 'pacifists, Jews, democrats, black-red-gold and the French are all the same. They all want the destruction of Germany'.[87]

The term 'Jewish Bolshevik', which was to later become a key phrase in Nazi propaganda, was already in use among radical right-wing German officers in 1918.[88] This was centred upon a belief that the German revolutionaries must have been Jewish, since there were a number of prominent Russian Bolsheviks who were Jewish. It also sprang from the military's recent experiences in the East, in which Jews were said to be more likely to be under the influence of Bolshevik ideas.[89]

The belief in an ostensibly Jewish-instigated defeat, and a new state that was allegedly heavily influenced by Jews, played a part in setting the tone within the armed forces for much of the Weimar era. Antisemitism increased due to the insinuation that the Jews were the common factor behind the pain of defeat, the threat of revolution and the spectre of Bolshevism.[90] It should be noted, however, that not all German troops shared the views of those who propagated the 'Stab in the Back' myth. Many working-class soldiers, for instance, had been members of the Social Democratic Party (SPD), which had long stood in opposition to antisemitism, and continued to do so after the war.[91] There were also important points of divergence between the military and the Nazi Party. Perhaps the most important ideological differences were related to religion; Christianity had long played, and continued to play, an important role within the military, and traditional Christian beliefs helped to offset radical influences.[92] However, many officers did hold antisemitic, anti-democratic and anti-socialist views, and the experiences of Jewish soldiers at the front had indicated that ordinary soldiers also openly expressed antisemitic sentiments, making it exceedingly difficult for Jewish soldiers to join and fit in.[93] Furthermore, some of the organisations associated with the army were officially racist: throughout the Weimar years, the most prominent war veterans' organisation, the Stahlhelm, introduced a clause forbidding Jewish veterans from membership.[94]

A further aspect of the developments in antisemitic rhetoric during this period was not only its association with Marxism, but also the depiction of an enemy that was not definitive or firm, but instead constituted an entity that was blurry, ambiguous and flexible enough to include any groups targeted. This rendered antisemitism a convenient tool for manipulation, and illustrated that alongside the more obvious features of ideological accord with the Nazi Party, many notable members of the military had developed a tendency to define and view their 'enemy' in racial and ideological, as well as in military terms.[95] This provided an indication of the shape that future indoctrination, and in turn conflicts, were to take, and confirmed the degree of ideological common ground that later was to exist between the Nazi Party and the German armed forces.

The prevailing political attitudes that existed within the military give an indication of the kind of reception that Nazi ideological schooling would encounter once it began. While it is difficult to assess the question of reception of indoctrination due to a lack of direct evidence such as opinion surveys in the military (although sources such as letters that soldiers sent home from the front, as well as internal correspondence within the military, will be discussed later), it is useful to look to Ian Kershaw's work on the broader implementation and successes of Nazi propaganda within the public sphere as an analytical framework. Kershaw has argued that Nazi propaganda was most successful in building on areas in which established prejudices already existed than when it attempted to either reverse existing beliefs or create an entirely new belief system.[96] Since it is clear that the military and the Nazi Party had many prejudices in common, Nazi political schooling needed only to build on and radicalise prejudices against Jews, socialism, democracy and Slavs that were already common within the armed forces, rather than to manufacture, or indeed to reverse opinions. Much of the political schooling that soldiers encountered fell into this category, due to pre-existing attitudes within the armed forces, or, in later years, the prior socialisation of young men in Nazi society, along with membership of the Hitler Youth and Reich Labour Service. Some areas of indoctrination, however, fell into the latter category of training that ran against entrenched beliefs, and were less successful, most notably in the area of religion.

Notes

1. Jürgen Förster, *Die Wehrmacht im NS-Staat: Eine strukturgeschichtliche Analyse* (Munich, 2007), 19.
2. Richard Bessel, *Nazism and War* (London, 2004), 1.
3. Förster, *Die Wehrmacht im NS-Staat*, 19–22. See also Ian Kershaw, *Hitler* (London, 2010), 256; Klaus Jürgen Müller, 'The Army and the Third Reich', in Neil Gregor (ed.), *Nazism* (Oxford, 2000), 168; Wilhelm Deist, 'The *Gleichschaltung* of the Armed Forces', in Militärgeschichtliches Forschungsamt (ed.), *The Build-Up of German Aggression* (Oxford, 1990), 550–52; Jochen Böhler, *Auftakt zum Vernichtungskrieg: Die Wehrmacht in Polen 1939* (Frankfurt, 2006), 27–34; Wolfram Wette, *The Wehrmacht: History, Myth, Reality* (Cambridge, MA, 2006), 2; Richard J. Evans, *The Coming of the Third Reich* (London, 2004), 316–17.
4. Ute Frevert, *A Nation in Barracks: Modern Germany, Military Conscription and Civil Society* (New York, 2004), 239.
5. Karl Demeter, *The German Officer Corps in Society and State 1650–1945* (London, 1965), 190.
6. Bessel, *Nazism and War*, 24; Robert O'Neill, *The German Army and the Nazi Party 1933–1939* (London, 1966), 4–5; Frevert, *A Nation in Barracks*, 239–41; Gordon A. Craig, *The Politics of the Prussian Army 1640–1945* (Oxford, 1955); Michael Salewski, 'Wehrmacht und Nationalsozialismus 1933–1939', in Militärgeschichtliches Forschungsamt (ed.), *Handbuch zur Deutschen Militärgeschichte 1648–1939* (Munich, 1978), 35.
7. Frevert, *A Nation in Barracks*, 241.
8. Wette, *The Wehrmacht*, 62; Frevert, *A Nation in Barracks*, 242.
9. Wette, *The Wehrmacht*, 67–69; F.L. Carsten, *The Reichswehr and Politics, 1918–1933* (Oxford, 1966), 30–31, 131–32.
10. Robert M. Citino, *The Path to Blitzkrieg: Doctrine and Training in the German Army, 1920-1939* (London, 1999), 7; Evans, *The Coming of the Third Reich*, 97–98.
11. Citino, *The Path to Blitzkrieg*, 7.
12. Frevert, *A Nation in Barracks*, 241–42; Salewski, 'Wehrmacht und Nationalsozialismus', 35; Michael Berger, *Eisernes Kreuz und Davidstern: die Geschichte jüdischer Soldaten in deutschen Armeen* (Berlin, 2006), 209.
13. Berger, *Eisernes Kruez und Davidstern*, 209.
14. Institut für Zeitgeschichte (hereafter IfZ), Da 033.176a, Reichswehrministerium (ed.), *Reichswehr* (Berlin, 1932).
15. Ibid.
16. Salewski, 'Wehrmacht und Nationalsozialismus', 35; Manfred Messerschmidt, *Die Wehrmacht im NS-Staat: Zeit der Indoktrination* (Hamburg, 1969), 19; idem, 'Die Wehrmacht als tragende Säule des NS-Staates (1933–1939)', in Walter Manoschek (ed.), *Die Wehrmacht im Rassenkrieg: der Vernichtungskrieg hinter der Front* (Vienna, 1996), 39; Wette, *The Wehrmacht*, 69.
17. O'Neill, *The German Army and the Nazi Party*, 4.
18. Wette, *The Wehrmacht*, 69; Messerschmidt, *Die Wehrmacht im NS-Staat*, 19; Förster, *Die Wehrmacht im NS-Staat*, 21; Böhler, *Auftakt zum Vernichtungskrieg*, 27–28.
19. Richard J. Evans, *The Third Reich in Power* (London, 2006), 9–10; Klaus Jürgen Müller, *The Army, Politics and Society in Germany, 1933–45: Studies in the Army's Relation to Nazism* (Manchester, 1987), 29–35; Deist, 'The Rearmament of the Wehrmacht', 520–22; Demeter, *The German Officer Corps*, 193–96.

20. Craig, *The Politics of the Prussian Army*, 482.
21. General Hans Oster, quoted in Demeter, *The German Officer Corps*, Appendix 32, 360–61.
22. O'Neill, *The German Army and the Nazi Party*, 5.
23. Ibid., 5–6.
24. Evans, *The Third Reich in Power*, 24–26; O'Neill, *The German Army and the Nazi Party*, 5–6.
25. See Wilhelm Deist, 'The *Gleichschaltung* of the Armed Forces', in Militärgeschichtliches Forschungsamt (ed.), *The Build-Up of German Aggression* (Oxford, 1990), 550–52; Förster, *Die Wehrmacht im NS-Staat*, 21–22; Bessel, *Nazism and War*, 23–37; Manfred Messerschmidt, '*Die Wehrmacht im NS-Staat: Zeit der Indoktrination* (Hamburg, 1969); Frevert, *A Nation in Barracks*, 249.
26. Bessel, *Nazism and War*, 24.
27. Frevert, *A Nation in Barracks*, 243.
28. Messerschmidt, 'The Wehrmacht in the National Socialist State', 174.
29. Kershaw, *Hitler*, 265; Messerschmidt, 'Die Wehrmacht als tragende Säule des NS-Staates', 40; Evans, *The Coming of the Third Reich*, 316–17; Hans-Erich Volkmann, 'Von Blomberg zu Keitel: Die Wehrmachtführung und die Demontage des Rechtsstaates', in Rolf-Dieter Müller and Hans-Erich Volkmann (eds), *Die Wehrmacht: Mythos und Realität* (Munich, 1999), 52–53; Kirstin A. Schäfer, *Werner von Blomberg: Hitlers erster Feldmarschall* (Paderborn, 2006), 441–46.
30. Bessel, *Nazism and War*, 35–37.
31. Deist, 'The Rearmament of the Wehrmacht', 550–52.
32. Schäfer, *Werner von Blomberg*, 100–13.
33. Jürgen Förster, 'Die Politisierung der Reichswehr/Wehrmacht', in *Das deutsche Reich und der Zweite Weltkrieg Band 9/1: Der deutsche Kriegsgesellschaft 1939 bis 1945* (Munich, 2004), 486.
34. Wette, *The Wehrmacht*, 69–70; Messerschmidt, 'Die Wehrmacht als tragende Säule des NS-Staates', 46–47; Schäfer, *Werner von Blomberg*, 122–25.
35. Brian Rigg, *Hitler's Jewish Soldiers* (Lawrence, 2002), 76–81.
36. Evans, *The Third Reich in Power*, 25.
37. Kershaw, *Hitler*, 318; Evans, *The Third Reich in Power*, 43; Schäfer, *Werner von Blomberg*, 152.
38. IfZ, Da 033.176a, Reichswehrministerium, *Reichswehr*.
39. Evans, *The Third Reich in Power*, 43.
40. O'Neill, *The German Army and the Nazi Party*, 39; Salewski, 'Wehrmacht und Nationalsozialismus', 57–58.
41. Salewski, 'Wehrmacht und Nationalsozialismus'.
42. Jürgen Förster, 'Complicity of Entanglement? Wehrmacht, War and Holocaust', in Michael Berenbaum and Abraham Peck (eds), *The Holocaust and History: The Known, the Unknown, the Disputed and the Reexamined* (Bloomington, 1998), 268–69.
43. Salewski, 'Wehrmacht und Nationalsozialismus', 57–58; Wette, *The Wehrmacht*, 73–75.
44. Wette, *The Wehrmacht*, 96.
45. O'Neill, *The German Army and the Nazi Party*, 55; Evans, *The Third Reich in Power*, 43.
46. Klaus Jürgen Müller (ed.), *Armee und Drittes Reich 1933–1939: Darstellung und Dokumentation* (Paderborn, 1989), 47–53.
47. Kershaw, *Hitler*, 304.

48. Messerschmidt, *Die Wehrmacht im NS-Staat*, 19; Salewski, 'Wehrmacht und Nationalsozialismus', 52; Wette, *The Wehrmacht*, 70–71; Schäfer, *Werner von Blomberg*, 122.
49. Jürgen Förster, '"Aber für die Juden wird auch noch die Stunde schlagen, und dann wehe ihnen!". Reichswehr und Antisemitismus', in Jürgen Matthäus and Klaus-Michael Mallman (eds), *Deutsche, Juden, Völkermord: Der Holocaust als Geschichte und Gegenwart* (Darmstadt, 2006), 28–29.
50. Frevert, *A Nation in Barracks*, 194–95, 252; Wette, *The Wehrmacht*, especially chapters one and two, 'Perceptions of Russia: The Soviet Union and Bolshevism as Enemies' and 'Anti-Semitism in the German Military'; Förster, '"Aber für die Juden wird auch noch die Stunde schlagen, und dann wehe ihnen!"'; Volker Berghahn, *Imperial Germany 1871–1914: Economy, Science, Culture and Politics* (Providence, 1994), 102–8; Messerschmidt, 'Die Wehrmacht als tragende Säule des NS-Staates', 44–45; Berger, *Eisernes Kreuz und Davidstern*, 182, 207–10.
51. Wette, *The Wehrmacht*, 31–32. See also Hans-Ulrich Wehler, *The German Empire 1871–1918* (Oxford, 1985), 102; John Horne and Alan Kramer, *German Atrocities, 1914: A History of Denial* (London, 2001), 153–61; Peter Pulzer, *Jews and the German State: The Political History of a Minority, 1848–1933* (Oxford, 1992), 115; Vejas Gabriel Liulevicius, *The German Myth of the East: 1800 to the Present* (Oxford, 2009), 149; Helmut Berding, 'Der Aufstieg des Antisemitismus im Ersten Weltkrieg', in Wolfgang Benz and Werner Bergmann (eds), *Vorurteil und Völkermord: Entwicklung des Antisemitismus* (Freiburg, 1997), 289–92.
52. Ben Shepherd, *Terror in the Balkans: German Armies and Partisan Warfare* (Cambridge, MA, 2012), 13.
53. Horne and Kramer, *German Atrocities*, 153–55; Frevert, *A Nation in Barracks*, 194–95.
54. Frevert, *A Nation in Barracks*, 194–95.
55. Ibid., 241.
56. Wette, *The Wehrmacht*, 42–69; Carsten, *The Reichswehr and Politics*, 37–132; Müller, *The Army, Politics and Society in Germany*, 25–27; Frevert, *A Nation in Barracks*, 241–44.
57. Frevert, *A Nation in Barracks*, 241–42; Shepherd, *Terror in the Balkans*, 57–58.
58. Carsten, *The Reichswehr and Politics*, 58–99.
59. Messerschmidt, 'Die Wehrmacht als tragende Säule des NS-Staates', 44–45; Frevert, *A Nation in Barracks*, 252; Wette, *The Wehrmacht*, 31–32; Martin Kitchen, *The German Officer Corps, 1890-1914* (Oxford, 1968), 46.
60. Pulzer, *Jews and the German State*, 23.
61. Evans, *The Coming of the Third Reich*, 31.
62. Berghahn, *Imperial Germany*, 102–6; Peter Pulzer, 'Die Jüdische Beteilung an der Politik', in Werner E. Mosse and Arnold Paucker (eds), *Juden in Wilhelmischen Deutschland 1890–1914* (Tübingen, 1976), 169–72; idem, *Jews and the German State*, 115.
63. Berghahn, *Imperial Germany*, 102–6; Wette, *The Wehrmacht*, 31–32; Berger, *Eisernes Kreuz und Davidstern*, 92; Pulzer, *Jews and the German State*, 115.
64. Messerschmidt, 'Die Wehrmacht als tragende Säule des NS-Staates', 44–45.
65. Berger, *Eisernes Kreuz und Davidstern*, 172; Pulzer, *Jews and the German State*, 205.
66. Berding, 'Der Aufstieg des Antisemitismus im Ersten Weltkrieg', 286–89; Noah Isenberg, *Between Redemption and Doom: The Strains of German-Jewish Modernism* (Lincoln, 1999), 54–55; Roger Chickering, *Imperial Germany and the Great War, 1914-1918* (Cambridge, 2004), 130.
67. Quoted in Berding, 'Der Aufstieg des Antisemitismus im Ersten Weltkrieg', 290.

28 • The Indoctrination of the Wehrmacht

68. Pulzer, *Jews and the German State*, 205. See also Wolfgang Benz and Werner Bergmann, 'Antisemitismus: Vorgeschichte des Völkermords?', in idem, *Vorurteil und Völkermord*, 21; Berding, 'Der Aufstieg des Antisemitismus im Ersten Weltkrieg', 291.
69. Wette, *The Wehrmacht*, 36–37; Berger, *Eisernes Kreuz und Davidstern*, 172–73; Pulzer, *Jews and the German State*, 205; Berding, 'Der Aufstieg des Antisemitismus im Ersten Weltkrieg', 291–92; Edgar Feuchtwanger, *Imperial Germany 1850–1918* (London, 2001), 182.
70. Wette, *The Wehrmacht*, especially chapters one and two, 'Perceptions of Russia: The Soviet Union and Bolshevism as Enemies', and 'Anti-Semitism in the German Military'; Förster, '"Aber für die Juden wird auch noch die Stunde schlagen, und dann wehe ihnen!"'; Chickering, *Imperial Germany and the Great War*, 130; Liulevicius, *The German Myth of the East*, 114–15; idem, *War Land on the Eastern Front: Culture, National Identity and German Occupation in World War I* (Cambridge, 2000), 1, 278–79; Benz and Bergmann, 'Antisemitismus: Vorgeschichte des Völkermords?', 12–21; Berding, 'Der Aufstieg des Antisemitismus im Ersten Weltkrieg', 302.
71. Berghahn, *Imperial Germany*, 106; Wette, *The Wehrmacht*, 34.
72. Liulevicius, *The German Myth of the East*, 115; Benz and Bergmann, 'Antisemitismus: Vorgeschichte des Völkermords?', 12; Pulzer, *Jews and the German State* , 3, 23; Wehler, *The German Empire*, 105–6; Shepherd, *Terror in the Balkans*, 18.
73. Liulevicius, *War Land on the Eastern Front*, 120.
74. Isenberg, *Between Redemption and Doom*, 55.
75. Ibid., 55–56.
76. Liulevicius, *War Land on the Eastern Front*, 1–5, 247.
77. Ibid., 25; idem, *The German Myth of the East*, 114; Wehler, *The German Empire*, 110.
78. Wehler, *The German Empire*, 140. See also Boris Barth, *Dolchstoßlegenden und politische Desintegration: Das Trauma der deutschen Niederlage im Ersten Weltkrieg 1914–1933* (Düsseldorf, 2003), 255.
79. Shepherd, *Terror in the Balkans*, 45–46.
80. Liulevicius, *War Land on the Eastern Front*, 9, 252–59.
81. Barth, *Dolchstoßlegenden und politische Desintegration*, 167, 223, 324–26; Chickering, *Imperial Germany and the Great War*, 189.
82. Chickering, *Imperial Germany and the Great War*, 190; Liulevicius, *War Land on the Eastern Front*, 219; Benz and Bergmann, 'Antisemitismus: Vorgeschichte des Völkermord?', 21–22.
83. Förster, '"Aber für die Juden wird auch noch die Stunde schlagen, und dann wehe ihnen!"', 30; Wette, *The Wehrmacht*, 40; Messerschmidt, 'Die Wehrmacht als tragende Säule des NS-Staates', 44–45; Pulzer, *Jews and the German State*, 271; idem, *The Rise of Political Anti-Semitism in Germany and Austria*, (Cambridge, 1968), 193.
84. Benz and Bergmann, 'Antisemitismus: Vorgeschichte des Völkermords?', 21–22.
85. Wette, *The Wehrmacht*, 40–41.
86. Förster, '"Aber für die Juden wird auch noch die Stunde schlagen, und dann wehe ihnen!"', 30.
87. Ibid., 22.
88. Wette, *The Wehrmacht*, 42–43; Förster, '"Aber für die Juden wird auch noch die Stunde schlagen, und dann wehe ihnen!"', 30.
89. Wette, *The Wehrmacht*, 43; Liulevicius, *War Lands on the Eastern Front*, 210; Shepherd, *Terror in the Balkans*, 49.
90. Förster, '"Aber für die Juden wird auch noch die Stunde schlagen, und dann wehe ihnen!"', 21; Berger, *Eisernes Kreuz und Davidstern*, 182.

91. Evans, *The Coming of the Third Reich*, 29–30, 70; Pulzer, *Jews and the German State*, 261; Werner Jochmann, 'Struktur und Funktion des deutschen Antisemitismus 1878–1914', in Wolfgang Benz and Werner Bergmann (eds), *Vorurteil und Völkermord* (Freiburg: Herder, 1997), 214–15.
92. Demeter, *The German Officer Corps*, 220; O'Neill, *The German Army and the Nazi Party*, 75; Frevert, *A Nation in Barracks*, 187–88; Shepherd, *Terror in the Balkans*, 27.
93. Evans, *The Coming of the Third Reich*, 75; Berding, 'Der Aufstieg des Antisemitismus im Ersten Weltkrieg', 290; Berger, *Eisernes Kreuz und Davidstern*, 209.
94. Wette, *The Wehrmacht*, 67–69; Messerschmidt, 'Die Wehrmacht als tragende Säule des NS-Staates', 44.
95. Wette, *The Wehrmacht*, 40.
96. Ian Kershaw, 'How Effective was Nazi Propaganda?', in David Welch (ed.), *Nazi Propaganda: The Power and the Limitations* (London, 1983), 182–83; see also David Welch, *The Third Reich: Politics and Propaganda* (London, 1993), 59.

Chapter 2

THE GOALS AND EFFECTS OF INDOCTRINATION

Ian Kershaw's assertion about the potential success of Nazi propaganda raises an important issue. To analyse the programme of ideological education that the German military was to implement, as well as the impact that it may have had upon soldiers, it is important to establish a theoretical framework. The focus of this framework is the process of indoctrination: the ways in which an organisation imposes and inculcates its ideology. This chapter will examine studies on indoctrination itself, particularly those concerning military organisations. Many of the theoretical concepts and practical examples raised provide important insights into the methods used by militaries to condition people to act in a manner conducive to the aims of the organisation they serve. The studies cited also investigate how specifically trained subjects act under the psychological and physical stresses of battle.[1]

There are a number of common features of studies of indoctrination and combat psychology. These include the control over information and communication, the loading and manipulation of language, the destruction or nullification of one's individuality, and the dehumanisation of both the enemy and those being indoctrinated.

Robert Jay Lifton carried out one of the best-known studies on indoctrination in his book *Thought Reform and the Psychology of Totalism*, which examined the indoctrination that American prisoners of war underwent during the Korean War.[2] Lifton asserted that control over communication is the most important feature of 'thought reform'. He argued that this is the 'psychological current upon which all else depends'.[3] One of the goals of a totalitarian organisation is to produce an environment in which it has as much control as possible over what its subjects hear, read and experience. This, according to Lifton, exerts an inordinate amount of pressure upon people's independence of thought and action. It deprives them of any external, independent information they can use to question what they are being told, and makes it extremely difficult to maintain an independent and separate sense of identity.[4]

The notion of a controlled environment in which access to information is strictly regulated is plainly visible within the German military. The military was situated within the totalitarian environment of Nazi Germany, where the regime placed a heavy emphasis upon propaganda, and also placed severe restrictions on the content of radio broadcasts, newspapers, film and magazines.[5] Within the closed-off world of the army barracks, and indeed while away at the front, soldiers were isolated from civilian society, as well as their friends and families, for extended periods of time. The military, as this book will demonstrate, exerted control over all forms of education on political matters. It also controlled, to a great degree, the media available to soldiers through its distribution of heavily propagandised, compulsory newspapers and magazines that presented a censored, blinkered view of the world and the soldier's role in it, insulating them from outside opinions and information that could challenge what they were being taught by the army. Within such an environment, people's opinions are more likely to become influenced by indoctrination than otherwise, particularly the young, who are constantly bombarded with the dominant ideology.[6] Furthermore, people finding themselves in such a situation have little or no recourse to validate the information they continually encounter, since no other veritable and competing sources of information are present.[7]

A further aspect that exerts pressure on individuals is the group setting. Adam Lankford adds a number of factors that further support Lifton's theory of the importance of 'milieu control', arguing that insulated environments help to accentuate the importance of the group setting. The segregation of military recruits from society meant they would often have had day-to-day contact only with other members of the military. This makes life particularly difficult for anyone placing themselves outside the social norms of the group. Lankford argues that 'new recruits to almost any organisation have a strong desire to fit in' and that this 'craving for social approval ... can make them more willing to adopt the group's prejudicial norms'.[8]

Denise Winn concurs with this notion, asserting that such an environment creates a situation where the pressure for consensus within the group often inhibits dissent. Psychologist Irving Janis agrees, with the military unit a prime example of such a group.[9] In such a setting, group norms can easily be established and adhered to, even when the members of the group have no connection with each other.[10] People's need to be one with a group in such contexts is often a way of gaining social approval, particularly within a segregated, unfamiliar and harsh setting like the military.[11]

Hugo Slim also argues that group and institutional environments influence behaviour among individuals, contending that they often 'lose their grip on their individual moral preferences and submit to wider social pressures'.[12] Such conformity is often a type of coping process. Winn argues that such settings often lead to individuals undergoing changes in attitudes and behaviour in order to measure up. In her study *An Intimate History of Killing*, Joanna Bourke argues that being part of a group, particularly in a military setting, can 'reduce inhibitions about the expression of aggression' and encourage a 'return to primitive forms of behaviour'.[13]

The importance of conformity leads to the process of breaking down the individual. This involves nullifying as much as possible the individual's sense of self, and side-lining personal values. In their place, the norms of the organisation become dominant. The individual no longer matters; only the group, and its ideology, does. Lankford uses the term 'deindividuation' to describe this process. Military organisations place particular emphasis on this process in order to foster obedience and accord in attitudes towards notions like the state, ideology and the enemy. By discouraging the capacity of soldiers to act as thoughtful individuals with the willingness to question authority and act independently, it intends to immerse soldiers in their duties within a collective force, taking away their sense of individuality and subjugating them to the organisation of which they are to become a tool.[14]

Many of the activities undertaken in militaries are about inculcating such an attitude. Individuals are broken down to be rebuilt into efficient fighting men, through the use of uniforms, lack of privacy, strict schedules and arbitrarily harsh regulations and punishments.[15] One British soldier described his training during the First World War as consisting of constant abuse that sought to 'reduce each man to a condition where he was amenable to any command'.[16] Frevert's study of the German military reveals that abuse and humiliation were a common feature of training from well before the Third Reich. She asserts:

> nearly all biographical accounts contain reports of humiliations and personal abasement, particularly in the first year. The army approach followed precisely the same method used in all other 'total institutions' where' ... individuals are cut off from points of reference to their lives outside and prior to the institution. Immediately after entering the army, a process began in trimming and programming, stripping and levelling, leaving the newcomers devoid of the previous identity ... [the recruits] then started on complex procedures that were to transform the civilian into a member of the armed forces'.[17]

Claudia Koonz has argued that before the Second World War, members of Nazi organisations experienced an environment that combined the above-described 'rigorous Prussian military traditions' and a 'distinctively Nazi concept of racial war'. This resulted in people becoming 'resocialised' and 'disinhibited', with many of them taking on numerous elements of Nazi ideology.[18] This is part of a process that leads to the dehumanisation of soldiers, which was a prominent feature of training within the Wehrmacht. The end effect of this is the creation of psychological distance between soldiers and their actions. In the Wehrmacht, not only was the individual broken down, but people were actively trained to forget or ignore their humane instincts (which were portrayed as signs of weakness and cowardice, and even as a betrayal to one's *Volk* and nation) and to replace them with instincts that National Socialism championed, like ruthlessness and brutality, particularly against certain racial groups.

The dehumanisation process is, however, a bilateral one. Military training also involves a systematic attempt to dehumanise the enemy. This process is also linked to the notion of group mentality. Since members of organisations become part of a collective, people who are outside of, and indeed enemies of the group, must be made to appear as different to the group as possible.[19] In the case of Germany's war on the Eastern Front, dehumanisation of the enemy 'allowed all the other steps for the regression of warfare to take place'.[20]

The very objective of a soldier is to kill the enemy. Yet it is not easy for people to kill, unless they feel they are somehow threatened, or that the enemy is less human than they are: 'the first step in getting human beings to kill people is to make them think that they are killing something else'.[21] Dehumanising the enemy aims to convince soldiers that they are fighting an adversary that is less human, and as different as possible to them. This creates a psychological distance between soldiers and the enemy. Soldiers are less able to identify with, and thus empathise with those whom they view as being completely different or inferior. This makes it easier to act violently towards the 'enemy', since they would not feel as though they were engaged with real human beings.[22] Soldiers behave much more aggressively in conflicts where they see the enemy as being fundamentally 'different'. The conduct of Allied soldiers in the Second World War is a prime example. Their behaviour towards Japanese soldiers was very different to when they faced Germans or Italians.[23] During the war in the Pacific, Allied propaganda sought to capitalise upon the obvious physical and cultural differences between Allied and Japanese troops and emphasised the 'otherness' of the Japanese. In a classic example of an 'extreme construction of enmity that dehumanises the enemy group',[24] it referred to them as sub-human 'vermin' in need of extermination, and alleged that they possessed a completely alien mind-set.[25] Dower argues that this profoundly affected the behaviour of Allied troops, who were involved in countless cases of wanton violence against Japanese troops and, later, civilians.[26] Shalit and Bourke also point to the Vietnam War, arguing that the numerous atrocities that US soldiers committed were related to the notion of psychological distance existing between American soldiers and the racially alien, supposedly uncivilised Vietnamese enemy who was fighting for a political system seemingly antagonistic to the American one.[27] One Marine who was involved in atrocities recalled:

> It wasn't like they were humans. We were conditioned to believe that this was for the good of the nation … and anything we did was okay. And when you shot someone you didn't think you were shooting at a human. They were a gook or a commie and it was okay.[28]

The enemy's status as 'outsiders' to the group is often presented as an existential threat.[29] Such thinking places all members of an 'enemy' people within a 'single and very general identity as a member of a group – an absolute and undifferentiated enemy'.[30] While dehumanising the enemy and inculcating the attitude required to kill enemy soldiers without hesitation is a common feature of almost all military training,[31] ideological schooling within the Wehrmacht went further. It made no distinctions between enemy soldiers and civilians, and as we will see, soldiers were trained to take part in a conflict in which unarmed civilians and prisoners of war, who could not have posed a physical threat to them, were perceived as legitimate targets due to their ethnicity or political beliefs.

A further aspect of the indoctrination process is the manipulation of language. This feature connects all other aspects of indoctrination. The exaggerations, illusions and subterfuge upon which indoctrination and propaganda depend are themselves reliant upon the careful structuring of language.

A common characteristic of language in a totalitarian setting is the 'thought terminating cliché'. In this context, complicated, multi-faceted issues are often spoken about, but never carefully analysed. They are condensed into 'brief, highly reductive, definitive sounding phrases, easily memorised and easily expressed', acting as 'interpretative shortcuts' that become representative of either ultimate good or ultimate evil.[32] The purpose of such loaded language is to bypass critical thinking and to steer thoughts towards the simplistic representation endorsed by the indoctrinating organisation. Such language is often repetitive, jargon-based and ultimately constrictive. Lifton argues that since language is so central to thoughts and experiences, one's capacity for thinking and feeling is narrowed in such a totalitarian environment.[33] Wehrmacht ideological education provided numerous examples demonstrative of the 'thought terminating cliché', as well as the categorisation of issues and people using 'ultimate terms', most prominently 'Jewish Bolsheviks' or simply 'Jewry'.

A further linguistic facet of the German military's communication was the vagueness of language that characterised many aspects of its indoctrination and command of its men. While there was a definite and easily recognisable tone and message behind the educational curriculum of the German military, it very rarely made explicit, specific commands. Furthermore, the image of the enemy, particularly the enemy that Germany was fighting in the East, was not made clear and specific. While the military made countless statements about the enemy, their identity was somewhat blurred and open to broad interpretation. Military propaganda did not precisely define who was a legitimate target for elimination, or who exactly the enemy was and who they were not. Nor did it set any boundaries for what was acceptable behaviour.

Ambiguity in orders and training can be a deliberate component of the military command structure that helps to shape the behaviour of soldiers in the field. Shalit argues that ambiguity of information is a tool used by militaries to influence outcomes, since vague information provided by commanders adds to the confusion that soldiers feel in the chaos of battle. Military training is based upon the notion that many situations in which soldiers find themselves will be new, confusing and unstructured. Within this context, a soldier needs to make sense of the situation and react to it as quickly as possible, often with reference only to their military training. This training is fashioned so that it shapes responses to such unfamiliar situations in a particular way, creating reference points for soldiers to refer to in chaotic situations that they would never encounter in civilian life. The more ambiguous and stressful the situation, 'the more important are the general belief systems of a soldier in determining the appraisal process ... when there is a perceived lack of objective information it is supplemented by subjective information'.[34]

Within the context of the Wehrmacht, this framework suggests that indoctrination provided soldiers with reference points in relation to a number of situations that they were likely to encounter. This may have included encounters with ethnically unfamiliar people, with local civilians engaged in unconventional forms of resistance regarded as 'underhand', or with people designated as enemies due to their physical appearance or political associations. For many, the reference points provided by their training would often have been the only ones, or at least the most familiar and relevant ones, that they would have had for such situations.

***

The method by which indoctrination is conducted is also a crucial aspect of this discussion. How is the dehumanisation of the enemy, the manipulation of language, the breaking down of the individual and, ultimately, the influencing of beliefs and behaviour made more effective? Importantly, to what extent can indoctrination shape attitudes? Psychiatrist James A.C. Brown believes that while people's deepest attitudes, which develop during childhood, rarely alter, less entrenched attitudes, which he denotes as 'opinions', are subject to change:

> Opinions are but briefly held and likely to reflect current public feeling; in many cases they reflect rather what the individual thinks he should feel than what, in fact, he does feel. They are readily changeable and may be susceptible either to propaganda or to reasoned argument.[35]

Brown further asserts that social forces have a powerful effect, particularly in totalitarian societies:

> The individual will accept a belief … because the belief has become orthodox and it is natural to conform, unless he is prepared to become a social outcast. Thus in a communist community brainwashing is likely to work but is hardly necessary, since in the long run people tend to conform because they are social.[36]

Indoctrination itself can, according to I.A. Snook, appear very similar to teaching. However, a number of the methods involved in indoctrination set it apart, as do the differences in the effects between teaching and indoctrination. Both teaching and indoctrination can involve questions and discussion, even debate and argument between teachers and pupils. However, in indoctrination, such conversations are held only in order to arrive at conclusions predetermined by those in charge. Indoctrination is also conducted in an environment in which the instructor has a high level of authority over their subjects. While almost all forms of teaching involve some level of authority, indoctrination takes this to another level. Instructors usually have physical control and are possessed of a status that would incline people to regard them as authorities that are worth listening to on particular subjects.[37] Ideological instructors in the German armed forces displayed all of these traits. They were higher in rank and more experienced in the military than the young recruits were, and they had complete coercive authority and physical control over them as authority figures, being military men in a nation in which the military had traditionally held an exceptionally prestigious and revered position.[38] Furthermore, in many cases, supposed 'experts' were brought in to deliver specific lessons; for instance, high-ranking SS officials and doctors would deliver lectures on race relations and racial hygiene.[39]

Numerous theorists argue that the effects of teaching and indoctrination also differ, albeit in surprisingly subtle ways. According to Thomas F. Green, those who form their beliefs by indoctrination will be able to explain the reasoning and evidence behind their opinions. Green contends, however, that this is not because the subject has thought deeply about their opinions or the reasoning behind them, having weighed up numerous sources of possibly conflicting evidence. Instead, their reasoning and evidence is merely a regurgitation of the reasoning and evidence involved in the indoctrination process.[40] This is often reflected by the subject's ignorance of the thinking behind other opinions, or indeed unwillingness to consider any other opinion.[41]

Numerous aspects of Nazi indoctrination resembled 'teaching'. While they were a constant presence, it was not a case of merely repeating slogans and clichés. Nor was it a matter of simply stating beliefs without providing evidence and reasoning behind them. It was more sophisticated than that. For many of the tenets of Nazi ideology, an abundance of 'evidence' was cited, and military recruits were encouraged to learn more about the wider context of political questions, and to become as 'informed' as possible about them. In the official training syllabus, this often took the form of 'historical evidence' that justified the Nazi positions relating to *Lebensraum*, ethnic cleansing, the destruction of the terms of the Treaty of Versailles and the fervent hatred and fear of Slavs, 'Jewish Bolshevism' and the Soviet Union. Tracts of 'scientific evidence', in the form of articles, lectures or presentations delivered by high-ranking scientists, justified the various forms of racism that existed in policies relating to eugenics and antisemitism.[42] Koonz has also argued that 'racial propaganda had to emanate from apparently objective sources'; 'knowledge' or 'science' were better able to influence people than 'propaganda'.[43]

The indoctrination process is also greatly assisted if it begins early. An individual's upbringing and socialisation help to instil a set of beliefs while they are too young to question them. Younger people often have limited perceptions and restricted sources of information, making them more vulnerable to outside influence. A childhood and youth that involves indoctrination further assists this process, as it strengthens and narrows one's point of view at a crucial stage of life. This can often create a dependence on the belief system in which a person grows up.[44] The Nazi regime targeted German youth from a very young age and, in effect, did not leave them alone throughout their childhood, youth and early adulthood. In this way, by the time those who grew up during the Third Reich had reached maturity and been conscripted into the military, they had undergone a socialisation strongly influenced by Nazi institutions. The regime intended to 'envelop the individual at every stage of development within a single organisation by subjecting him to a planned course of indoctrination'.[45]

The vulnerability of children extends beyond their increased susceptibility to propaganda itself; young people are particularly vulnerable to pressure to conform by peers and older authority figures.[46] Moreover, they are also likely to be less certain of their beliefs and the facts that inform them, making them more vulnerable to influence.[47] Indeed, the very process of growing into adulthood involves gaining a sense of self and a sense of individuality, which helps to make people more certain and secure about their beliefs. It also involves developing the ability to think critically. The Hitler Youth, the Reich Labour Service and the German armed forces deliberately sought to hinder these processes through their active use of methods that 'deindividualised' and dehumanised members of the organisation. The notion of the younger, or 'Hitler Youth generation' of soldiers being more likely to embrace Nazi ideology has been strongly argued by Omer Bartov in his work on the armed forces.[48]

The theoretical framework set out above gives an outline of the aspects of indoctrination and combat psychology that are relevant to this study. The following chapters will demonstrate that these characteristics were present in the educational methods and content utilised by the Wehrmacht in the political schooling of its troops.

Notes

1. Robert J. Lifton, *Thought Reform and the Psychology of Totalism: A Study of 'Brainwashing' in China* (London, 1961); E.S. Williams (ed.), *The Soviet Military: Political Education, Training and Morale* (Basingstoke, 1987); Denise Winn, *The Manipulated Mind: Brainwashing, Conditioning and Indoctrination* (London, 1983); Claudia Koonz, *The Nazi Conscience* (Cambridge, MA, 2006); Ben Shalit, *The Psychology of Conflict and Combat* (New York, 1988); Eyal Ben-Ari, *Mastering Soldiers: Conflicts, Emotions and the Enemy in an Israeli Military Unit* (London, 1998); Hugo Slim, *Killing Civilians: Method, Madness and Morality in War* (London, 2007); Joanna Bourke, *An Intimate History of Killing: Face-to-Face Killing in Twentieth Century Warfare* (London, 1999); Kathleen Taylor, *Brainwashing: The Science of Thought Control* (Oxford, 2004); Adam Lankford, *Human Killing Machines* (Plymouth, 2009); Gregory G. Dimjian, 'Warfare, Genocide, and Ethnic Conflict: A Darwinian Approach', *Baylor University Medical Center Proceedings* 23(3) (July 2010), 292–300; Ian Kershaw, 'How Effective Was Nazi Propaganda?', in David Welch (ed.), *Nazi Propaganda: The Power and the Limitations* (London, 1983), 180–205; David Welch, *The Third Reich: Politics and Propaganda* (London, 1993).

2. Lifton, *Thought Reform and the Psychology of Totalism*.
3. Ibid., 420.
4. Ibid., 421.
5. Richard J. Evans, *The Third Reich in Power* (London, 2006), 120–49; see also Welch, *The Third Reich*.
6. Lifton, *Thought Reform and the Psychology of Totalism*, 420.
7. Hans Toch, quoted in Winn, *The Manipulated Mind*, 37–38.
8. Lankford, *Human Killing Machines*, 17.
9. Ibid., 34–37, 112–14.
10. Winn, *The Manipulated Mind*, 112–14.
11. Ibid., 110–12.
12. Slim, *Killing Civilians*, 221.
13. Bourke, *An Intimate History of Killing*, 98–99.
14. Lankford, *Human Killing Machines*, 130.
15. Bourke, *An Intimate History of Killing*, 79.
16. Ibid., 80.
17. Ute Frevert, *A Nation in Barracks: Modern Germany, Military Conscription and Civil Society* (New York, 2004), 182–83.
18. Koonz, *The Nazi Conscience*, 221–22.
19. Shalit, *The Psychology of Conflict and Combat*, 48–68.
20. Mary R. Habeck, 'The Modern and the Primitive: Barbarity and Warfare on the Eastern Front', in George Kassimeris (ed.), *The Barbarisation of Warfare* (London, 2006), 85.
21. Slim, *Killing Civilians*, 217.
22. Lankford, *Human Killing Machines*, 24; Shalit, *The Psychology of Conflict and Combat*, 48–68; Dimjian, 'Warfare, Genocide, and Ethnic Conflict', 293–94.
23. Shalit, *The Psychology of Conflict and Combat*, 48.
24. Slim, *Killing Civilians*, 217.
25. John W. Dower, *War without Mercy: Race and Power in the Pacific War* (New York, 1993), 71, see also 86–89, 19–20.
26. Ibid.
27. Ibid., 48.
28. Bourke, *An Intimate History of Killing*, 205.
29. Lankford, *Human Killing Machines*, 19–24.
30. Slim, *Killing Civilians*, 125.
31. Koonz, *The Nazi Conscience*, 221.
32. Lifton, *Thought Reform and the Psychology of Totalism*, 429.
33. Ibid., 430.
34. Shalit, *The Psychology of Conflict and Combat*, 20.
35. James A.C. Brown, quoted in Winn, *The Manipulated Mind*, 29–30.
36. Ibid., 34.
37. I.A. Snook, 'Indoctrination and Moral Responsibility', in idem (ed.), *Concepts of Indoctrination: Philosophical Essays* (London, 1972), 152–54.
38. Frevert, *A Nation in Barracks*.
39. See, for example, Bundesarchiv/Militärarchiv, Freiburg (hereafter BA/MA) RW6/161, *Erster nationalpolitischer Lehrgang für Lehrer der Kriegsschulen, Akademien usw vom 17.1.37 bis 23.1.37 in Berlin* and BA/MA RW 6/V. 166, *Sommer-Lehrgang für Offiziere in Bad Tölz:* 'Vortragsreihe über nationalsozialistische Weltanschauung und Zielsetzung vom 11.-17.6.1939 in Bad Tölz'.
40. Thomas F. Green, 'Indoctrination and Beliefs', in Snook, *Concepts of Indoctrination*, 38.

41. Ibid.
42. See BA/MA RW 6/V. 166, *Sommer-Lehrgang für Offiziere in Bad Tölz*.
43. Koonz, *The Nazi Conscience*, 13.
44. Green, 'Indoctrination and Beliefs', 37–38.
45. Welch, *The Third Reich*, 61.
46. Lankford, *Human Killing Machines*, 52; Snook, *Concepts of Indoctrination*, 154–55.
47. Winn, *The Manipulated Mind*, 36–37.
48. See Omer Bartov, *Hitler's Army: Soldiers, Nazis and War in the Third Reich* (Oxford, 1991).

Chapter 3

The Beginnings of Nazi Ideological Education in the Wehrmacht

From the beginning of the Third Reich, the German military became an increasingly politicised organisation. The process by which this occurred has been well documented in some of the standard works on the armed forces during this period.[1] These studies are, however, relatively uninterested in how these developments affected the experience of the lower ranks, or in their possible connection to the participation of members of the Wehrmacht in atrocities during the Second World War. Fostering a 'Nazified' military was a process that involved, to differing degrees, all levels of the armed forces, not just the higher-ranking members of the officer corps who dealt with the Nazi Party.

A critical part of this process was the programme of political schooling that the armed forces implemented for its troops. It was perhaps the clearest indication of the intentions of the armed forces minister, General Werner von Blomberg. Blomberg wanted the army's Nazification to go well beyond its alignment with the party at the level of the high command and the ministry, as well as its adoption of numerous Nazi laws and symbols. As this chapter will illustrate, he wanted the army to become a highly politicised fighting force, and he viewed the education of the rank and file as the most crucial step in achieving this goal.

It is, in fact, unsurprising that Blomberg should look to education as a key area. He was highly experienced in the matter of military training. He had spent many years as chief of the army's educational department, having been appointed by Hans von Seeckt in 1925.[2] As the Nazi Party would be responsible for the indoctrination of the civilian population (although as we will see, civilian and military propaganda efforts were to overlap and complement each other), Blomberg saw that the military leadership would have to take responsibility for training its soldiers and officers in the supposed virtues of Nazism. It also had to ensure that they were aware of how Nazism impacted their own role; their support of the Nazi regime and its ideology was to become an important part of their duty as members of the armed forces.[3]

In one sense, the notion of implementing political training was not a radically new concept in the German military. While the new regime required a much more intense engagement with politics than in previous contexts, knowledge of the political and legal aspects of the regime they served had long been an essential part of training in the German army, for officers in particular.

Jörg Muth carried out an extensive study of officer training in the German armed forces during the first four decades of the twentieth century. While his work focuses primarily upon tactical effectiveness, rather than ideological schooling and war crimes, he does reveal that officers received in-depth instruction and testing on political and legal matters well before 1933.[4] So wide-ranging was the education they received that Muth argues that officer training more closely resembled a university than a strictly military school.[5] During the Weimar Republic, for instance, officer candidates were trained and tested in civics and history, and were required to be well versed in the constitutional law of both the Weimar Republic and Imperial Germany. In compulsory testing that decided whether a candidate would advance further towards becoming an officer, civics questions had a multiplier of two, compared to four for military tactics.[6] One exam in 1931, for instance, asked officers to answer questions such as, 'How is the idea of the rule of the people realised in the constitution?', as well as writing about the implications for German national security of the eastern German borders set by the Versailles Treaty. If a German officer wanted to be commissioned, and then to rise up the ranks, he had to be not only tactically and organisationally adept, but also politically knowledgeable.[7]

It was therefore not unprecedented for German military training to include the teaching of non-military topics. Nor was it unprecedented for officers to be required to have deep and extensive knowledge of political topics. Indeed, the fact that many of the officers who were members of the armed forces during the period of changeover between the Weimar Republic and the Third Reich had undergone such extensive political training indicates that many, if not all, would have been aware of what Nazi ideological training would mean for the military, and how it could potentially affect the way in which the army operated. Furthermore, as Muth points out, this education's presence during the Weimar Republic demonstrates that German officers would have been well aware of the implications of Hitler's policies once he came to power. This in itself suggests much about the support or acquiescence that so many of them displayed.[8]

It did not take long for Blomberg's efforts in establishing political training to play a role in the lives of those ranked well below him. A few months after the Nazis assumed power, soldiers needed only to pick up the armed forces weekly newspaper to become conscious of the expectations that the military leadership had of their role under the new regime. The 18 August 1933 edition of the military weekly contained the lead article 'The Soldier and the National Revolution'. The article stated that 'an understanding of National Socialism is a must for every officer. It is completely out of the question for an officer not to have read the Führer's book, *Mein Kampf*.[9]

The most important aspect of the politicisation of the lower ranks of the military was established soon afterwards in the form of a political training programme for troops. In April 1934, Blomberg ordered that frequent lessons about 'political questions' were to become compulsory for the entire military. The high command would regularly distribute guidelines and lessons in the military districts, which were directly responsible for the training of soldiers, as well as their recruitment. Ideological training was to become another part of the regular, planned training of officers and soldiers. Company commanders and officers in charge of recruits were to draw upon the materials distributed by the high command to train their men.[10] A year later, Blomberg issued a directive stating that the content of this educational material was 'just as binding as any other official instruction',[11] and as critical as any other kind of training that soldiers were to receive during their period of service, stating:

> The Wehrmacht can only fulfil its responsibilities within our race and state if, with complete inner conviction, it possesses and achieves spiritual unity with National Socialism, the guiding force of German racial and national life. I therefore place great importance upon the coherent political education and instruction … of the three branches of the armed forces.[12]

In turn, the lower ranks received regular political schooling as part of their training. Blomberg's war ministry edited and distributed booklets and manuals that served as the main source of teaching material in the barracks. Senior military officers, as well as SS officers and doctors, and other officials from various branches of the party, such as the Hitler Youth or Reich Labour Service, authored the articles within them. Likewise, the subjects were taught by officers or members of other Nazi organisations. Anyone who taught in the Wehrmacht schools, even those who taught non-ideological subjects, had, by order of General von Blomberg, to be a member of the National Socialist Teachers' League.[13]

In keeping with the goals set out by the new 'guiding force of German racial and national life', the 'leadership responsibilities' that the high command viewed fit for the Wehrmacht to carry out were reflected in the material distributed to officers in charge of training courses on military bases. As early as 1935, the content of the curriculum covered topics such as 'The National Socialist world-view' and 'The military as the instrument of the Führer's political will'.

It had also begun the process of dehumanising those considered by the Nazi regime to be 'outsiders'. The educational material sought to foster aggression towards those considered different, presenting these 'others' as existential threats. Manuals typical of this effort included 'The Protection of the German Race' and 'The Ordering of the German People's Land',[14] which propagated the need to conquer *Lebensraum* in the East,[15] indicating an effort to instil the idea of viewing Eastern Europe in terms of '"races and spaces" to be ordered by German mastery'.[16] Many manuals targeted Jews in particular. Examples included 'The Destructive Influence of Jews' and 'The Genocidal Jewish Bolshevist Regime in Moscow'. They referred to Jews as 'parasites' who needed to be 'radically eliminated from the sphere of German life'. The curriculum also spoke of the soldiers' task of combating 'World Jewry' beyond Germany's borders, and of their task of implementing a 'new, radical solution to the Jewish question'.[17]

In 1936, for example, the war ministry set out the topics to be covered during a course of 'national political lessons', illustrated in this excerpt from a booklet distributed in May of that year:

> The content of a national political course for a class of military trainees is to be divided into four main sections:
>
> 1. The National Socialist Movement
> 2. The protection of the German race
> 3. The rebuilding of the Reich
> 4. The securing of the economy.[18]

A military instructional course that placed as much emphasis upon a political movement and its pseudo-scientific racial theories as it did upon the nation's foreign policy and economic security indicated the type of military that the war minister was setting out to create, and the type of role that a German soldier was being trained to carry out.

The war ministry, as well as leaders of the regime, made efforts to stress the extent of political responsibility that the armed forces were to have under the new government. Indeed, it was to constitute a role that would run parallel to the efforts of the Nazi Party's paramilitary wings, the SS and SA. To indicate this, the 23 May 1936 edition of *Wehrmacht Guidelines for Lessons in Everyday Political Questions*[19] featured a speech that Hermann Göring delivered to a gathering of SS, SA and Wehrmacht soldiers and officers. Perhaps in an attempt not only to stress the unity of purpose of the three organisations, but also to encourage them to move past the deep fissures between the SA and military that occurred in 1934, Göring asserted that:

> Our Führer's idea, our ideology ... gives us a strong feeling of belonging together, we soldiers of the Wehrmacht and we men of the black and brown orders [the SS and SA]. We belong together ... the mighty idea of National Socialism unites us, it binds us together. The military ... stands with us in the movement ... we are all filled with the knowledge of National Socialism.[20]

The reintroduction of conscription in 1935 saw important developments in the role that the armed forces were to play in indoctrinating their men. Since all young men would now be undertaking military service, Blomberg saw this as an opportunity for the armed forces to become not only the nation's defence force, but also its most important indoctrinator of the German people in the merits of Nazism,[21] announcing in a directive in April 1935 that the military was to become 'the nation's great educational school'.[22] Military service became designated as the 'last, and highest step' in the education and development of young men that took place within the wider framework of Nazi society, which began at home, and progressed through school, the Hitler Youth and the Labour Service.[23]

The military sought to customise the role that it would come to play in indoctrinating young recruits and longer-serving officers alike within this broader context. It tailored training in order to build upon earlier indoctrination, and sought to avoid excessive overlap and repetition of the curricula of the Hitler Youth and Labour Service, which many of the recruits would have passed through before being drafted into the military. Some correspondence within the military indicates that many recruits showed enthusiasm for both military service and Nazism itself:

> We receive recruits who come to the armed forces full of the best intentions, ready for action, enthusiastic, and also politically educated ... These German youths have a strong trust in the army, they see in it an ideal training ground, and expect to gain the last step in their education in the service of the new national community.[24]

This may have been overly optimistic, however. It soon became apparent that significant variations in political consciousness existed and that the military would have an important role to play in the socialisation of young men. This belief came about when many entrants to the armed forces, particularly once conscription had begun, displayed a disappointing lack of ideological conviction, or even the most basic knowledge of the principles of Nazism.[25] The wide cross-section of society represented by conscripts produced variations in social class, religious denomination and regional background. This presented a significant challenge. It would not be a case of the military simply furthering the training of an influx of eager young followers of Nazism. Evidence of this is present in a speech during a military conference on ideological training in Berlin, in January 1937. In the speech, an officer named Major Streit stated that the military should not be complacent about incoming recruits: 'It is not true, as is often remarked, that all of today's youth come into our ranks with an enthusiastic belief in National Socialism. It is more often the case that a portion of the youths must be trained by us in order to become convinced by National Socialism'.[26]

In another piece that prefaced a political education manual, a senior Reich Labour Service official justified the volume and intensity of indoctrination carried out in the military by writing of his experience with conscripts coming to the Reich Labour Service for the first time:

> Neither the youth organisations nor the schools have prepared all of these young people properly. After all, people come to our camp who, on their way here, are travelling on a train for the first time ... and the most curious things happen. When they see a picture of the Führer, they will ask, 'Who's that?' There are young people who don't know who the Führer is. But they seem to know about other supposedly important personalities. The question has often been asked, 'Why is the only important man missing? Where is the picture of the pope?'[27]

Such statements were supported by internal surveys conducted within the Reich Labour Service, which illustrated that such ignorance of Nazism was widespread. One survey revealed that one in four members of the Reich Labour Service could not answer the most basic questions about the Nazi regime.[28] A further Reich Labour Service report, dated 18 January 1936, stated:

> ... political immaturity and inexperience is ... sometimes staggering. Many have hardly any knowledge or concern over the events that followed the year 1918; and about the events of the past 3 years, for the most part the men have only a vague idea; a worryingly large portion of the men know very

little of National Socialist ideology ... The low level of political knowledge becomes clear through the numerous cases of recruits who do not recognise a picture of the Führer, or who do not know the names of the most prominent National Socialists.[29]

The most likely explanation for large numbers of youths displaying an ignorance of Nazism is that they were members of a cohort joining these organisations before the onset of compulsory service in the Hitler Youth and the Labour Service. In effect, the age group dominant in the earliest Wehrmacht recruitment drives may not have had experience in either organisation. While many boys were compelled to join the Hitler Youth, with around 30.5 per cent of those between the ages of ten and eighteen being members in 1933, and around 64 per cent in 1937, it was not compulsory until early 1939.[30] This posed a problem for the military during this early stage of its effort to impart Nazi ideology within its ranks. The Reich Labour Service presented a similar problem. A year of labour service became compulsory for all young men in 1935. This reveals that while practically all recruits in the later years of the regime, and particularly during the war years, would have served in these organisations, and thus experienced considerable ideological indoctrination, the earliest conscripts to the military were not necessarily former members of these organisations.

Those who voluntarily joined the military before conscription was reintroduced, however, did not reflect this trend of ideological ignorance. During the early stages of the Third Reich, before the regime had introduced compulsory service for youths in Nazi organisations, the military began rapidly increasing its membership. While doing so, it sought out information about the kind of men who were entering the military. More specifically, it sought to determine how they might react to Nazi ideological education. In order to gauge this, senior officers carried out personnel surveys of incoming recruits.

One such survey was undertaken at the end of 1934.[31] The timing of this survey allows an insight into the demographic of recruits who were joining the army voluntarily, and during a period before the onset of compulsory Hitler Youth and Reich Labour Service membership. Wishing to know what kind of men the Wehrmacht would be training, war minister Werner von Blomberg sent out a directive to the leaders of the three branches of the armed forces, ordering them to conduct a survey of their men to gather information about their backgrounds. The survey was to cover all those who had joined the armed forces from 1 October 1933 until 1 November 1934, a time in which a large recruitment drive took place and, importantly, the year before conscription was instated.[32] It posed six questions:

- How many of the men came from the occupied Saar region?
- How many came from a previous career, and how many of them were unemployed?
- And, most importantly in terms of the possible ideological persuasions of the recruits,
- How many of the men are the sons of members of the Nazi Party, or the sons of members of the SA or SS?
- How many of the men were themselves members of the party, the SA or SS?
- How many of the men were in the Reich Labour Service?
- What is their religious denomination?

The responses to the survey reveal much about the kind of people who were joining the military during this period. The navy replied with surveys of its Baltic and North Sea fleets. Of the 7,100 sailors surveyed, approximately 60 per cent were members of the party, the SA or the SS (4,386 out of 7,119), and around 20 per cent were former members of the Reich Labour Service, or were the sons of party, SS or SA members.[33]

Interestingly, the air force missed the deadline for responding, with Hermann Göring apparently 'not in the position' to respond to the request in time. When they eventually did reply, the statistics were patchy, since, according to Göring, some units had not yet completed their surveys. However, of the approximately four thousand men who were surveyed, more than 2,336 were former SS, SA or party members, 1,214 were sons of party members, and 767 had been members of the Reich Labour Service.[34]

The army provided the largest and most detailed response to Blomberg's request. For our purposes, the army is the most important branch of the military, as its members were the most likely to have become involved in atrocities during the Second World War. The army surveyed the 182,842 men who had chosen to join in the period in question, and it provided a more thorough response than requested. The army broke down the memberships of the men and their fathers into separate categories for the SA, SS and Nazi Party, as well as supplying information on prior membership of the Hitler Youth.

In providing this information, the army revealed that its intake of recruits in 1934 consisted overwhelmingly of men who had links to Nazi organisations, either through their own voluntary membership or through the membership of their parents. Of the 182,842 men surveyed, over ninety-three thousand had been members of the SA, more than thirty-two thousand were members of the Nazi Party, nearly ten thousand had been members of the SS, around thirty thousand had been members of the Labour Service, and over twelve thousand had been in the Hitler Youth. Over forty thousand recruits were the sons of members of the Nazi Party, SS or SA.[35]

The survey did not indicate how many of the men fell into more than one category, so it is impossible to know precisely how many recruits had links to Nazi organisations. Yet if we make a conservative estimate, by assuming that the men who were members of the Nazi Party and SA had also served in the Labour Service, the survey indicates that over 50 per cent, and probably many more of the recruits, were members of Nazi organisations prior to joining the army. Moreover, considering that the army numbered around 240,000 by October 1934, the influx of these 182,842 recruits during 1934 makes up a considerable proportion of the total number of army members at that stage.

The significance of the backgrounds of these men is that they previously had identified with the doctrines of Nazi ideology, and/or had already encountered considerable political indoctrination, or at least the less formal but still significant influence of their Nazi Party-member fathers. This is not to say that these men had joined the military purely because of their political persuasions; we cannot know this from the information provided. What is interesting to note, however, is that relatively few had joined due to unemployment; the vast majority had come from previous careers, or straight from school or university. Only 14 per cent of recruits to the army and 19 per cent of naval recruits had been out of work before joining. While we cannot know precisely why the majority of men joined the armed forces, we can be confident that those who had links to Nazi organisations would have been more receptive to the military's attempts at indoctrination, and thus more likely to become the ideologically conscious soldiers that the military sought to produce.

The presence of such large numbers of men with such backgrounds is also significant because it indicates the makeup of the force into which many more young men were to be conscripted from 1935 onwards. It indicates that these conscripts, who were to serve for one year, extended to two years in 1936,[36] regardless of their own ideological awareness and leanings (as indicated earlier in this chapter, many were not convinced Nazis, or even remotely politically conscious), were entering an organisation in which Nazism was present at all levels. Nazism was the official political doctrine of the armed forces, as imposed from above by the high command and as embodied by its programme of ideological education, and Nazi ideology was also alive in the lower ranks, down to the newest volunteers. For the period of 1934–35, this ideology was preached to an intake of men of which at least half could already be described as Nazi followers, or at the very least, men familiar with Nazi ideology.

This has implications beyond the probability of these men eagerly taking to their ideological training. When considering the implementation and reception of ideological education, one must consider whether there was a significant disconnect between the official doctrine being instituted by the war ministry and the rank and file; whether the lower ranks chose to ignore the directives from above concerning ideological training, whether they took it less than seriously or if they opposed the notion of Nazism in the military. The presence of so many young soldiers who were, by choice, members of Nazi organisations casts doubt upon these notions and suggests that Nazism would have found significant support within the rank and file.

These statistics also raise the possibility of peer pressure being a further factor beyond formal indoctrination. Young men who were conscripts in the years following this survey, many of whom had no prior experience in Nazi organisations or identification with Nazi values, were entering an organisation in which a large percentage of their immediate superiors and their peers were convinced Nazis. It is thus likely that young draftees entering the army would have encountered encouragement from their peers to take on the tenets of Nazism present in ideological education, and that ideological influences existed beyond initial training, when soldiers entered their respective regiments. This also suggests that young entrants to the military would have felt the need to fit in with their cohort to make life easier in the potentially alienating and distressing context of being a newcomer in the barracks.

These statistics also indicate that the army was dealing with an intake of volunteers that was large enough to represent a significant proportion of the membership of the army itself. This further suggests that from the earliest years of the Third Reich, the military conducted ideological education within an environment that was very well suited for its reception. Not only was the military able to restrict access to information and exert pressure from above, but the politics it was trying to impart had the support of many of those within the cohort that it sought to influence, which has the added effect of increasing the level of peer pressure in such a situation. It was not a matter of indoctrinating a majority of ideologically oblivious recruits from scratch, nor was it a case of attempting to win over a majority of sceptical opponents of Nazi ideology. Instead, during the recruitment drive of 1934, the military was dealing with an influx of men of which a significant number were already predisposed to agree with Nazi ideology. This would have made the military's task of indoctrination easier for this group of men, creating a generation of soldiers that would have helped to lay the foundation for the indoctrination of the men who were conscripted into the army from 1935 onwards, particularly the earliest intakes of conscripts, who often showed far less prior knowledge of National Socialism.

The military high command was not only interested in educating new recruits. Concerns also existed about the need to train officers in the tenets of National Socialism, particularly those who had spent a long period of time in the military and had therefore missed out on the Hitler Youth and Labour Service. In order to resolve this, along with the steady stream of booklets and training manuals issued by the high command, on Blomberg's orders, hundreds of officers were invited to numerous training camps and conferences that sought to offer further ideological training, as well as instruction on how best to implement the curriculum within their regiments.

The concern over officers also included responding to reports of any supposedly anti-Nazi activities. This suggests that the implementation of Nazi ideological training was not a token gesture to gain favour with the regime, and was instead being taken seriously. An instance that was illustrative of the pressure exerted in the prewar period occurred in Mecklenburg Schwerin in 1936. Local party officials, unnamed in the report, made a number of complaints to a locally based officer about their concerns at the conduct of a local army lieutenant, Karl Hahn. The accounts of the lieutenant's behaviour, according to both military and government officials, cast doubt upon his National Socialist credentials, and the complaint was deemed important enough to pass on to the armed forces high command for deliberation. The file contained dozens of sworn statements from local Nazi Party members that told of numerous instances of questionable behaviour. Sixteen Nazi Party members testified that Lieutenant Hahn had continually failed to give the 'German greeting'. Another party member stated that Hahn had flown the old imperial black, white and red flag right up until the day the government had decreed that only the swastika was to be flown. After this change in law, he had not flown a flag at all. Further indicative of his suspect ideological convictions, Hahn had refused to allow his daughters to join the League of German Girls. Hahn's reasoning for this was that it would distract the girls from their schoolwork and, perhaps more revealing of the reason behind Hahn's aversion to National Socialism, because the League of German Girls was not sufficiently Christian for his daughters.[37]

In light of these transgressions, the investigating officer requested that the war ministry seriously consider whether Lieutenant Hahn should be thrown out of the army. In this instance, the military decided that Hahn should be allowed to continue serving. He was, however, summoned to Berlin and given a 'stern warning' that such behaviour was unbecoming of a German officer, and that continued misconduct would mean dismissal.[38]

Other such incidents, even trivial matters, occurred in which the behaviour of members of the armed forces, particularly officers, caused concern and reached the desks of the highest-ranking commanders. An episode that took place in Hanover early 1938 involved a major who had displayed 'un-National Socialistic behaviour' by failing to donate to the government's Winter Aid appeal, and was brought to the attention of the Supreme

Command of the Wehrmacht. The officer in question, Major Guercke, was subsequently prevented by the party's regional branch from becoming head of the local tennis club, since 'only men who had shown, over a long period that they had actively served the movement' were desired in such positions. In this case, however, higher authorities within the military decided to take no formal action, arguing that Guercke's years of service for 'Führer, People and Fatherland' were indicative of his political reliability.[39]

These cases indicate that the military abilities of officers were not the only criteria for serving in the armed forces under the Nazi regime. The rhetoric disseminated by the Wehrmacht stressing the importance of becoming an army permeated by the tenets of Nazi ideology, and indeed of using Nazi ideology as its guiding principle, was not simply for show. The idea of becoming a National Socialist army was being monitored at all levels, with even seemingly minor transgressions causing concern. As Blomberg had indicated early on, officers were to lead by example in creating a highly politicised military. The case of Lieutenant Hahn in particular also indicates the coercive elements that were present in the politicisation of the military. It was not a question of merely trying to persuade members of the armed forces to adhere to Nazism. Instead, National Socialist beliefs and behaviours became official duties. This is crucial when analysing the behaviour of members of the Wehrmacht once they were in the field, where the only reference points they had in chaotic situations were their military training and the often imprecise directives of their commanders.

In keeping with efforts to educate officers, a conference that sought to bolster ideological training and cohesion in the officer corps was held over one week in Berlin in January 1937. Notices that the ministry distributed to the military in advance stated that those who were to take part in the forum would be the army, navy and air force officers who were responsible for implementing ideological training within their units or academies.

General Wilhelm Keitel, a particularly strong supporter of Hitler, opened the conference, which was to have a 'special focus on racial problems'.[40] The next speaker was Alfred Rosenberg, the leading racial theorist within the Nazi Party, who spoke about the 'Ideological foundations of Nazism'. Other speakers included Rudolf Hess, Joseph Goebbels and Heinrich Himmler. Topics covered included 'The racial and eugenic laws of the Third Reich', 'The origins and tasks of the Nazi Party' and 'The national political duties of commanders'.[41] The conference not only dealt with the ideology to be covered during military training, but also focused on making sure that the curriculum was being taught and implemented effectively. Officers took part in seminars that included 'The content of national political lessons' and 'Methods of national political teaching'.[42] In the latter seminar, an army officer argued that political schooling, along with the virtues of Nazism, must be closely linked to military training itself, particularly the notion of the soldier as the embodiment of the nation, and the idea of Nazism being born from this concept.[43]

The vigorous approach to Nazification on display at this conference was reflected in the educational curriculum, particularly its 'special focus on racial problems'.[44] During another conference in January 1938, in a speech that was later printed and distributed within the military as a training manual, a Nazi official, Dr Gross, explained the emphasis placed upon race in training future soldiers and officers:

> The considerable amount of time that is devoted to biological questions in this training programme fully corresponds with the importance of … race and ethnicity in our political and historical situation. It is not an exaggeration when we say that all of our present problems and tasks … relate back to biology. Therefore, racial politics stands as the middle point of our educational and instructional work.[45]

In turn, soldiers received intensive instruction on so-called biological questions, and, significantly, what an adoption of National Socialist attitudes to race was to mean in practical terms. Racial threats were posed both within and outside of Germany. The Slavs posed a particular danger. Worse still, 'Slavic' countries, including Poland, the Ukraine and Russia, were increasing their birth rates at such an 'unbelievably high rate' that the statistics were not known, which would cause further danger in the future. The numbers, particularly in Russia, presented an 'unimaginable ethno-political threat' to Germany and to Europe.[46]

It was 'Jewry', however, that was depicted as the most dangerous racial threat. The time dedicated to the 'Jewish Question' within the curriculum is striking. In another speech printed within a separate military training manual, the aforementioned Dr Gross stated that for the military, the 'Jewish problem is a special case within the context of the basic racial problem … the Jewish problem takes first position'.[47] In early 1937, a further educational booklet issued by the war ministry contained the following lessons: 'Jewry: A look back at the destructive influence of Jews since their emancipation in the early 19th century', 'The Jewish influence on certain areas of German economic, cultural and political life', 'The measures the National Socialist State has enacted to exclude the Jews from the German racial community' and 'The ban on intermarriage between Jews and Germans'.[48] A booklet issued a year later contained lessons that sought to draw connections between Jews and other domestic racial 'enemies', linking Jews to the groups classified by the Nazis as *asozial*,[49] which included vagrants, habitual criminals and the 'work-shy'. It asked soldiers to compare the 'Jewish newspapers' of the Weimar era, with their ostensible support of *asozial* elements, to the policies implemented by the Nazi government.

Soldiers also received regular lessons on 'practical measures for maintaining racial hygiene'.[50] An interesting example of the depiction of race as the most important consideration of the dutiful German soldier is situated in the March 1936 edition of *Guidelines for Lessons in Everyday Political Questions*. The edition included a lesson on 'Population and Racial Policy', which recommended that soldiers read the latest documents on race and population policy issued by the Reich Committee for Public Health. The military guidelines then asserted that within these documents it was compulsory for soldiers to read issue six, which recommended having as many children as possible, as well as issue ten, 'The ten commandments for choosing a wife'.[51] The lesson also indicated that it was 'compulsory' for all members of the armed forces to see the play *Schwiegersöhne*. This theatrical production, produced at the behest of the Reich Committee for Public Health, was being performed in all major cities in Germany. The play ostensibly gave 'important lessons about race',[52] and where possible, officers were to arrange special performances of the play for viewing by soldiers.[53] The play, whose title translates as 'Sons in Law', evidently dealt with, and no doubt condemned, intermarriage between 'Aryans' and 'non-Aryans'. The guidelines referred to the play as providing 'important lessons about race, hereditary health, the law for the prevention of hereditarily diseased offspring and the law for the protection of German blood, and it makes clear the necessity of the regime's racial measures'.[54]

The content of this lesson is an interesting example of the use of theatre for propaganda purposes, and precedes the use of later, infamous films such as *Jew Süss* and *The Eternal Jew*, which were utilised for the antisemitic instruction of SS and police units.[55] It is also indicative of the similarities that existed between the ideological education, and therefore anticipated responsibilities, of the military and the SS, an issue that will be dealt with in more detail below.

Dedication to schooling soldiers in matters concerning racial hygiene shows that the military was not averse to mirroring the government's policy developments. At the very least, the regime's racial laws did not seem to cause the military to reconsider its position.[56] The war ministry issued the cited edition of political guidelines in March 1936, not long after the passing of the Nuremberg Racial Laws in September 1935. Alongside the order for soldiers to attend the play, the guidelines also instructed officers to pay particular attention to the latest developments in the Nazi government's population and racial policies. The March 1936 guidelines specifically instructed troops to 'read the Nuremberg laws and take notice of them'.[57] These included the 'Law for the Reconstitution of the Civil Service' in 1933 and the banning of

Jews from serving in the military in 1935. According to the aforementioned booklet issued in 1937, the two laws were based upon the most important concept: only 'Aryans' could lead the German people. 'Foreign races' were not desired in the civil service, or in the German military itself.[58] The Nazi Party enacted the Nuremberg Laws in order to prevent intermarriage and sexual contact between 'Aryans' and Jews, which would facilitate the exclusion of the 'hostile Jewish race from the German racial community'.[59]

Ideological indoctrination material issued by the war ministry boasted that these anti-Jewish policies had resulted in a number of 'successful' outcomes. Soldiers were informed that the government's ban on intermarriage and other measures to exclude the Jewish population from the national community meant that 'Jewry in Germany [was] no longer proliferating. It is dying out';[60] the regime had implemented policies that effectively 'condemned Jewry to extinction within the borders of the Reich'.[61]

Even at this early stage, Wehrmacht educational material also placed emphasis on the ostensible link between Judaism and Bolshevism. In October 1936, for example, a set of guidelines that were to 'provide the young German soldier with a consciousness of the life and death struggle of his people' contained a lesson of the threat that the 'Jewish Bolshevists' posed to the world.[62] The 'Jewish Bolshevists' were fostering worldwide revolution and sought to 'exploit the German people and use them as cannon fodder in the quest for world domination'. These 'Jewish Communist leaders' were also attempting to turn peaceful people against each other and to organise civil wars.[63] These statements perpetuated the link between Jews and Bolshevism and propagated the Nazi myth of a 'Jewish regime' in Moscow, employing the vague expression 'Jewish elements', a turn of phrase that blurred the image and scope of exactly who was to be considered an 'enemy'.

This is strongly reminiscent of the rhetoric employed by the Nazi Party and military during the 1941 invasion of the Soviet Union. While not providing proof of the intentions of the regime or the military at this early stage, it indicates that as early as 1936, soldiers were being prepared for the possibility of the kind of war that later took place against the Soviet Union, not to mention the racially charged campaigns that took place in Poland and Yugoslavia. While this did not strictly 'preview' the worst of the atrocities committed by the Wehrmacht during the Barbarossa, Balkans and Poland campaigns, to paraphrase Ian Kershaw, without such a mentality, such atrocities would not have been possible.[64]

The notion that the military would be engaged in a battle against biological and political enemies, rather than a strictly military adversary, was propagated well before the Barbarossa campaign, and put into practice in the German invasion of Poland in 1939. As we will see, members of the armed forces in Poland did not need the orders of 1941, nor did they need to become brutalised by the horrific conditions of the Eastern Front, in order to feel as though it was within the scope of their role to target civilians on racial and ideological grounds. The next chapter will demonstrate that the Wehrmacht's programme of political schooling continued, and in some cases sharpened its racial and political tone in the period preceding the Second World War. It will then examine the involvement of the army in atrocities during the invasion of Poland. In doing so, it will show that there is much to suggest that a link exists between the military's educational programme and the behaviour of German soldiers and officers during the Poland campaign.

Notes

1. Militärgeschichtliches Forschungsamt (ed.), *Das deutsche Reich und der zweite Weltkrieg* (Munich, 2004). In particular, see Jürgen Förster's essay, 'Geistige Kriegführung in Deutschland 1919 bis 1945', in Volume 9, Part 1, 469–621; Manfred Messerschmidt, *Die Wehrmacht im NS-Staat: Zeit der Indoktrination* (Hamburg, 1969); Klaus Jürgen Müller (ed.), *Armee und Drittes Reich 1933–1939: Darstellung und Dokumentation* (Paderborn, 1989); Robert O'Neill, *The German Army and the Nazi Party, 1933–1939* (London, 1966); Michael Salewski, 'Wehrmacht und Nationalsozialismuz 1933–1939', in Militärgeschichtliches Forschungsamt (ed.), *Handbuch zur Deutschen Militärgeschichte 1648–1939* (Munich, 1978); F.L. Carsten, *The Reichswehr and Politics, 1918–1933* (Oxford, 1966); Jürgen Förster, *Die Wehrmacht im NS-Staat: Eine Strukturgeschichtliche Analyse* (Munich, 2007).
2. Jörg Muth, *Command Culture: Officer Education in the US Army and the German Armed Forces, 1901–1940, and the Consequences for World War II* (Denton, 2011), 136–37.
3. Jürgen Förster, 'Die Politisierung der Reichswehr/Wehrmacht', in *Das deutsche Reich und der Zweite Weltkrieg Band 9/1: Der deutsche Kriegsgesellschaft 1939 bis 1945* (Munich, 2004), 486.
4. Muth, *Command Culture*.
5. Ibid., 193.
6. Ibid., 155.
7. Ibid., 155–60.
8. Ibid., 155.
9. Müller, *Armee und Drittes Reich*, 165.
10. Ibid., 168; Kirstin A. Schäfer, *Werner von Blomberg: Hitlers erster Feldmarschall* (Paderborn, 2006), 123–24; Wolfram Wette, *The Wehrmacht: History, Myth, Reality* (Cambridge, MA, 2006), 85; Ben Shepherd, *Hitler's Soldiers: The German Army in the Third Reich* (London, 2016), 11.
11. O'Neill, *The German Army and the Nazi Party*, 71.
12. Institut für Zeitgeschichte, Munich (hereafter IfZ), Da 033.158-1937a, 'Erlaß des Reichskriegsministers und Oberbefehlshabers der Wehrmacht vom 30 Januar 1936', in

Oberkommando der Wehrmacht (ed.), *Nationalpolitischer Lehrgang der Wehrmacht vom 15 bis 23 Januar 1937* (Berlin, 1936).
13. IfZ, MA 241, *Vereinbarung über die Eingliederung der Lehrer an Wehrmachtschulen in den NSLB* (Berlin, 12 May 1934).
14. 'Deutsches Volksbodens'. *Volksboden* is difficult to translate. Another way of expressing it in English could be 'land belonging to the German people', but due to the racial connotations of 'Volk' it could also be translated as 'German ethnic land'. Either way, it has a meaning that is suggestive of lands lost under Versailles and considered to be German by virtue of their populations of ethnic Germans and their past status as being under German rule.
15. IfZ, Da 33.60, *Richtlinien für den Unterricht über politische Tagesfragen. Nur für den Dienstgebrauch der Wehrmacht*, 17 May 1936, 2–4.
16. Vejas Gabriel Liulevicius, *War Land on the Eastern Front: Culture, National Identity and German Occupation in World War I* (Cambridge, 2000), 8.
17. IfZ, Da 033.158-1937a, 'Erlaß des Reichskriegministers und Oberbefehlshabers der Wehrmacht vom 30 Januar 1936'.
18. IfZ, Da 33.60, Oberkommando der Wehrmacht (ed.), *Richtlinien für den Unterricht über politische Tagesfragen*, 23 May 1936, 247.
19. IfZ, Da 33.60,*Richtlinien für den Unterricht über politische Tagesfragen*, 23 May 1936, 5–6.
20. Hermann Göring, quoted in Ibid.
21. Ute Frevert, *A Nation in Barracks: Modern Germany, Military Conscription and Civil Society* (New York, 2004), 242.
22. Förster, 'Die Politisierung der Reichswehr/Wehrmacht', 488.
23. Ibid., 488–89.
24. Bundesarchiv/Militärarchiv (hereafter BA/MA) RW 6/V. 159, Wehrmachtsamt/Abt. Inland: (nr. 600/35g.J IVa): *Erziehung in der Wehrmacht*, Berlin, 16 April 1935, 2.
25. BA/MA RW6/161, *Erster nationalpolitischer Lehrgang für Lehrer der Kriegsschulen, Akademien usw vom 17.1.37 bis 23.1.37 in Berlin*, 23.
26. Ibid., 23–24.
27. BA/MA 6/v.420, *Nationalpolitischer Lehrgang der Wehrmacht vom 12. bis 21. Januar 1938. Nur für den Dienstgebrauch in der Wehrmacht* (Berlin, 1938), 204.
28. Förster, 'Die Politisierung der Reichswehr/Wehrmacht', 502–3.
29. Quoted in Kiran Klaus Patel, *Soldaten der Arbeit: Arbeitsdienste in Deutschland und den USA* (Göttingen, 2003), 259.
30. Michael H. Kater, *Hitler Youth* (Cambridge, MA, 2004), 28–29.
31. IfZ, MA 34, OKW 853, *Geheime Kommandosache*, 26 October 1934.
32. Richard J. Evans, *The Third Reich in Power* (London, 2006), 341.
33. IfZ, MA 34, OKW 853, *Geheime Kommandosache*, 26 October 1934.
34. Ibid.
35. Ibid.
36. Evans, *The Third Reich in Power*, 342.
37. IfZ, MA 33, OKW 861, *Leutnant Karl Hahn, Grevesmühlen*.
38. Ibid.
39. Ibid.
40. BA/MA RW6/161, *Erster nationalpolitischer Lehrgang für Lehrer der Kriegsschulen*.
41. Ibid.
42. Ibid.
43. Ibid., 23–28.

44. Oberkommando der Wehrmacht (ed.), *Nationalpolitischer Lehrgang der Wehrmacht vom 12-21 Januar, 1938*, 21–39.
45. Ibid., 21.
46. IfZ, Da 033.158-197a, 'Dr Gütt, Praktische Maßnahmen der Gesundheits- und Rassenpflege', in *Nationalpolitischer Lehrgang der Wehrmacht vom 15 bis 23 Januar 1937. Nur für den Dienstgebrauch in der Wehrmacht* (Berlin, 1937), 52.
47. BA/MA RW 6/V. 421, OKW/1619b, *Nationalpolitischer Lehrgang der Wehrmacht vom 29. November bis 2. Dezember. Nur für den Dienstgebrauch in der Wehrmacht* (Berlin, 1938), 29.
48. BA/MA RW6/161, *Erster nationalpolitischer Lehrgang für Lehrer der Kriegsschulen*, 249.
49. *Asozial* translates loosely as 'antisocial', or can be applied to somebody considered a 'social outcast'.
50. BA/MA 6/v.420, 'Praktische Maßnahmen der Gesundheits- und Rassenpflege', in *Nationalpolitische Lehrgang der Wehrmacht vom 12. bis 21. Januar 1938*, 52–71.
51. IfZ, Da 33.60, Heft 6, 'Kinderreichtum – Volksreichtum' and 'Zehn Gebote für Gattenwahl', in *Richtlinien für den Unterricht über politische Tagesfragen*, 26 March 1936, 12.
52. 'Den Soldaten der Wehrmacht ist der Besuch dieses Stückes zu befehlen', in *Richtlinien für den Unterricht über politische Tagesfragen*, 26 March 1936, 12.
53. 'Auf die Möglichkeit, das Stück in den einzelnen Standorten in Sondervorstellungen für die Wehrmacht zur Vorführung zu bringen, wird hingewiesen', in *Richtlinien für den Unterricht über politische Tagesfragen*, 26 March 1936.
54. Ibid., 12.
55. Jürgen Matthäus, 'Die "Judenfrage" als Schulungsthema von SS und Polizei', in Jürgen Matthäus et al. (eds), *Ausbildungsziel Judenmord? Weltanschauliche Erziehung von SS, Polizei und Waffen SS im Rahmen der Endlösung* (Frankfurt, 2003), 66.
56. Manfred Messerschmidt, 'Die Wehrmacht als tragende Säule des NS-Staates (1933–1939)', in Walter Manoschek (ed.), *Die Wehrmacht im Rassenkrieg: Der vernichtungskrieg hinter der Front* (Vienna, 1996), 45–47.
57. *Richtlinien für den Unterricht über politische Tagesfragen*, 26 March 1936, 12.
58. IfZ, Da 033.158-197a, *Nationalpolitischer Lehrgang der Wehrmacht vom 15 bis 23 Januar 1937*, 74.
59. Ibid., 248.
60. IfZ, Da 033.158-1938.1, Reichshauptamtsleiter Dr Gross, 'Die Leitgedanken der NS Rassenpolitik', in *Nationalpolitischer Lehrgang der Wehrmacht vom 12. bis 21. Januar 1938*, 39.
61. Ibid.
62. IfZ, Da 33.60, 'Die Bolschewistische Weltgefahr', in Reichskriegsministerium (ed.), *Richtlinien für den Unterricht über politische Tagesfragen*, 15 October 1936, 3–6.
63. Ibid., 1–5.
64. Ian Kershaw, *Hitler* (London, 2010), 468–69. In this context, Kershaw was speaking of the links between the mentality evident in a passage in *Das Schwarze Korps*, the SS magazine, which spoke in 1938 of the 'annihilation' of Jewry in Germany, and the later atrocities of Auschwitz and Treblinka.

Chapter 4

THE LEAD-UP TO WAR AND THE POLAND CAMPAIGN

~~~~

Notions of race and ideology playing a central role in the conduct of the Wehrmacht have long been familiar when dealing with the war against the Soviet Union.[1] The crimes that German soldiers perpetrated in Poland in 1939, however, only began to attract closer attention more recently.[2] German troops carried out the harassment, humiliation, torture and murder of thousands of civilians, and cooperated with the *Einsatzgruppen*, the specialised mobile killing squads of the SS and the police, in their extermination efforts against Polish elites and Jewish civilians. These crimes occurred well before the notorious criminal orders handed down by army generals during the Barbarossa campaign in 1941, and before the 'barbarisation of warfare' that occurred in the Soviet Union.[3] They occurred in 1939, in keeping with a number of ideologically driven, yet less specific, orders from above, and due to soldiers taking the initiative in carrying out extreme violence against civilians, with Jews often the most commonly targeted group. These events indicate the importance of the Polish campaign as a first step in the involvement of the armed forces in atrocities, and as a campaign whose conduct was influenced by, among other things, the military's prior ideological education of its soldiers and officers.

The explanations that scholars have utilised to account for German atrocities during the Barbarossa campaign are insufficient to explain the crimes of the Wehrmacht in Poland. Although the war had, from the start, a racial component, German soldiers who committed atrocities were not, by and large, acting on orders that were as specifically racially and ideologically driven as those handed down during the invasion of the Soviet Union, which directed them to behave in a manner that disregarded any considerations of limiting violent conduct towards civilians and prisoners.[4] Additionally, the 'situational factors' involved in the Soviet campaign are not compelling within the Polish context. It is unlikely that at this very early stage of the war soldiers could have become 'brutalised' by long-term exposure to extreme violence. The Polish campaign took place under favourable conditions against a relatively weak enemy,[5] was a short and, for German soldiers, a more successful and less traumatic campaign than their later experience of war against the Soviet Union.[6]

Jochen Böhler is persuasive when he argues that the inhumane behaviour that soldiers directed against civilians was due largely to virulent anti-Polish and antisemitic attitudes.[7] While Böhler has documented such attitudes prevalent among members of the military, he has not closely examined the kind of ideological education to which these men had been exposed as part of their military training. In fact, Böhler highlights the fact that 'the socialisation of soldiers … during their basic military training and education that occurred before the beginning of the war has not yet been well researched'.[8] He is correct in pointing out that a closer investigation of the 'socialisation' of soldiers is crucial in order to better comprehend the actions of the Wehrmacht in Poland.

This chapter will go some way towards investigating the socialisation of troops by looking at the training that took place in the period leading up to the invasion of Poland. It will demonstrate that the high command intensified its efforts to foster values that, when combined with other factors, particularly a pre-existing tradition within the German army of brutal treatment of partisan resistance, later manifested themselves in criminal behaviour in the field. This will help to account for the ideological motivations cited by Böhler, as well as the tendency of troops to go beyond the letter of their orders in carrying out violence against civilians, and of lower-ranking officers to tolerate or even encourage such behaviour.

***

In 1938, the year before the start of the Second World War, a number of developments took place that were to prove critical in the continuing politicisation of the German armed forces. Klaus Jürgen Müller has argued that 1938 was the year that represented the 'decisive break in the relationship between the military and politics in Germany'.[9] The command structure of the Wehrmacht underwent a number of key changes. While I have primarily been concerned with the lower levels of the armed forces, it is nonetheless important to understand the effect that developments at the top might have had on the rest of the organisation. A chain of events that became known as the Blomberg-Fritsch crisis took place at the highest level of the German armed forces early in 1938. The crisis and its aftermath resulted in a restructuring of the military that led to an increase in the influence of Nazism, and of Hitler himself, within the armed forces. The events resulted in the war minister, Werner von Blomberg, as well as commander-in-chief of the army, Werner von Fritsch, being pushed out of their positions and replaced by officers who were regarded by Hitler as being more ideologically committed. This reshuffle was to foreshadow further changes within the upper echelons of the armed forces, and ultimately served to place more power in the hands of Hitler.[10]

The first crisis came about when it was discovered that Blomberg had married a young woman who had allegedly worked as a prostitute and appeared in nude photographs. In light of the potential problems this could cause, Hitler asked him to annul the marriage or to resign. Blomberg refused. He relented, however, when Göring threatened to publicise his wife's past, resigning his post. That Blomberg would be forced out of his position, in light of the key role he had played in implementing the Nazification of the army, particularly in the area of political schooling, indicates the degree of dismay and embarrassment that his marriage had the potential to arouse. Hitler, as well as Göring, had been witnesses at the wedding. Additionally, the woman's reputation was further tainted by allegations that the photographs had been taken by a Jew. The humiliation would be too much for Hitler, even for someone as politically reliable as Blomberg.[11]

There is evidence to suggest, however, that there were other factors involved in Blomberg's dismissal. A few months prior to the scandal, Blomberg had shown that even his commitment to Hitler and his agenda had its limits. In a move that would not have aided him, in January 1938 Blomberg had expressed disagreement regarding some of Hitler's foreign policies, in particular over the nature and timing of his plans for conflict with France, Britain and Czechoslovakia.[12] According to O'Neill, this led Hitler to suspect that Blomberg would 'panic' in the face of escalating tensions, particularly with France.[13] Regardless of how important Blomberg's objections may have been as a factor in his dismissal, his removal meant there would be one less dissenting voice in the upper echelon of the military, a voice that could be replaced with someone more devoted to Hitler's foreign policy agenda.

Having refused to annul his marriage, Blomberg resigned his position and left for Italy, albeit with a full pension and a further pay-off.[14] Significantly, Hitler was able to accomplish Blomberg's removal without resistance from the officer corps.[15] His prior loyalty to Hitler counted against him in one respect; he was, according to Kershaw, 'not popular in the top leadership of the army. He was seen as too much Hitler's man and too little the army's. When his personal life led to professional trouble … he had no friends to count upon'.[16]

The drama surrounding Blomberg led to another crisis, this time involving the commander-in-chief of the army, Werner von Fritsch. Hitler, worried about further scandal in the military, remembered accusations of homosexuality made against Fritsch in 1936. As noted in the Hossbach Memorandum, Fritsch had also been critical of Hitler's plans for war, and Hitler was suspicious of his conservative leanings and disdain for the Nazi Party.[17] He had also made enemies within the SS, particularly Heinrich Himmler and Reinhard Heydrich, who had contrived to make the most out of the accusations; Heydrich produced the file on the seemingly forgotten matter almost immediately.[18] In spite of his vigorous denial of the accusations, Fritsch was forced to resign on 4 February 1938.[19]

The immediate result of the Blomberg-Fritsch crisis was a change in leadership in the military. In the face of Göring's desire to succeed Blomberg as war minister, Hitler decided instead that he himself would take over Blomberg's role and gain direct command of the Wehrmacht, with General Wilhelm Keitel as his advisor.[20] Keitel, who did not stand out as being particularly qualified for the position, was appointed chief of the Supreme Command of the Wehrmacht mainly due to his political persuasions and support of Hitler.[21] Walther von Brauchitsch, an admirer of Hitler and a man who had, in a meeting with Keitel in Berlin on 28 January 1938, confirmed that he was willing to bring the army closer to the state and its ideology, took over from Fritsch as head of the army.[22] A few months after his appointment, Brauchitsch articulated his own viewpoint on Nazism's place in the military in an order that stated the following:

> The armed forces and National Socialism are of the same spiritual stem. They will accomplish much for the nation in the future if they follow the example and teaching of the Führer … The officer corps must not be surpassed by anybody in the purity and genuineness of its National Socialist outlook.[23]

The most important consequence of the crisis was that it fundamentally altered the relationship between Hitler and the military. According to Kershaw, 'Just when Hitler's adventurism was starting to cause concern, the army showed its weakness and allowed him to take a position of dominance'.[24] Hitler was now in command of the military and used the crisis as an excuse to make numerous further changes within the organisation. He forced out many of the more conservative officers who had stood for an independent army within the state and who had questioned or were not committed enough to Hitler's domestic and foreign agendas. He filled the leading positions with officers who were more 'ideologically reliable'.[25] Some officers, including Generals Halder, Oster, von Stülpnagel and Rundstedt, considered taking action to protect the honour of the army and to confront the SS and Gestapo, but others, including Ludwig Beck, were against it as it would constitute mutiny, which would only make the situation worse.[26] The end result of this was the end of an independent army, making the officer corps a 'purely executive agent of the state under political control', something that had not existed in the Prusso-German Empire or in the Weimar Republic.[27] The Wehrmacht had become 'an instrument of the Führer'.[28]

Did these personnel changes at the top of the chain of command change the level or intensity of ideological education that ordinary soldiers and officers experienced in the armed forces? It is difficult to state categorically the effect that it had, since Blomberg had already been so enthusiastic in his implementation of Nazi ideological education. However, the drive towards war, along with the intensity of racially driven rhetoric, did become more pronounced in the lead-up to the invasion of Poland in 1939. For instance, one booklet issued by the Supreme Command of the Wehrmacht, now headed by Keitel, in early 1939 stated that 'more emphasis will be placed upon lessons about the National Socialist world-view and national political goals'.[29]

There is also evidence of efforts to justify the change in personnel at the top of the chain of command, including the assumption of supreme command by Hitler himself. The Supreme Command of the Wehrmacht (OKW) issued one training manual, for example, which sought to rationalise the new organisation of the military as actually being part of existing convention. It informed soldiers that the military's politicisation, its subordination to the head of the state and their own role as ideological combatants was in fact no more than a continuity of military tradition: 'The soldier is, and always has been, an instrument of politics. This was so during the First, Second and Third German Reich'.[30] It went on to explain the normality of the idea of soldiers carrying out a political role by quoting Carl von Clausewitz, the iconic figure of Prussian military theory: 'War is merely the continuation of politics through other means'.[31] The lesson drew heavily upon apparent historical precedents, particularly relating to the Kingdom of Prussia, evoking order, discipline and, most importantly, military success. The example below, which incorporates all these elements, is drawn from the article 'The Officer and Politics: Then and Now' in the *Educational Booklet for Lessons on the National Socialist World-View and Orientation Towards Political Goals*, which was issued to soldiers undergoing training in early 1939. The links to the developments within the military during the previous year are clear:

The officers of the Prussian army of the nineteenth century and during the Second Reich were also political. They lived in the tradition of that army as supporters of the Crown. They were monarchical. Their political objective was thus 'With God for King and Fatherland', as it stood inscribed on their helmet … The officers of the new German Wehrmacht are political. They have sworn an oath to the Führer and supreme military commander, who is also the political leader of the German *Volk*. The German Wehrmacht is the instrument of his political will. This political objective is anchored in the National Socialist world-view … The binding of weapon and world-view is the precondition for the strength of this military; the education of the Wehrmacht will be directed in light of this knowledge … In the army the young recruit will receive the necessary weapons training, and he will also be further formed for the other areas of his life … The highest values of National Socialism, formed in the experience at the front in the World War and further developed in the struggle for the domestic and international liberation of the Reich, are also the highest values of the nation's weapon-bearers. Therefore the officer is also the political leader of his men and his ideology is forged alongside his weapon as his inspiration.[32]

***

'The training programme carried out in Bad Tölz was in every way a complete success', reported Captain Hermann Kraus, an officer of the 99th Artillery Regiment, enthusiastically informing his regiment of the course he had just completed, noting in particular that 'the lectures were outstanding'.[33] Kraus was referring to a week-long 'Summer Course for Officers', in the Bavarian resort town of Bad Tölz in early June 1939. Its central feature was a 'Lecture series about National Socialism's world-view and goals', which included presentations on racial and population policies, as well as on the enemies of the 'movement'. The training week, not unlike previously mentioned officers' conferences, was to have a 'special focus on race', and its goal was to ensure that 'the ideology of the Nazi Party would become second nature to every officer'. Nazi Party officials were also seemingly pleased with the course, with the national treasurer, Franz Xaver Schwarz, writing that he was 'convinced that the officer's course in Bad Tölz [would] lead to a further deepening of the bond between the party and the military in undertaking their common work'.[34]

The nature of the summer course, which took place from 11 to 17 June, just months before the start of the war, showed precisely what 'training' could involve for officers of the Wehrmacht in 1939. The course, which followed an identical course held earlier in the year, which also 'ran smoothly',[35] was attended by over 120 officers from all three branches of the armed forces, with lieutenants, captains and majors present.[36] It was made up of abstract political tracts, with little mention of military tactics or enemies, but instead of enemies of the Nazi movement. The activities in which participants took part included sightseeing trips to the nearby Bavarian Alps to engender greater love of the German Fatherland, along with outdoor activities with members of the Hitler Youth to cement relations between the two organisations and to help prepare the next generation of soldiers. The course also included visits to a mental asylum in Eglfing, as well as a trip to the elite Adolf Hitler School at Sonthofen.

The week allowed the officers' mass attendance at lectures delivered by, among others, SS doctors, approved academics, Nazi officials, and military and SA officers. Lecture topics, which were to place particular emphasis upon 'Race and *Lebensraum*', included 'The World-View of National Socialism', 'Racial and Population Policy' and 'Eastern Space'. Officers were also split up into smaller working groups to help supplement and reinforce the material heard in lectures. In these smaller classes, officers took part in informal discussions over the learning material, which covered subjects such as 'The enemies of the movement' (note the specific focus on enemies of the 'movement' [*Bewegung*]) and 'The origins of the capitulation of 1918'.[37]

The week also included activities that served to reinforce lectures and classes by demonstrating Nazi theory being put into practice. The most noteworthy of these trips were those taken to Eglfing, Sonthofen and Landsberg. The trip to Eglfing, the site of a hospital for the mentally and physically disabled, took place on the afternoon of Tuesday 13 June. The day's morning lecture was entitled 'The Prevention of Hereditarily Diseased Offspring'.[38] It was delivered by the director of the asylum at Eglfing, Dr Hermann Pfannmüller, a dedicated Nazi who had advocated involuntary euthanasia for many years, and who was to become heavily involved in the Nazi euthanasia programme (Action T4).[39] The officers took part in a tour of the facility, culminating in the patients being taken out and paraded before the officers in order for them to observe the mentally disabled up close. The group also travelled to Landsberg, where they visited the cell in which Hitler had been imprisoned, and where he had written *Mein Kampf*. The week culminated in a social event on the final evening of the course.

The specific objectives of this course are revealed by the make-up of those attending, as well as by written reports. The course consisted of lower and mid-ranking officers drawn from all three branches of the armed forces, showing that the course was not about fostering unity across the ranks within individual units. Nor was it merely an attempt to teach officers how better to indoctrinate the men serving under them. In an internal report dated a week after the course took place, one officer, Captain Hof, wrote under the headline 'Purpose and Objective of the Course' that:

> One often encounters those of the understanding that this course took place so that these officers could now school their own soldiers in the Nazi worldview and politics by way of similar lectures. But this is definitely not the thinking behind it. Such courses are for facilitating the ideological development of the officers themselves. The necessity of this becomes clear through the fact that our young soldiers, who have already been in the Hitler Youth, SA and such, come into the Wehrmacht with some background of political schooling. From this alone comes the need to secure the leadership of the military on ideological grounds. This will not be achieved through a few lectures, but instead through a systematic treatment of this question, which must ensure that the philosophy of the party becomes a given for every officer … these courses should serve to make National Socialism dominant in the thoughts of all our officers.[40]

This quotation echoes the military's earlier anxiety over the ideological reliability of its officer corps. However, examining the correspondence of some of the officers who attended the week in Bad Tölz reveals that perhaps the high command need not have been too concerned.

The existing reports and private letters of officers present at the summer training camp reveal that the course was, from the viewpoint of the military, a resounding success. Numerous officers filed reports or wrote letters that praised both the camps and the ideology that was espoused there. Captain Hermann Kraus, quoted earlier, was not the only officer who enthused about the content of the propaganda and welcomed the notion of intensive ideological schooling for the officer corps. On 20 June 1939, a Major Wizotski, in a letter to another officer, Major Pfeiffer, wrote the following about the camp, and other equivalent camps that had been held:

> They are a must for all officers that have a role to play in educating young German soldiers … This education extends the knowledge of the National Socialist world-view, and also plays a decisive role in bettering the understanding of the educational literature involved.[41]

Numerous officers expressed particular approval of lectures involving racial hygiene. The visit to the asylum at Eglfing was also written about favourably, and seemed to have served the purpose of reinforcing the racial propaganda. One captain wrote the following in his report:

> The lecture from Dr Pfannmüller about the prevention of hereditarily diseased offspring … which was bolstered by the presentation of a few invalids from the institution, along with statistical evidence, was convincing for all participants … We also generally agreed that such courses were necessary for officers. A leader of a company of troops that has had the foundations

of National Socialist thought conveyed to him in such a way will be able to answer questions that might be posed to him by members of his unit with greater clarity and certainty, since the goals and themes of the national political lessons will now be much clearer to him.[42]

Another officer expressed similar approval of the racial content of the course. Noting that although all talks were 'very good', he singled out the lecture delivered by Professor Gross, which covered the topic of racial and population policy. He also praised the decision to take the officers to Eglfing:

> The underpinning of the racial and population lectures through the display of diseased patients in Eglfing was particularly welcome. As a consequence of this, every participant will deepen the National Socialist body of thought in his unit by being able to speak about such things through real life experience. In this, he will be much more successful than merely by speaking about or repeating things that he had only heard or read.[43]

While the existence of correspondence that praises the training programme suggests an overall approval of both the establishment of such a course and the encroachment of Nazi ideology into the official doctrine of the military, questions arise as to whether such praise was indeed universal, or even genuine. Within a totalitarian society, and within a military itself, where questioning of instructions and decisions made from above is at best frowned upon, one queries whether officers were merely reluctantly acquiescing to this intrusion of politics into their profession. While it is impossible to know the attitudes and private thoughts of all officers, there are indications that the praise was genuine; there is evidence that shows that officers felt able to openly express dissent and disagreement over aspects of the programme.

In particular, numerous officers expressed reservations about the attacks on religion and the church. Within his account of the success of the programme, Captain Hof pointed out that, 'On this occasion as well, the question over the church led to lively debate'.[44] Other officers also wrote of such debates; one officer, after writing approvingly of the lecture on sterilisation and the associated visit to the Eglfing asylum, noted that 'some officers were indignant at the frequent and repetitive attacks that were made against the church'.[45] This hints at a connection between the Nazi Party's racial hygiene policy and the instances of opposition by the churches.

This is a good example of political schooling encountering problems when clashing with, and indeed trying to reverse rather than build upon, pre-existing opinions and beliefs.[46] In 1939, despite the party's best efforts, Christianity still played an influential role in German society. Nazi notions of racial hygiene stood in opposition to Christian morality, and sought to replace the Christian view of the sanctity of life with a system that rested importance only upon the perceived benefits to the German race.[47] As a reaction to this, religious organisations, which had provided opposition to the Nazi Party in other areas, had become a hindrance to the programme of racial hygiene.[48] The directors of some church-run missions had attempted to hinder the transfer of mentally and physically disabled patients to state-run institutions, and a number of church leaders had spoken out against the Nazi government's sterilisation of those deemed 'racially unfit'.[49] The churches therefore became a target for attacks by Nazi officials. Such attacks evidently took place repeatedly during the training camp. Clearly, however, numerous officers held reservations about such anti-Christian, anti-clerical rhetoric. The indignation at attacks on the church in relation to the lecture on racial hygiene and the subsequent tour of the asylum shows that although most officers were convinced of the merits of Nazi racial hygiene, some may have disagreed on religious grounds with the sterilisation of the physically and mentally handicapped, or at least took issue with the continual attacks on church leaders who did, and felt able to articulate their dissent. Moreover, this was apparently not forbidden, since the camp's organisers allowed, and even facilitated, group discussions and debates on such topics.

The most extensive account that relates to the reactions of officers to the training is a personal letter by an officer who took part in the course. Writing to another officer, Major Wolf Hermann gave a general overview of the week, writing approvingly of the training, albeit with an interesting take on the 'religious questions' that came up over the course of the week.

> I believe that these days in [Bad] Tölz provided a strong experience for most of us, and I believe that we will be able to adopt aspects of the fanatical conviction of the men who spoke to us, and will now speak to our soldiers about National Socialism in the same uncompromising manner ... I also found the lectures and associated visits to Eglfing and Sonthofen to be extremely valuable.[50]

Like other correspondents, Hermann mentioned the discussions that took place on religion. However, he had a slightly different take on the matter. While not personally offended by the attacks on the church or religion, he did question the logic of the constant assault on religion and religious institutions when National Socialism itself was being preached to the officers as if it were a type of religion. He worried that religious-style sermonising, paired with attacks on and suppression of religion and the very notion of religious belief, could lead to confusion among officers, who were supposed to be the future 'preachers' of the National Socialist 'faith', and possibly hamper their future efforts at indoctrinating soldiers under their command. After speaking of the fanaticism of the instructors, who, in direct contrast with their fervent anti-religious stance, imparted their National Socialist 'beliefs' in the manner of a religious faith, he wrote:

> The officer is a type of messenger of National Socialist ideology … Maybe it would be good if, in future, lecturers speak in less of a missionary, polemical manner. It is not really necessary in this circle, which is not just some public meeting. It has become known to me that it left a bad taste in the mouths of some participants.[51]

Evidently, not only was such missionary zeal paradoxical, confusing and even irritating, it was also not needed. Hermann's suggestion that such fervour was not required 'in this circle' implies that the officers present at the course, unlike other sectors of the public, did not need much convincing of the merits of National Socialism.

While these snippets of information do not give us a complete picture of the extent of the dissent, or of the exact problems that officers had with ideological education, they do show us that officers did not blindly or uncritically accept indoctrination, nor did they agree with every aspect of it. The evidence also strongly suggests a generally positive attitude among officers towards Nazism, and the idea of moving away from the traditional role of soldiers and towards a new racially and ideologically motivated form of conflict. It also indicated the widespread acceptance of an ideology that viewed humanity in terms of stark biological differences, and which called for the elimination of those who were deemed racially unfit. The presence of instances of criticism suggests that had the officers any other issues with elements of the course, they would have mentioned them, and similar discussions would have taken place.

In this sense, it is perhaps more significant what is not present in the reports. There is no mention of any officer questioning the constant attacks on Jews in the lecture series, nor of any dissent or reservations expressed at the general notion of being trained to take part in conflicts that would target enemies, often civilians, on racial, biological and ideological grounds. Nor are there reports of disagreement with the notion of Germany's right to conquer 'living space' at the expense of Slavic populations in the East. Furthermore, other aspects of the Nazification of the military that were taking place, through the lectures delivered by SS members, the interaction with the Hitler Youth, or even more banal factors like the base itself being run by the SS, seemed to be unworthy of questioning or protest. The overwhelming impression gained from the correspondence among officers who took part in the course is that the officers approved of most aspects of the training they were receiving, along with many of the ideas that the training imparted.

***

At the same time as the military was running ideological training camps in 1939, the training that was carried out across the country in the barracks also displayed a concentration of racially driven rhetoric. The Supreme Command of the Wehrmacht, the successor of the war ministry, produced a number of booklets that provided 'lessons on the National Socialist world-view and national-political goals' for men passing through military training during 1939 that were representative of this.[52] Like the officers' course in Bad Tölz, the educational material's special focus was upon race, particularly on Jews. One example of this programme was an educational manual entitled 'The Jew in German History', written by Dr C.A. Hoberg.[53] This piece employed a Nazi reading of German history to encapsulate the party's views on the 'Jewish question'. It contained many of the elements of the rhetoric that normally are only associated with the Barbarossa campaign. It informed soldiers that Jews were nothing less than their enemy, and sought to foster aggression towards them. It dehumanised Jews, it emphasised their 'otherness' and their status as an existential threat, and it attempted to place as much psychological distance as possible between soldiers and members of the 'Jewish race'.[54]

The role of Jews in German history, according to Hoberg, was essentially negative and destructive. The article reinforced antisemitic stereotypes and legitimised them by drawing upon observations that influential German thinkers had supposedly made centuries earlier. In order to bolster the notion of the cheating, deceitful Jew, particularly in matters relating to money, Hoberg referred to a quotation he alleged was made by Johann Wolfgang von Goethe, the most significant figure in German literature:

> Behind the mask of the honest petty bourgeois lies the lurking face of the eternal Jew. Few saw this as clearly as Goethe, who in 1778 wrote that 'this cunning people sees only one way: as long as there is order, they have no hope; even when there seems to be stability and the fires of chaos are nearly extinguished, the entire land can go up in flames again before we know it'.[55]

Hoberg further underlined his point by citing Karl Marx, which in itself is indicative of the cynical and opportunistic nature of Nazi propaganda. Himself Jewish and a founder of socialist thought, Marx was designated by Nazism as both a racial and ideological enemy, and a personification of the link between communism and Jews. Nevertheless, Hoberg took the step of pointing out Marx's famous article on the 'Jewish Problem', in which he had proclaimed: 'What is the secular basis of Judaism? Practical need, self-interest. What is the secular religion of the Jews? Huckstering. What is his secular God? Money'.[56]

Concentrating on racial differentiation, Hoberg elaborated on the concept of the Jews being excluded from the German community on biological grounds. He cited the 'mass conversion of Jews to Christianity in the nineteenth century',[57] during which Jews were able to convert and take on Christian names that concealed their Jewish origins. Because there were so many 'baptised Jews', religion had become worthless as a means of classifying the German population. Race could be the only way to decide who was a Jew.[58] As a result of this method of classification, modern antisemitism was to be a 'racial antisemitism', with soldiers instructed that since only those of German blood could be citizens, no Jew was a German citizen.[59]

Soldiers were subsequently informed of the measures that the National Socialist regime was taking to solve the 'Jewish question'. Hoberg praised Hitler's 'extermination of Jewish influence in Germany' and his 'solution of the Jewish question', calling it a 'colossal task … that has filled the German *Volk* with a new spirit'.[60] What is most significant about this article, however, is that it made an explicit call for a 'completely new, original solution of the Jewish question',[61] suggesting that the measures taken to exclude Jews from the German racial community through social and cultural segregation were merely laying the foundations for more radical developments:

> National Socialism does not wish to preserve the Jewish people, as the old Reich did. It also does not wish to absorb them into the German *Volk*, as was done during the nineteenth century. Instead, it wishes to radically eliminate them from the sphere of German life, as it is the only thing for a foreign body, a parasite and carrier of disease.[62]

The use of such rhetoric is suggestive of the radical outcomes that may have come about in dealing with the 'Jewish question', indicating an attempt to prepare soldiers for any possible path that Nazi policy might have taken. While the language of this phrase may suggest that it merely endorses the forced emigration of Jews from Germany, the call for a 'completely new, original solution to the Jewish question', along with the equating of Jews with 'parasites', suggests that it was encouraging troops to think beyond the boundaries of removal. In any case, by 1939 the forced emigration of Jews was not a particularly 'radical' idea. Removal had been the objective of anti-Jewish policy since 1933, with measures taken to compel Jews to leave the Reich, preferably leaving their assets behind.[63] Further statements made within Hoberg's essay support this contention, as it explicitly instructed troops that the eradication of Jews from Germany would not signal the end of the battle:

> The battle against Jewry will go on, even when the last Jew has left Germany. Two great and important tasks will remain.
> 1. The eradication of all the after-effects of the Jewish influence.
> 2. The struggle against world Jewry, that seeks to turn all peoples of the world against Germany.[64]

This indicates that the Nazi regime would carry on efforts to solve the 'Jewish question' outside Germany's borders. Hoberg wrote that 'world Jewry' had infiltrated and now controlled the governments of the West, as well as that of the Soviet Union. In London, Paris, Moscow and New York, Jews supposedly filled positions of authority, and he asserted that all of these influential Jews sought to instigate a European war in order to ensure the destruction of Germany.[65] In effect, the armed forces supreme command had instructed soldiers that Jews were responsible for all existing opposition to Germany, insinuating that every Jew, foreign and domestic, was to be regarded as an enemy. This was a particularly dangerous notion to be giving to soldiers, whose role is to engage with and kill their enemies. The lesson ended with an ominous instruction to soldiers that was in keeping with the idea of a life and death, racial struggle against 'world Jewry':

> We combat world Jewry in the way one must combat a poisonous parasite; we engage it not only as an enemy of our *Volk*, but instead as a plague on all peoples. The struggle against Jewry is a moral crusade for the purity and health of the peoples created by God, and for a new, more just world order.[66]

These statements echo Hitler's notorious Reichstag speech of 30 January 1939, which he made shortly before the armed forces high command issued the cited booklet to troops. As in Hoberg's essay, Hitler asserted that the Western democracies were controlled by Jews, and were engaging in a 'shameful spectacle … oozing sympathy for the poor tormented Jewish people'. Hitler went on to characterise Jews as possessing 'nothing except infectious political and physical diseases', stating that 'the sooner this problem is solved the better; for Europe cannot settle down until the Jewish question is cleared up', famously pronouncing that 'if the international Jewish financiers in and outside Europe should succeed in plunging the nations once more into a world war, then the result will not be the bolshevisation of the earth, and thus the victory of Jewry, but the annihilation of the Jewish race in Europe!'.[67] Unlike the popular postwar myth, military education and training was keeping in step with the most radical progressions in Nazi anti-Jewish rhetoric, rather than attempting to distance itself from Hitler and his political aspirations.[68]

During the period leading up to the invasion of Poland, there also existed a strengthening in the links between the German military and the armed SS that went beyond the armed forces' incorporation of SS-style racial and ideological indoctrination into their training. Indicative of this is a document issued to the 19th Infantry Regiment, which was to take part in the invasion of Poland. From the high command of the army in Berlin, on 20 June 1939, General Walther von Brauchitsch issued a directive entitled 'Co-operation of the Army with the Armed SS'.[69] In the directive, Brauchitsch, the commander-in-chief of the army,[70] stated that the formation of such SS units would result in the military and the armed SS working more closely together than ever before, with the real possibility that the two organisations would be deployed in the same fields of operations. In order to address this, he ordered a number of measures that were to foster a 'mutual relationship of trust and camaraderie that will promote favourable conditions for the common struggle, shoulder to shoulder', and to 'deepen as much as possible the cooperation … in both official and unofficial capacities … between army and armed SS troops'.[71] Brauchitsch announced that he, in partnership with the leader of the SS, Heinrich Himmler, was ordering a new focus on a number of areas of collaboration. The instructions included the following:

- Armed SS troops are to play a more comprehensive part in the army's manoeuvres and exercises over the summer, as well as in the army's upcoming autumn exercises.
- Close unofficial connections between the officer corps and the SS officer corps are to be fostered through their taking part in social and comradely events.
- SS officers are to take part in the training of army officers on the bases.
- Emphasis is also to be placed upon the cooperation of the army and SS troops through the two organisations' respective publications.[72]

The army wanted its men to view the armed SS as an important partner in the area of deployment. Brauchitsch also regarded it as an organisation with similar values and tasks. Along with the more practical measures of taking part in field exercises together in order to bolster the operational effectiveness of the two organisations during wartime, the army's high command was looking beyond military cooperation and towards ideological cohesion, and aligning the military ever more closely with the SS ideal of ideologically and racially motivated soldiers. This is particularly evident in Brauchitsch's directives to allow SS officers to take part in the training of army officers; the military was encouraging its officers to undergo ideological education from armed SS men, who, as Jürgen Förster has pointed out, received intensive indoctrination in Nazi racial policy that aimed to foster the 'political soldier' and sought to, among other things, normalise and legitimise the murder of

Jews.[73] Brauchitsch's instruction that the army's publications were to place special emphasis on the cooperation with the SS, as well as his instructions to officers to interact socially with SS men, also points to the overall effort to encourage friendship and cross-organisational bonds with the SS, and to help ensure that the two organisations would support each other's operations in any upcoming deployment.

The commander-in-chief of the army issuing such instructions to a regiment that was to take part in the invasion of Poland is further evidence that helps explain the numerous instances of soldiers cooperating with the SS in carrying out atrocities. Members of the military had taken on the ideological training of the armed SS, which along with the specially formed SS task forces (*Einsatzgruppen*) took part in massacres of civilians during the Poland campaign.[74] Most importantly, they had been encouraged to see themselves as organisations that were taking part in the same struggle. This document is also significant in a historiographical sense, as it helps to further counter the postwar myth that the military always viewed the SS with suspicion and stood against its activities.[75]

***

Having established the ideological foundations of the German armed forces, it is important, before we look at its participation in military conflict, to examine certain elements of its tactical basis that, when placed alongside ideological factors, may have influenced its behaviour while deployed in the field.

The most relevant element of the Wehrmacht's mode of operations within this context was its command principle, which was known as *Auftragstaktik*. *Auftragstaktik* is difficult to translate into English in a precise way. In a literal sense, its translation is 'task-based tactics', but perhaps a more accurate way of putting it, in terms of its meaning, would be 'tactics focused on achieving a task'. One scholar has described *Auftragstaktik* as a system of 'directive command', whereby officers were 'guided by directives' in a decentralised command system, which contrasts with the highly centralised system of 'restrictive control' that is based on very specific, restrictive and detailed orders, which has long been favoured by many other armies, including the British army.[76] *Auftragstaktik* is a doctrine in which decision-making is decentralised, giving officers and soldiers in the field as much latitude and responsibility as possible in deciding for themselves how to implement tasks assigned by higher-ranking officers.[77]

Auftragstaktik was based upon flexibility, initiative and taking advantage of circumstances as they presented themselves. It remained a core tenet of the army's approach to training and fighting during the implementation of Nazi indoctrination, and closely examining it allows a clearer understanding of the training that took place and the way in which the army was to function once it took part in armed conflict. The most important insight we can draw from analysing this doctrine is the influence it had on the relationship between training, orders and situational factors, which leads to a clearer understanding of ideological education and the Wehrmacht's involvement in war crimes.

Under the system of *Auftragstaktik*, orders from above were brief and usually verbal, and open to interpretation. Senior officers would assign a task to be carried out, but would not give specific instructions as to *how* to accomplish it, leaving it up to those on the ground to use their judgement and training to decide.[78] Subordinates were always to focus on the overall intent of the orders. In order for the system to function successfully, upon being given a mission, lower-ranking officers, and even soldiers, had to fully understand what their commander intended without him necessarily articulating it.[79] This has implications for the notion of ideological education playing an important role in the behaviour of the Wehrmacht. This is because the crucial factor in successfully implementing the doctrine of *Auftragstaktik* during wartime is the way in which an army trains its soldiers during peacetime.[80] According to Jörg Muth, *Auftragstaktik* fostered a military organisation in which even those towards the bottom of the chain of command understood what was required of them: 'Because of his training, a German officer simply did not require detailed instructions'.[81]

Auftragstaktik was developed well before the time of the Third Reich. The notion of 'directive command' was present in Prussian army circles from the early nineteenth century, when notions of set-piece battle were being done away with.[82] A more developed doctrine of *Auftragstaktik* then later arose as a response to the Austro-Prussian War of 1866 and the Franco-Prussian War of 1870–71. Finding that advances in technology were forcing the dispersion of armies, commanders could no longer observe or control their forces as closely and directly as they had done in previous campaigns. This meant that lower-ranking officers were in the position of having to either make quick decisions in the absence of detailed orders from above, or simply delay action until orders could be received.[83] Since Prussian junior officers were not trained for such scenarios, the results were often disastrous. In turn, the army sought ways to better prepare lower-ranking officers for such situations.

Among the most influential officers in developing the principles of *Auftragstaktik* were Field Marshal Helmut von Moltke and General Sigismund von Schlichting. Both wished to allow officers, at all levels, a greater degree of independence in choosing how to act on the battlefield. Moltke saw the key principle of the doctrine as the subordinate acting, without specific instructions, in a way that achieved his superior's intent:

> Diverse are the situations under which an officer has to act on the basis of his own view of the situation. It would be wrong if he had to wait for orders at times when no orders can be given. But most productive are his actions when he acts within the framework of his commander's intent. It is absolutely necessary that subordinate headquarters recognise the object of what has been ordered. This enables them to strive for that object even if conditions make it necessary to act differently from what has been ordered.[84]

Schlichting, who himself was influenced by von Moltke, further stressed that modern command required general directives, while officers on the ground should use their own judgement to act within the overall intent of their superiors' directives. Schlichting viewed this as far superior to the alternative system of officers having to follow detailed, rigid orders from superiors who were not familiar with the immediate situation, arguing that this would better allow for responses to the unknown circumstances that would arise in the chaos and confusion of battle.[85]

In turn, from the late nineteenth century onwards, *Auftragstaktik* became the command philosophy that guided the training of officers in the German military. A field manual issued in the German army in 1908 indicated its influence:

> In issuing orders, detailed instructions should be especially avoided in cases where circumstances may have changed before the order can be carried out … The general view of the commander for the conduct of the intended operation should be given, but the method of execution must be left open. An order thus issued assumes the nature of a directive.[86]

According to Dennis E. Showalter, this system achieved mixed results during the First World War.[87] While *Auftragstaktik* was successful in launching offensives and achieving quick tactical gains, it was a less successful method in allowing for comprehensive strategic planning, or for industrial and economic mobilisation. Showalter cites Ludendorff's spring offensive of 1918 as a telling example, citing his typically open-ended orders as 'punch a hole and see what happens', as demonstrative of the spirit of *Auftragstaktik*.[88] Ludendorff's strategy is also reminiscent of the views of J.F.C. Fuller, the British general and military historian, who remarked that Moltke 'brought his armies to the starting point and then abdicated his command and unleashed them'.[89]

The postwar period saw a continuation in this command principle. In spite of the enormous structural and personnel changes that the German armed forces underwent as a result of defeat and the Versailles Treaty, their commitment to the doctrine of *Auftragstaktik* remained in place throughout the Weimar Republic era.[90] In 1925, the army chief of staff, Hans von

Seeckt, conveyed the importance of the doctrine to the *Reichswehr*, writing in his 'Observations of the Chief of the Army Command' that 'the principle' of tactical instruction was to 'increase the responsibilities of the individual man, particularly his independence of action, and thereby increase the efficiency of the army'.[91]

The establishment of the Third Reich saw significant changes in the structure, doctrine and training of the German armed forces. *Auftragstaktik*, however, remained in place. Its presence was evident when the military issued a training manual in 1933, which was entitled 'Truppenführung', or 'Leadership of Troops'.[92] It contained many similarities to previous regulations issued during both Weimar and Imperial Germany, with regulations directing that 'lower commanders must be given considerable freedom as to aggressive conduct'.[93] The document set out in clear terms what this would mean. It emphasised individual initiative. It also placed particular weight upon decisiveness of action, even in the absence of specific orders or clear information: 'The first criterion in war always remains decisive action. Everyone, from the highest commander down to the youngest soldier, must constantly be aware that inaction and neglect incriminate him more severely than any error in the choice of means'.[94]

Captain Albert C. Wedemeyer, an American officer who took part in an exchange programme with the German army in 1936, summed up the overriding attitude to making decisions on the battlefield as such: 'Better a faulty plan or decision permeated with boldness, daring, and decisiveness than a perfect plan enmeshed in uncertainty'.[95] In other words, speed and aggression were more important than accuracy; it was better to take the wrong course of action quickly and forcefully than to act with too much consideration or hesitation. A common refrain of military instructors was that 'the officer who waits until he has clear information always acts too late'.[96] Furthermore, a lack of specificity in orders was, in many circumstances, seen as a desired trait:

> If changes in the situation are anticipated before an order can be executed, the order should not go into detail. This is especially important in larger operations, when orders must be issued several days in advance. The general intent is stated and the end to be achieved must especially be emphasised. The general intent must be stated for the execution of impending operations, but the method of execution is left to the subordinate commanders.[97]

The above quotations demonstrate the essence of *Auftragstaktik*. In achieving the goals outlined by their commanders, subordinates had to focus upon the *intent* of the order, and all their actions were to conform to this intent. It did not matter how they went about carrying out their orders.

It only mattered that they achieved the end they thought was desired by superiors. The means to achieve such ends were open for interpretation and initiative,[98] and the more decisive and aggressive the interpretation, and the quicker the course of action was decided upon and taken, the better.

The training of soldiers during peacetime was the crucial factor in ensuring that the system of *Auftragstaktik* worked. In this sense, the interpretation, the initiative and the inferences that subordinates make in order to achieve the intent of their commanding officer are strongly shaped by their training, making detailed instructions superfluous.[99] Unlike more conventional military orders that specifically set out *how* to achieve an objective, while placing restrictions on what a commander may do, evident in the philosophy of 'restrictive control',[100] under the doctrine of *Auftragstaktik* there is a 'gap' where the 'how' of the order normally exists. Subordinate troops on the ground had to fill in this 'gap'. The clearest indication they received as to how to act in such situations was provided in their training. This principle is evocative of the notion of ambiguity in orders being a tool used by militaries to influence outcomes; when soldiers find themselves in the chaos of battle, they need to react as quickly as possible. In such situations, soldiers usually fall back upon their military training, which is fashioned with the intention of shaping their responses in a particular way.[101]

What made this system especially precarious is that it gave the impression that it was permissible for any course of action to be carried out, so long as it achieved the so-called 'intent' of superiors, and that it conformed to the training that soldiers and officers had undergone. Few, if any, boundaries were set.

If anything, the notion of the existence of boundaries was contrary to the spirit of the doctrine. The only guidelines provided were an emphasis on 'decisive action', along with a scorning of careful consideration over which course of action to take. In effect, this means that almost any means can be justified by stating that the officer was merely acting as quickly, aggressively and decisively as possible, using his initiative and his training to achieve the ends that he saw as desired by his superiors. The risk involved in such a doctrine is that it made the escalation and radicalisation of violence much more likely, and even expected, than under a system that encouraged restraint and careful consideration.[102] The system was 'self de-limiting, making it more likely to … produce greater policy drift towards greater violence, than to challenge it'.[103]

The existence of *Auftragstaktik* as a command principle has implications for this study. The doctrine itself, and the way in which it was implemented, was concerned primarily with tactical and strategic matters. *Auftragstaktik* sought to ensure flexibility on the battlefield in order to grant those on the ground the ability to make decisions based on their own first-hand observations. It also aimed to allow speed and improvisation in an era in which the notion of mobile, 'lightning war' was at the forefront of commanders' minds.[104] Yet this doctrine has wider repercussions when it is implemented as a principle of issuing and carrying out instructions and directives. This is relevant to actions that were carried out that fall under the category of war crimes. Regardless of the context, whether they were involved in battle against enemy soldiers, in anti-partisan conflict or in occupying or 'pacifying' civilian populations, the rank and file had to interpret general orders from above, and take action that they regarded as conforming to the intent of their superiors. In the German armed forces, both the subordinate and commanding officer were serving within a military that trained its men in the tenets of Nazism, with the aim of ensuring that they would always act according to Nazi ideology, even when it was not explicitly set out in orders.[105]

This style of command was very similar to the standard Nazi Party technique that was explained in a document relating to the 1938 *Kristallnacht* pogrom. The document, a report of the Nazi Party Supreme Court, stated that it was

> ... obvious to active National Socialists from the *Kampfzeit* ... that orders for campaigns ... need not be completely clear and detailed. They are also accustomed to reading more into such an order than is written or said, just as the issuer of this order has often become adept, in the Party's interest ... at leaving the order unclear and at merely sketching out its aim.[106]

Ben Shepherd points out the relevance of this style of command in his work on the Wehrmacht in Yugoslavia, arguing that:

> The style of command within the Third Reich ... was more open ended than one might expect. This meant that directives often resembled not so much clear cut orders as general guidelines for action. In this way they embodied the National Socialist 'leadership principle'.[107]

Looking closely at *Auftragstaktik* and its relationship with ideological training in the Wehrmacht helps to demonstrate that soldiers and officers had a relatively high degree of independence. Yet this independence was to take place within the context of what they understood the 'intent' of their commanders to be. Training of soldiers was the key factor in implementing *Auftragstaktik* in a manner that would ensure that soldiers' initiative was exerted in ways that their training would help to shape. Ceaseless ideological indoctrination that constantly taught soldiers that they were to engage with ideologically and ethnically defined enemies, and a new type of racial war that only one ethnic group would survive, ensured that soldiers interpreted their orders in a way that furthered the goals of Nazi ideology. The fact that soldiers' training was designed to ensure that they would act according to the tenets of Nazi ideology regardless of whether it was expressed in their orders illustrates how the notion of *Auftragstaktik* fitted in well with the ideological education that took place. In effect, the military's familiarity with the concept of *Auftragstaktik* was an important factor in the army's wartime implementation of the Nazi ideology that was so prominent in its training. It also indicates that not only had the military taken on elements of Nazi ideology, but it also had a command structure in place that was very similar to that of the Nazi Party itself.

***

The invasion of Poland displayed many facets of the war of extermination that began two years later in the Soviet Union. As Jochen Böhler asserted, the Poland campaign represented the 'prelude to the war of extermination'.[108] From the beginning, alongside the territorial goals of revising the Treaty of Versailles and securing *Lebensraum*, the campaign was an ideological one. Hitler made this clear to numerous generals on 22 August 1939 at his mountain retreat near Berchtesgaden. He instructed them that they were not to think of the upcoming campaign in traditional terms, and instead were to concentrate on the 'elimination of living forces, not the arrival at a certain line', and that the campaign was to be carried out with the 'greatest brutality and without mercy'. Hitler then proclaimed that the SS stood ready to 'mercilessly send to their death men, women and children of Polish descent', indicating his decision to eliminate the Polish upper class, clergy, intelligentsia and Jews.[109]

Numerous examples of directives to troops in the immediate lead-up to the invasion alerted them to the racial nature of the upcoming struggle, with an emphasis on the threat posed by the Polish civilian population. This included proclamations relating to the so-called Polish 'ethnic character', described as 'cruel and sly', as well as the danger of Polish Jews, who were 'Bolshevist friendly and anti-German'[110] and who 'see in the Germans their personal enemy'.[111] In effect, the military sought to instil the attitude that all Polish civilians were treacherous and deceitful, with the local Jews said to be whipping them into an anti-German frenzy. The directions justified harsh measures taken against civilians, as Poles, and especially Jews, were always hostile and suspect.[112]

In a 'Leaflet for the Conduct of German Soldiers in the Occupied Territory of Poland', the commander-in-chief of the army, Walther von Brauchitsch, alerted German soldiers that they would 'confront inner enmity from all civilians who are not members of the German race'. He also told them that 'the behaviour towards Jews needs no special mention for the soldiers of the

National Socialist Reich'.[113] Instructions given to the 208th infantry division provide a further example of how German soldiers were instructed to act: 'Treatment of the population should be severe ... and should the need arise, drastic measures should be taken'.[114] While not explicitly ordering soldiers to murder civilians, it effectively gave them permission to do so. When placed within the context of the long-term ideological education within the army that continually depicted the enemy, particularly regarding the East and Jews, such directives help to account for instances of atrocities. Ideological education had laid the foundations for the normalisation of such orders, and for them to be taken to the furthest degree. Images of certain types of enemies had become blurred, since racial classifications did not distinguish between civilians and military personnel.

Letters and diary entries that soldiers penned during the Poland campaign provide an insight into the attitudes of some of those in the field. Extensive studies of Wehrmacht letters, carried out by Walter Manoschek[115] and Stephen G. Fritz,[116] have shown that many servicemen, particularly the younger soldiers who, due to their age group, were of the generation that experienced prior indoctrination not only in the army but also in schools, the Hitler Youth and the Reich Labour Service, adopted numerous aspects of the National Socialist view of the world.[117] Numerous letters suggest that ideological instruction had an effect upon many soldiers, particularly in relation to the 'Jewish question'. Many soldiers fighting in Poland regarded the Jews they encountered as the enemy. Even the very sight of Jews, particularly the unfamiliar *Ostjuden* (Eastern, often Orthodox Jews) provoked negative perceptions, and seemed to confirm the destructive stereotypes that ideological education promoted. A letter from a soldier of the 111th Mountain Artillery Regiment, Corporal G., during the early phase of the campaign illustrated such views:

> In Bircza we recognised the necessity of a radical solution of the Jewish question. Here one could see these beasts in the flesh ... With their beards and kaftans, with their devilish grimaces they made a ghastly impression upon us. Anyone who was not already a radical antisemite must become one here. In comparison to the Polish caftan-Jews, our own Jewish bloodsuckers are lambs. No wonder that after twenty years the Polish state has become victim to these parasites.[118]

What is striking about this letter is not only the virulent antisemitism on display, but also the language employed. The terms used are identical to those found within the educational material, particularly the call for a 'radical solution' to the 'Judenfrage'. The branding of Jews as 'parasites' echoed Hoberg's article, which referred to Jews in the same terms. Furthermore, Corporal G.

saw the radical solution as a 'necessary' action, reflecting the emphasis placed upon scientific, pragmatic 'necessity' present in propaganda relating to the 'Jewish question'. In turn, the combination of virulent antisemitism and its expression in strikingly similar language gives the impression of a soldier schooled in a particularly National Socialist style of antisemitism, one that viewed Jews within the context of a 'Jewish question' and sought a 'radical solution' to a problem rooted in racial rather than religious differences.

Another soldier, from the 35th infantry division, wrote a letter home that further suggested adherence to the ideas espoused in the Wehrmacht's educational programme:

> The Jew has always been a plague on Europe's soil. Historical documentation has confirmed that since the first intrusion of Jews and their religion in Europe, Europeans have been fighting each other … They have succeeded in destroying world peace, and, today, 2000 years later, the first reaction is taking place to make Europe Europe again, and Germany into a Reich of all those of Germanic origins.[119]

While antisemitism in itself may have existed prior to these soldiers' enlistment in the military, the expression of it in such terms is strongly evocative of military ideological education. The parallels between the second letter and Hoberg's 'The Jew in German History' are striking. It is difficult to say how representative these letters were of the broad mass of soldiers that took part in this campaign. Indeed, we will probably never be able to know for certain due to the number of soldiers, and therefore letters, involved in such a study. Questions arising from the use of letters from the front as a source will, however, be dealt with in greater detail later in this study.

Harassment, theft and acts of extreme violence against Polish civilians became a common feature of the invasion. Orders that called for 'drastic measures' against the population 'should the need arise', alongside a deep suspicion and hatred of the supposedly inferior and deceitful Polish race that was propagated by military commanders, resulted in numerous instances of massacres of civilians.[120] Alongside these orders, antisemitic sentiments produced a tendency to implicate Jews in cases of partisan warfare conducted against German forces, even taking for granted that all Jewish men, women and children were armed and presented a threat to the invading army.[121] In the Polish town of Bilgoraj, for instance, the commander of the third battalion of the 63rd Infantry Regiment noted the appearance of partisan activity in his report as *Judengefahr* (translated as 'Jewish threat' or 'Jewish danger').[122] Consequently, German soldiers often made Jewish inhabitants of Polish towns collectively responsible for guerrilla attacks. It was often the case that entire Jewish populations of towns were detained.[123]

The looting of Jewish homes and property, as well as the arbitrary humiliation of Jewish men by cutting off their beards, or by forcing them to scrub the streets, were also common events,[124] and many were the subject of photographs taken by soldiers. Many of these pictures were supplemented with mocking captions. One such picture, of a German soldier cutting a Jewish man's hair, was accompanied by the caption 'The locks fall. Jewish crook at the mobile barber shop'. Two photographs taken by a member of the army's alpine division (*Gebirgsjäger*) show Jews lining up and being made to carry out forced labour, with the derisive commentary: 'The "Chosen People"', and 'Even they can learn how'.[125] This spirit of triumphalism over apparently vanquished and humiliated 'enemies', who were no more than civilians, suggests that ideological considerations played a significant role in shaping soldiers' views of their sanctioned role in this conflict.

Polish citizens could do little to counter the treatment they encountered at the hands of the invading Wehrmacht. In November 1939, shortly after the invasion had taken place, a number of Polish citizens, on behalf of the populations of Warsaw and Lodz, wrote a letter to German army commanders in order to protest against the behaviour of its men and plead with German generals to intervene. The Poles were stunned that soldiers of the German army could behave in such a manner. The letter outlined the numerous crimes that German soldiers had committed.

> Are you aware that German soldiers are carrying out outrageous atrocities against the Polish and Jewish populations? The soldiers are robbing and plundering, and any protest results in them turning their weapons on defenceless, unarmed people. Even daylight robbery on the streets is an everyday occurrence. Travelling salespeople who have come here are being robbed of their money and cars, and numerous murders of Jewish and Polish business owners have been carried out.[126]

German soldiers were behaving 'like wild hordes', particularly support troops who were in the rear echelons.[127] The attempts by some generals to bring such behaviour under control, fearing a breakdown in discipline, clearly had little effect on many soldiers. Soldiers were 'ignoring the orders that they are not to murder or plunder'.[128]

The activities of other German organisations during the occupation of Poland also helped to create an environment that was conducive to such behaviour. The German police were in no position to intervene, due to a 'lack of united leadership'. Indeed, the police did not seem to want to put a stop to the violence and theft. Most German police were turning a blind eye to the conduct of the army: 'only a few … have tried to prevent these horrendous crimes', while others refused to interfere, telling people that they 'might be punished' if they did. Even those policemen who did try to intervene made little impact, with soldiers simply ignoring them. The SS was also helping to set the tone for the undisciplined behaviour of the military: 'The SS ... has given the signal that Germans can do anything they like with Jews and Poles ... The SS leaders cover for the brutality of their men. Everyone can do whatever they want ... No wonder that the soldiers do what they want to as well'.[129]

Such behaviour was one consequence of the environment fostered within the military prior to and during the invasion and occupation of Poland. The soldiers who engaged in such activities were treating the people they encountered in a way that was not inconsistent with their training. Military training had not set boundaries that governed who could and could not be entangled in armed conflict. In short, there was no sense of 'limited warfare', which 'encourages reasonable use of force and compassionate conduct towards the unarmed enemy' and 'sets boundaries to organised human violence'.[130] Instead, there was a consistent repudiation of such a notion. Nor did the troops' orders prior to the campaign set strict boundaries. German soldiers and lower-ranking officers were interpreting these orders, which decreed that they treat the population, who were 'not members of the German race', 'severely' and that they should take 'drastic measures' 'should the need arise',[131] with 'the behaviour towards Jews [needing] no special mention'[132] in a way that was, again, in no way inconsistent with their training.

Such orders effectively sanctioned criminality, and soldiers acted in such a manner even when, later on, their commanders explicitly forbade them from taking part in activities like lootings and executions, prohibitions that contrasted with the spirit of the initial orders soldiers received from the highest levels of the army's command structure. Such behaviour is also partially explainable by the fact that in contrast to the harsh discipline handed out for desertion or 'cowardice' in battle, such unauthorised activities against the enemy rarely resulted in punishment.[133] All of this fits into a broader context in which the 'accepted rules of war ... did not apply to the political and racial categories deemed by the regime, and thus by the Wehrmacht, as undeserving'.[134] When such orders and training existed, it was difficult for the military to prevent and then punish soldiers for doing what, in effect, they had been trained and then instructed, or at the very least encouraged, to do.

The notion of German soldiers being able to 'do whatever they want' leads to an important aspect of the violence that took place against civilians. It often took place spontaneously at the behest of soldiers and junior officers.[135] While the orders at the start of the campaign contained harsh language and insinuations about ruthless behaviour, they were not explicit in setting out exactly what soldiers were to do. Those on the ground still had to take the final step, on their own initiative, if they were to commit war crimes. The way in which members of the German armed forces behaved strongly suggests that it was a matter of soldiers and junior officers interpreting their orders from higher-ranking commanders in a certain manner. The attitude fostered by military indoctrination, typified by documents such as 'The Jew in German History', supplemented their orders and effectively provided soldiers and officers with an idea of the kind of behaviour that was expected of them. Men who had continually received instruction about the danger posed by foreign races to the survival of the German nation, and the need to 'radically eliminate' the Jews like a 'poisonous parasite', could be expected to act in the ways they did in Poland when ordered to take 'drastic measures' against civilian populations, particularly when told by the commander-in-chief of the army that their 'behaviour towards Jews needs no special mention'.

It is within this framework that the examination of the military's educational material is important. While historians have documented army atrocities in Poland, using pre-existing antisemitic and anti-Polish prejudices as an explanation for these acts, scholars have largely overlooked the role the military itself played in reinforcing and propagating them during training, and making them a part of military doctrine, as well as a duty of soldiers at the lowest levels. It is therefore critical to consider the Wehrmacht's ideological education programme, and, in turn, view the directives given and the actions carried out during the Polish campaign within this context.

In fact, making such acts of personal initiative likely was one of the very purposes of the programme of ideological education in the armed forces. It was also closely related to the army's command doctrine of *Auftragstaktik*.[136] Indicative of this premise, one year before the beginning of the Poland campaign, the high command of the army issued a statement clarifying what the ideological education of troops would mean during wartime: 'It is a given that the officer, in every situation, acts according to the ideology of the Third Reich, even when such ideologies are not explicitly expressed in official regulations and decrees or in orders while on active duty'.[137] When an educational programme with such objectives was implemented, under the umbrella of the command doctrine of *Auftragstaktik*, it is little wonder that German troops went beyond the letter of orders, and interpreted and carried out instructions in a manner that advanced the racial and ideological aims of the Polish campaign.

There are, of course, numerous other factors involved in accounting for German war crimes in Poland. Aspects of the conduct of German soldiers in Poland had clear parallels in previous campaigns. One important element is the German army's history of brutal treatment of civilian populations during war, particularly those suspected of being involved in armed resistance.

During the Franco-Prussian War of 1870–71, German troops often encountered attacks from volunteer French civilian units known as *Francs-Tireurs*, or 'Free-Shooters'.[138] The image of the *Francs-Tireurs* lingered in the German mentality long after the Franco-Prussian War, causing a particular hatred of irregular warfare. This manifested itself decades later during the German invasion of France and Belgium in 1914, where German troops reacted with extreme brutality to the slightest civilian resistance, resulting in thousands of civilians being shot.[139] Such behaviour was not restricted to France and Belgium in 1914. During the German campaign on the Eastern Front during the First World War, collective punishment was often imposed upon villages or towns in which German troops were shot at, and civilians caught in possession of firearms were executed.[140] German war crimes also took place during numerous other conflicts in the imperial era, with harsh treatment of enemies, including civilians in cases of resistance, a hallmark of the conduct of the German army.[141]

The German army's brutal reactions in such situations were not solely the result of their hatred of irregular warfare. The fear of *Francs-Tireurs*, often further fuelled by myths and rumours that spread throughout the army, meant that troops were often particularly edgy and prone to panic and overreaction.[142] Furthermore, senior German commanders believed that the *Francs-Tireurs* had attributes in common with elements that they viewed as Germany's internal enemies: they were Catholic and working class. While this may not have been a motivating factor for regular troops, many of whom were Catholic and/or working class, Ben Shepherd has argued that it is notable that senior officers were 'advocating a reprisal policy that fused "security" needs with ideological ones', which had the long-term effect of ingraining the idea of an association between 'combating insurgency and combating ideological enemies'.[143]

Of course, alongside the aversion to partisan warfare, and closely related to the notion of merging ideological goals with security goals, was the presence of pre-existing anti-Slavic attitudes. Such sentiments had long existed within German society, as well as within the military itself, with the popular stereotype portraying Slavs as primitive, backward and barbaric.[144] The Nazi regime sought to exploit these sentiments in the lead-up to the outbreak of war, launching a barrage of anti-Polish propaganda upon the German public.[145] More specific to the military, the experience of the German army in Eastern Europe during and immediately after the First World War had a profoundly negative effect on the views that it had of the lands and people of the East. The army's occupation was characterised by 'colonial style condescension and casual brutality' towards the Slavic populations they encountered; locals were required to bow to Germans, and unchecked violence towards civilians became common.[146] The legacy of the German occupation and its experience there was that the East was regarded as primitive and threatening, and viewed in terms of '*Raum* and *Volk*' that needed to be conquered and ordered by German forces. These pre-existing ideas were ripe for Nazi ideology to build upon and radicalise in its approach to the upcoming war in the East,[147] with Shepherd arguing that the experience of Eastern Europe during the First World War was an 'incubator of the ideological harshness Nazism would later come to exploit in military servants a quarter of a century later'.[148]

A further precedent for the German military's targeting of civilians in Poland, which displayed aspects of both the aversion to irregular warfare and the brutal treatment of racial 'others', was set in German South West Africa in 1904, in which a rebellion of the indigenous Herero people against German rule was brutally suppressed by the army in a campaign of attempted extermination. This campaign displayed parallels with the Nazi programme in Eastern Europe in that it sought to annihilate a supposedly inferior 'race' in order to secure *Lebensraum* for Germans.[149] The strategy of military leaders, in what they labelled a 'race war', was based upon wiping out the enemy. The German commander, General Lothar von Trotha, received an instruction from Kaiser Wilhelm II to 'crush the rebellion by all means necessary', indicating that he, as the commander on the ground, had the power to decide how to enact the Kaiser's orders.[150] Trotha thought that 'no war may be conducted humanely against non-humans' and set in motion a 'race war', which involved an 'annihilation order' that decreed that 'within the German borders, every Herero, with or without weapons … will be shot'.[151] While the German army was by no means unique among Western armies in carrying out a brutal colonial campaign, this campaign nonetheless helped to remove limitations to violence, particularly against civilians. It also helped create a link between the notions of a military defeat of an enemy force and the extermination of a people.[152]

The conduct of German soldiers in Poland in 1939 was therefore not the first situation in which German soldiers had responded brutally against suspected insurgents, nor was it the first time that their behaviour had indicated a blurring of the lines between civilian and military targets. Instead, there had previously existed a particular fear of, and harsh attitude towards, unconventional warfare, as well as collective punishment that made no allowances for the status of civilians, and which amalgamated security and ideological goals.[153] In turn, precedents had been set in allowing the military's prevailing doctrines to be enacted in dealing with enemy populations. Horne and Kramer argue that in 1914, the response of the German army to the fear of *Francs-Tireurs* reflected the prejudices and canons that existed within the German army. In the case of Poland in 1939, the behaviour of German troops very much reflected the official doctrines of the German military regarding alien races, and the form of warfare that Germans had been trained to carry out when facing such enemies.

The environment in which the troops found themselves was also a contributing factor. German soldiers were in a place that was unfamiliar, and seen by many as being primitive and backward.[154] This hostile and alien environment made for confusion, nervousness and bouts of panic.[155] It is here that an insight into the nature of military training is instructive, and supportive of Horne and Kramer's notion of the predominant doctrines of the military influencing behaviour. As noted earlier, military training seeks to shape soldiers' responses to confusing and chaotic situations in a way that is based upon the information that the military provides them.[156]

The involvement of German troops in atrocities in Poland in 1939 was the result of numerous factors. Negative, pre-conceived notions of the people and lands of Eastern Europe existed, and past mistreatment of civilians during German military campaigns had set important precedents for acceptable behaviour. Training within the Wehrmacht made such behaviour even more likely in the future. Had the official doctrine of the military been different, had soldiers been trained to engage in 'limited warfare', which encouraged reasonable use of force and compassionate conduct towards the unarmed enemy, and which set clear boundaries to violence,[157] and nonetheless behaved the way that so many did in Poland, prewar training could indeed be discounted as a contributing factor within this debate. But this was far from the case. It is instructive that, in general, the Wehrmacht's behaviour in the West in 1940 was not as bad as in Poland in 1939, despite the military's past experiences with *Francs-Tireurs* in France and Belgium. In fact, the most notable instances of German atrocities in France, for instance, were when they encountered black French soldiers serving in colonial units.[158]

***

Jochen Böhler asserts that while the military campaign in Poland lasted, the German army was responsible for as many executions of Polish civilians, including Jews, as were the police and SS.[159] In the aftermath of the campaign, the head of the security police and the SD, Reinhard Heydrich, noted that, 'If one compares the cases of excesses and looting carried out by the army with that of the SS and police, on this occasion, the SS doesn't come out too badly'.[160] The soldiers and officers of the Wehrmacht had played a significant role in this 'prelude to the war of extermination'[161] despite not, unlike the SS and the police, having been officially, explicitly ordered to carry out the liquidation of Germany's racial and ideological enemies, an objective delegated to the SS and the police. The campaign displayed many of the features of the Barbarossa campaign: the Wehrmacht executed non-combatants and prisoners in large numbers, based upon racial and ideological considerations, and generally, with a few exceptions, allowed the SS task forces a free hand in carrying out Nazi ethnic policy.[162]

Some senior officers did, however, disapprove of the behaviour of the SS and the police. These included General Johannes Blaskowitz, head of the Eighth Army, who was the most outspoken in protesting against the massacres of civilians, arguing that as well as being morally outrageous, such activities would not quell Polish resistance, and instead assist enemy propaganda and convince more people to resist the occupation.[163] He also worried about the possible effect of the killings on discipline among his own men, fearing 'immeasurable brutalisation and moral debasement'.[164] Other senior officers had similar concerns, worrying about a breakdown in military discipline, and became anxious to preserve the military's executive authority over other organisations,[165] with one senior officer, Walter Petzel, concerned that the SS was behaving like a 'state within a state'.[166] Nevertheless, the majority of military commanders agreed with the basis of the roles of the SS and the police, and even those who displayed hesitancy soon recognised that their actions provided an important security function in cleansing 'resistance' behind the army's front line.[167] The uncovering of the previously cited document issued by the army's high command to units that were to take part in the invasion of Poland, which ordered the fostering of better relations with the SS, helps to account for the cooperation of the army and the SS, which 'functioned smoothly and without friction, particularly when it came to the deportation of Jews'.[168] Heydrich confirmed this when he noted that securing the military's assistance in such tasks was not difficult, and that this early cooperation helped to establish the roles that each organisation would play later on in the Soviet campaign.[169]

The actions of the German army during the Poland campaign suggest that ideological education within the military is an important factor in accounting for the involvement of the military in atrocities during the Second World War. While the influences of membership in the Hitler Youth, as well as exposure to National Socialist attitudes in German society, are undoubtedly important when investigating the socialisation of German troops, this framework does present a number of problems in the context of the Poland campaign.[170] The most significant problem arises due to the fact that the combat troops involved in the invasion, according to regimental personnel surveys, were generally born in 1915 or 1916. Alexander Rossino has argued that this meant they were of an age group whose 'socialisation was complete by the time Hitler came to power in 1933',[171] and most of them were too old to have belonged to the Hitler Youth.[172]

Böhler is more thorough, however, when he points out that while many who took part in the invasion of Poland had reached adulthood before or during the earliest stages of the Nazi era, they had come of age during the turbulent, often violent Weimar era. He also shows that one in seven soldiers of an average infantry division was at one stage a member of the SA, around half had been members of the Reich Labour Service, and one in five had been in the Hitler Youth.[173] Such statistics are supported by the previously mentioned survey (see chapter three) of Wehrmacht recruits during the recruitment drive of 1934.[174]

The examination of the Wehrmacht's systematic programme of ideological instruction moves the historiography beyond the current level of understanding, which, while recognising that National Socialist ideology played an important role in influencing the actions of Wehrmacht troops during this campaign, does not adequately account for the role that the military itself played in this process. The systematic ideological indoctrination of soldiers and officers exposes the responsibility of the military itself, alongside other institutions like the Hitler Youth and the Reich Labour Service, in instilling the values of National Socialism into its members and, just as importantly, training them to implement them. As Böhler points out, while not all soldiers had previous membership, and thus indoctrination, in other Nazi organisations, all had undergone training in the military.[175]

The analytical framework outlined in this chapter also allows a more comprehensive explanation for the tendency of soldiers to go beyond the letter of their orders and take the initiative in carrying out the murder of Germany's racial and ideological enemies. The army's efforts to indoctrinate lower-ranking officers provide an insight into why so many officers agreed with the racial nature of the campaign, and why they tolerated the actions of both the SS and the men under their command. A deeper appreciation of the relationship between official orders and actual occurrences enables a more thorough understanding of the crimes of the Wehrmacht in Poland. It exposes the unspoken expectations that went with official orders, and, in turn, allows us a clearer understanding of how those on the ground were likely to have interpreted such directives.

Notes

1. See, for example, Christian Hartmann, Johannes Hürter and Ulrike Jureit, 'Verbrechen der Wehrmacht: Ergebnisse und Kontroversen der Forschung', in idem, *Verbrechen der Wehrmacht: Bilanz einer Debatte* (Munich, 2005), 21–28; Omer Bartov, *The Eastern Front, 1941–45: German Troops and the Barbarisation of Warfare* (Basingstoke, 1985); idem, *Hitler's Army: Soldiers, Nazis and War in the Third Reich* (Oxford, 1991); idem, 'Operation Barbarossa and the Origins of the Final Solution', in David Cesarani (ed.),

The Final Solution: Origins and Implementation (London, 1996), 119–36; idem, 'Soldiers, Nazis and War in the Third Reich', *The Journal of Modern History* 63(1) (March 1991), 44–60; Jürgen Förster, 'Operation Barbarossa as a War of Conquest and Annihilation', in Berel Lang and Simone Gigliotti (eds), *The Holocaust: A Reader* (Carlton, 2005), 184–97; idem, 'Der Weltanschauungs- und Vernichtungskrieg im Osten', in *Das deutsche Reich und der Zweite Weltkrieg Band 9/1: Der deutsche Kriegsgesellschaft 1939 bis 1945* (Munich, 2004), 519–538; idem, 'Geistige Kriegführung in der Phase der ersten Siege', in *Das deutsche Reich und der Zweite Weltkrieg Band 9/1*, 506–19; Stephen G. Fritz, '"We Are Trying … to Change the Face of the World" – Ideology and Motivation in the Wehrmacht on the Eastern Front: The View from Below', *The Journal of Military History* 60(4) (1996), 683–710; Ben Shepherd, *War in the Wild East: The German Army and Partisans* (Cambridge, MA, 2004); Christian Hartmann, *Wehrmacht im Ostkrieg: Front und militärisches Hinterland 1941–1942* (Munich, 2009); Hans Safrian, 'Komplizen des Genozids: Zum Anteil der Heeresgruppe Süd an der Verfolgung und Ermordung der Juden in der Ukraine 1941', in Walter Manoschek (ed.), *Die Wehrmacht im Rassenkrieg: Der Vernichtungskrieg hinter der Front* (Vienna, 1996), 90–115; Wolfram Wette, *The Wehrmacht: History, Myth, Reality* (Cambridge, MA, 2006), 90–138; Richard Bessel, *Nazism and War* (London, 2004), 108–26; Richard J. Evans, *The Third Reich at War* (London, 2009), 175–77, 239, 255–56; Ian Kershaw, *Hitler* (London, 2010); Stephen G. Fritz, *Ostkrieg: Hitler's War of Extermination in the East* (Lexington, 2011), 67–70, 94–104.
2. See Jochen Böhler, *Auftakt zum Vernichtungskrieg: Die Wehrmacht in Polen 1939* (Frankfurt, 2006); idem, *"Grösste Härte …": Verbrechen der Wehrmacht in Polen, September, Oktober 1939* (Warsaw, 2005); idem, *Der Überfall: Deutschlands Krieg gegen Polen* (Frankfurt, 2009); Alexander B. Rossino, *Hitler Strikes Poland: Blitzkrieg, Ideology, and Atrocity* (Lawrence, 2003).
3. Bartov, *Hitler's Army*, 12–28.
4. Böhler, *Auftakt zum Vernichtungskrieg*, 18.
5. Evans, *The Third Reich at War*, 101–2.
6. Ibid.
7. Ibid., 20; see also Böhler, *Der Überfall*.
8. Böhler, *Auftakt zum Vernichtungskrieg*, 36.
9. Klaus Jürgen Müller, 'The Army and the Third Reich', in Neil Gregor (ed.), *Nazism* (Oxford, 2000), 169.
10. Kershaw, *Hitler*, 397–98.
11. Karl-Heinz Janssen and Fritz Tobias, *Der Sturz der Generäle: Hitler und die Blomberg-Fritsch-Krise 1938* (Munich, 1994); Richard J. Evans, *The Third Reich in Power* (London, 2006), 643–46; Kershaw, *Hitler*, 391–94; Harold C. Deutsch, *Hitler and His Generals: The Hidden Crisis, January–June 1938* (Minneapolis, 1974), 80–121.
12. See the Hossbach Memorandum, Berlin, 10 November 1937, available at http://avalon.law.yale.edu/imt/hossbach.asp (accessed 17 September 2018). See also Evans, *The Third Reich at War*, 642; Robert O'Neill, *The German Army and the Nazi Party, 1933–1939* (London, 1966), 139; Michael Salewski, 'Wehrmacht und Nationalsozialismus 1933-1939', in Militärgeschichtliches Forschungsamt (ed.), *Handbuch zur Deutschen Militärgeschichte 1648-1939* (Munich, 1978), 194.
13. O'Neill, *The German Army and the Nazi Party*, 139.
14. Evans, *The Third Reich in Power*, 642–43; Kershaw, *Hitler*, 391–94.
15. Salewski, 'Wehrmacht und Nationalsozialismus', 195. See also Kirstin A. Schäfer, *Werner von Blomberg: Hitlers erster Feldmarschall* (Paderborn, 2006), 180–91.

16. Kershaw, *Hitler*, 391; Salewski, 'Wehrmacht und Nationalsozialismus', 196.
17. O'Neill, *The German Army and the Nazi Party*, 139.
18. Evans, *The Third Reich in Power*, 693; Kershaw, *Hitler*, 394.
19. Kershaw, *Hitler*, 391–98.
20. Ibid., 397–98; Salewski, 'Wehrmacht und Nationalsozialismus', 194–95; Manfred Messerschmidt, 'Die Wehrmacht als tragende Säule des NS-Staates (1933-1939)', in Manoschek, *Die Wehrmacht im Rassenkrieg*, 52; Müller, 'The Army and the Third Reich', 169; Evans, *The Third Reich in Power*, 644.
21. Gustav-Adolf Caspar and Herbert Schottelius, 'Die Organisation des Heeres 1933–1939', in Hans Meier-Welcker (ed.), *Handbuch zur deutschen Militärgeschichte 1648–1939* (Frankfurt, 1978), 328; Messerschmidt, 'Die Wehrmacht als tragende Säule des NS-Staates', 49–50.
22. Evans, *The Third Reich in Power*, 644; Kershaw, *Hitler*, 422; Manfred Messerschmidt, *Die Wehrmacht im NS-Staat: Zeit der Indoktrination* (Hamburg, 1969), 211–13; O'Neill, *The German Army and the Nazi Party*, 146.
23. Brauchitsch, quoted in O'Neill, *The German Army and the Nazi Party*, 68.
24. Kershaw, *Hitler*, 399–400.
25. Ibid., 398; Evans, *The Third Reich in Power*, 644–45; O'Neill, *The German Army and the Nazi Party*, 139; Salewski, 'Wehrmacht und Nationalsozialismus', 194–203; Müller, 'The Army and the Third Reich', 169.
26. Salewski, 'Wehrmacht und Nationalsozialismus', 202.
27. Müller, 'The Army and the Third Reich', 170.
28. Messerschmidt, 'Die Wehrmacht als tragende Säule des NS-Staates', 52.
29. Institut für Zeitgeschichte, München (hereafter IfZ), Da 33.59, Oberkommando der Wehrmacht (ed.), *Schulungshefte für den Unterricht über nationalsozialistische Weltanschauung und Nationalpolitische Zielsetzung, Erster Jahrgang, 1939*, 2.
30. IfZ, Da 33.59, Oberkommando der Wehrmacht (ed.), 'Offizier und Politik, Einst und Jetzt', in *Schulungshefte für den Unterricht über nationalsozialistische Weltanschauung und nationalpolitische Zielsetzung, Erster Jahrgang 1939*, 4–6.
31. Ibid.
32. Ibid., 6–8.
33. Bundesarchiv/Militärarchiv (hereafter BA/MA) RW 6/V. 166, 'Erfahrungsbericht von Hauptmann Hermann Kraus', in *Sommer-Lehrgang für Offiziere in Bad Tölz: 'Vortragsreihe über nationalsozialistische Weltanschauung und Zielsetzung vom 11.–17.6.1939 in Bad Tölz'*.
34. Letter from Franz Xaver Schwarz, in BA/MA RW 6/V. 166, *Sommer-Lehrgang für Offiziere in Bad Tölz*.
35. Ibid.
36. BA/MA RW 6/V. 166, *Sommer-Lehrgang für Offiziere in Bad Tölz*.
37. Ibid.
38. 'Die Verhütung des erbkranken Nachwuchses', in BA/MA RW 6/V. 166, *Sommer-Lehrgang für Offiziere in Bad Tölz*.
39. Evans, *The Third Reich at War*, 81.
40. Hauptmann Hof, Berlin, 25 June 1939: 'Zweck und Ziel der "Vortragsreihe"' in BA/MA RW 6/V. 166, *Sommer-Lehrgang für Offiziere in Bad Tölz*, 2–3.
41. Major Wizotski, 'Erfahrungsbericht über die Vortragsreihe für Offiziere', in BA/MA RW 6/V. 166, *Sommer-Lehrgang für Offiziere in Bad Tölz*.
42. BA/MA RW 6/V. 166, 'Erfahrungsbericht', Hauptmann 7./J.R. 13, 2–4.
43. BA/MA RW 6/V. 166, 'Erfahrungsbericht', Hauptmann 6./J.R. 12.

44. Hauptmann Hof, Berlin, 25 June 1939, 'Zweck und Ziel der "Vortragsreihe"', in BA/MA RW 6/V. 166, *Sommer-Lehrgang für Offiziere in Bad Tölz*, 8.
45. 'Erfahrungsbericht', Hauptmann 7./J.R in BA/MA RW 6/V. 166, *Sommer-Lehrgang für Offiziere in Bad Tölz*, 13, 2–4.
46. Ian Kershaw, 'How Effective Was Nazi Propaganda?' in David Welch (ed.), *Nazi Propaganda: The Power and the Limitations* (London, 1983), 182–83; see also David Welch, *The Third Reich: Politics and Propaganda* (London, 1993), 59.
47. Evans, *The Third Reich at War*, 546–51.
48. Ian Kershaw, *Popular Opinion and Political Dissent in the Third Reich: Bavaria 1933–1945* (Oxford, 1983), 156–223.
49. Evans, *The Third Reich at War*, 92–95.
50. Personal letter from Major Wolf Hermann, Berlin, 30 June 1939 in BA/MA RW 6/V. 166, Sommer-Lehrgang für Offiziere in Bad Tölz.
51. Ibid.
52. IfZ, Da 33.59, Oberkommando der Wehrmacht (ed.), *Schulungshefte für den Unterricht*.
53. Dr C.A. Hoberg, 'Der Jude in der deutschen Geschichte', in IfZ, Da 33.59, Oberkommando der Wehrmacht (ed.), *Schulungshefte für den Unterricht*, 3–42.
54. Hugo Slim, *Killing Civilians: Method, Madness and Morality in War* (London, 2007), 217; Adam Lankford, *Human Killing Machines* (Plymouth, 2009), 217; Ben Shalit, *The Psychology of Conflict and Combat* (New York, 1988), 48; Gregory G. Dimjian, 'Warfare, Genocide, and Ethnic Conflict: A Darwinian Approach', *Baylor University Medical Center Proceedings* 23(3) (July 2010), 293–94.
55. Hoberg, 'Der Jude in der deutschen Geschichte', in IfZ, Da 33.59, Oberkommando der Wehrmacht (ed.), *Schulungshefte für den Unterricht*, 10.
56. Quoted in ibid., 12. English translation of Marx from Andy Blunden and Matthew Grant (eds), Karl Marx, *On the Jewish Question* (London, 2010). Available at https://www.marxists.org/archive/marx/works/download/pdf/On%20The%20Jewish%20Question.pdf.
57. Hoberg, 'Der Jude in der deutschen Geschichte', in IfZ, Da 33.59, Oberkommando der Wehrmacht (ed.), *Schulungshefte für den Unterricht*, 36.
58. Ibid.
59. Ibid.
60. Ibid., 37.
61. Ibid.
62. Ibid.
63. Michael Burleigh and Wolfgang Wippermann, *The Racial State: Germany 1933–1945* (Cambridge, 1991), 88.
64. Hoberg, 'Der Jude in der deutschen Geschichte', in IfZ, Da 33.59, Oberkommando der Wehrmacht (ed.), *Schulungshefte für den Unterricht*, 40.
65. Ibid., 37.
66. Ibid., 41.
67. 'Hitler's Reichstag Speech, January 30, 1939', reproduced in Gigliotti and Lang, *The Holocaust: A Reader*, 240–42.
68. See Jürgen Förster, *Die Wehrmacht im NS-Staat: Eine Strukturgeschichtliche Analyse* (Munich, 2007).
69. BA/MA RH37/316, Abschrift – Auszug: Der OBH des Heeres. Berlin, den 20. Juni 1939 – von Brauchitsch. Betrifft: 'Zusammenarbeit des Heeres mit der SS Verfügungstruppe'.
70. Wette, *The Wehrmacht*, 102.
71. BA/MA RH37/316, 'Zusammenarbeit des Heeres mit der SS Verfügungstruppe'.

72. Ibid.
73. See Jürgen Förster, 'Weltanschauliche Erziehung in der Waffen SS', in *Ausbildungsziel Judenmord? Weltanschauliche Erziehung von SS, Polizei und Waffen SS im Rahmen der Endlösung* (Frankfurt, 2003), 87–113.
74. Peter Longerich, *Holocaust: The Nazi Persecution of the Jews* (Oxford, 2010), 145.
75. Wette, *The Wehrmacht*, 229–35.
76. Martin Samuels, *Command or Control? Command, Training and Tactics in the British and German Armies, 1888–1918* (London, 1995), 5.
77. Ibid.
78. Daniel J. Hughes, 'Schlichting, Schlieffen, and the Prussian Theory of War in 1914', *The Journal of Military History* 59(2) (April 1995), 275.
79. Bruce Condell and David T. Zabecki (eds), *On the German Art of War: Truppenführung* (London, 2001), 4.
80. Jörg Muth, *Command Culture: Officer Education in the US Army and the German Armed Forces, 1901–1940, and the Consequences for World War II* (Denton, 2011), 174–75.
81. Ibid., 174.
82. Colonel R.R. Davis, 'Helmuth von Moltke and the German-Prussian Development of a Decentralised Style of Command: Metz and Sedan 1870', *Defence Studies* 5(1) (2005), 85.
83. Samuels, *Command or Control*, 22.
84. Helmut von Moltke, quoted in Davis, 'Helmuth von Moltke and the German-Prussian Development', 86.
85. Hughes, 'Schlichting, Schlieffen, and the Prussian Theory of War', 269–75.
86. Quoted in Samuels, *Command or Control*, 7.
87. Dennis E. Showalter, '"No Officer Rather Than a Bad Officer": Officer Selection and Education in the Prussian/German Army, 1715–1945', in Gregory C. Kennedy and Keith Neilson (eds), *Military Education Past, Present and Future* (London, 2002), 46.
88. Ibid.
89. Hughes, 'Schlichting, Schlieffen, and the Prussian Theory of War', 269.
90. Condell and Zabecki, *On the German Art of War*, 3–4; Robert M. Citino, *The Path to Blitzkrieg: Doctrine and Training in the German Army, 1920–1939* (London, 1999), 223–28.
91. Quoted in Condell and Zabecki, *On the German Art of War*, 4.
92. Citino, *The Path to Blitzkrieg*, 223–28.
93. Ibid., 228.
94. Condell and Zabecki, *On the German Art of War*, 19.
95. Ibid., 23.
96. Citino, *The Path to Blitzkrieg*, 232.
97. Condell and Zabecki, *On the German Art of War*, 30.
98. Hughes, 'Schlichting, Schlieffen, and the Prussian Theory of War', 275.
99. Muth, *Command Culture*, 174.
100. Samuels, *Command or Control*, 3–5.
101. Shalit, *The Psychology of Conflict and Combat*, 20.
102. Jeffrey W. Legro, 'Military Culture and Inadvertent Escalation in World War II', *International Security* 18(4) (Spring 1994), 114–15.
103. Isabel Hull, *Absolute Destruction: Military Culture and the Practices of War in Imperial Germany*, (Ithaca, 2006), 116.
104. Hughes, 'Schlichting, Schlieffen, and the Prussian Theory of War', 277.
105. 'Geheimer Erlass des ObdH über die Erziehung des Offizierkorps, 18.12.1938', quoted in Böhler, *Auftakt zum Vernichtungskrieg*, 29.

106. Quoted in Longerich, 'From Mass Murder to the "Final Solution"', 214.
107. Ben Shepherd, *Terror in the Balkans: German Armies and Partisan Warfare* (Cambridge, MA, 2012), 10.
108. This is a translation of the title of Böhler's work, *Auftakt zum Vernichtungskrieg*.
109. Rossino, *Hitler Strikes Poland*, 9–10; Evans, *The Third Reich at War*, 10.
110. Rossino, *Hitler Strikes Poland*, 24.
111. Böhler, *"Grösste Härte ... "*, 60.
112. Rossino, *Hitler Strikes Poland*, 26–27.
113. Bartov, *Hitler's Army*, 64.
114. Böhler, *"Grösste Härte ... "*, 60.
115. Walter Manoschek (ed.), *"Es gibt nur eines für das Judentum: Vernichtung": Das Judenbild in deutschen Soldatenbriefen 1939–1944* (Hamburg, 1995).
116. Stephen G. Fritz, *Frontsoldaten: The German Soldier in World War II* (Lexington, 1995).
117. Ibid., 187–218.
118. Quoted in Böhler, *Auftakt zum Vernichtungskrieg*, 48.
119. Corporal A.M., 35th Infantry Division, letter dated 1 August 1940, in Manoschek, *"Es gibt nur eines für das Judentum: Vernichtung"*, 14.
120. Böhler, *Auftakt zum Vernichtungskrieg*, 40–52.
121. Ibid., 48–49.
122. Quoted in ibid., 49; see also Böhler, *Der Überfall*, 191.
123. Böhler, *Auftakt zum Vernichtungskrieg*, 49.
124. Evans, *The Third Reich at War*, 50–54.
125. Judith Levin and Daniel Uziel, 'Ordinary Men, Extraordinary Photos', *Yad Vashem Studies* 26, http://www.yadvashem.org/odot_pdf/Microsoft%20Word%20-%202290.pdf (accessed 26 September 2018).
126. IfZ, MA 261, *Die Bevölkerung von Lodz und Warschau*, 11 November 1939.
127. Ibid.
128. Ibid.
129. Ibid.
130. Slim, *Killing Civilians*, 6–12.
131. Böhler, *"Grösste Härte ... "*, 60.
132. Bartov, *Hitler's Army*, 64.
133. Ibid., 61.
134. Ibid.
135. Böhler, *"Grösste Härte ... "*, 116.
136. Muth, *Command Culture*, 174.
137. 'Geheimer Erlass des ObdH über die Erziehung des Offizierkorps, 18.12.1938', quoted in Böhler, *Auftakt zum Vernichtungskrieg*, 29.
138. John Horne and Alan Kramer, *German Atrocities, 1914: A History of Denial* (London, 2001), 1; Shepherd, *Terror in the Balkans*, 25–26.
139. Horne and Kramer, *German Atrocities*, 1, 15–19; see also Shepherd, *Terror in the Balkans*, 31.
140. Vejas Gabriel Liulevicius, *War Land on the Eastern Front: Culture, National Identity and German Occupation in World War I* (Cambridge, 2000), 79.
141. Hull, *Absolute Destruction*, 331.
142. Horne and Kramer, *German Atrocities*, 90–91.
143. Shepherd, *Terror in the Balkans*, 32–33.

144. Vejas Gabriel Liulevicius, *The German Myth of the East: 1800 to the Present* (Oxford, 2009), 114; idem, *War Land on the Eastern Front*, 25; Shepherd, *Terror in the Balkans*, 20; Hans-Ulrich Wehler, *The German Empire 1871–1918* (Oxford, 1985), 110.
145. Evans, *The Third Reich at War*, 8–13; Rossino, *Hitler Strikes Poland*, 1–28; Böhler, *Auftakt zum Vernichtungskrieg*, 36–41.
146. Liulevicius, *War Land on the Eastern Front*, 63; idem, *The German Myth of the East*, 140.
147. Liulevicius, *War Land on the Eastern Front*, 1.
148. Shepherd, *Terror in the Balkans*, 253.
149. Benjamin Madley, 'From Africa to Auschwitz: How German South West Africa Incubated Ideas and Methods Adopted and Developed by the Nazis in Eastern Europe', *European History Quarterly* 35(3) (2005), 457.
150. Tilman Dedering, '"A Certain Rigorous Treatment of All Parts of the Nation": The Annihilation of the Herero in German South West Africa, 1904', in Mark Levene and Penny Roberts (eds), *The Massacre in History* (New York, 1999), 209.
151. Madley, 'From Africa to Auschwitz', 442.
152. Dedering, '"A Certain Rigorous Treatment"', 209; Horne and Kramer, *German Atrocities*, 168–69; Madley, 'From Africa to Auschwitz', 458; Hull, *Absolute Destruction*, 119.
153. Böhler, *Auftakt zum Vernichtungskrieg*, 40–52; idem, *Der Überfall*, 191.
154. Liulevicius, *War Land on the Eastern Front*, 25; idem, *The German Myth of the East*, 114; Wehler, *The German Empire*, 110.
155. Böhler, *Auftakt zum Vernichtungskrieg*, 63.
156. Shalit, *The Psychology of Conflict and Combat*, 20.
157. Slim, *Killing Civilians*, 11–12.
158. Raffael Scheck, '"They Are Just Savages": German Massacres of Black Soldiers from the French Army in 1940', *The Journal of Modern History* 77(2) (June 2005), 325–44; idem, *Hitler's African Victims: The German Army Massacres of Black French Soldiers in 1940* (Cambridge, 2008).
159. Böhler, *"Grösste Härte ..."*, 141.
160. Reinhard Heydrich, quoted in ibid., 141.
161. Böhler, *Auftakt zum Vernichtungskrieg*.
162. Ibid., 141.
163. Bartov, *Hitler's Army*, 66.
164. Ibid., 66–67; Böhler, *Auftakt zum Vernichtungskrieg*, 238–39; Evans, *The Third Reich at War*, 25–27; Kershaw, *Hitler*, 524; Wette, *The Wehrmacht*, 100–103.
165. Wette, *The Wehrmacht*, 101–2.
166. Quoted in Bessel, *Nazism and War*, 96.
167. Rossino, *Hitler Strikes Poland*, 88.
168. Böhler, *Der Überfall*, 199.
169. Ibid., 100–101.
170. Rossino, *Hitler Strikes Poland*, 217–21.
171. Ibid., 220; see also Böhler, *Auftakt zum Vernichtungskrieg*, 33–36.
172. Rossino, *Hitler Strikes Poland*, 217.
173. Böhler, *Auftakt zum Vernichtungskrieg*, 33–35.
174. MA 34, OKW 853, *Geheime Kommandosache*, 26 October 1934.
175. Böhler, *Auftakt zum Vernichtungskrieg*, 33–35.

Chapter 5

THE HITLER YOUTH AND THE REICH LABOUR SERVICE

In a speech in 1933, Adolf Hitler informed the leaders of the army that they would have 'first-class recruitment material through the educational work of the movement, and this will guarantee that the spirit of National Socialism will remain with the recruits after their period of service'.[1] Some of the most significant 'educational work' carried out by the Nazi Party to provide 'first-class' recruits for the army took place in the Hitler Youth and the Reich Labour Service.

The possible influence of these organisations in the socialisation of those who became members of the Wehrmacht raises important questions. While many of those who were fighting in 1939 were too old to have belonged to the Hitler Youth (most having been born in 1915 or 1916),[2] some undoubtedly had been members of the Hitler Youth, and many would also have been members of the Reich Labour Service, as it became compulsory in 1935. More importantly, however, in later campaigns, particularly the invasion of the Soviet Union, and right up until the end of the war, on all fronts, a large majority of soldiers would have been members of both organisations.[3]

For these cohorts, ideological indoctrination in the Wehrmacht took place within a broader context, since military service was not the only place where political schooling occurred. As Werner von Blomberg stated in 1935, when conscription was reintroduced, 'Service in the Wehrmacht is the last and highest step in the general education process of any young German, from the home to the school, to the Hitler Youth and Labour Service'.[4] With such a statement in mind, if we are to understand the 'general education process' of German soldiers, it is important to closely examine what this socialisation process entailed during the formative years of youth. Boys from the age of fourteen to eighteen served in the Hitler Youth, which became mandatory in 1939, while six months of Reich Labour Service became compulsory for young men between the ages of eighteen and twenty-five from 1935 onwards.[5] Omer Bartov, who argues strongly in favour of ideology being a critical factor in the involvement of soldiers in atrocities, emphasises the importance of exposure to Nazi indoctrination at a young and impressionable age, in an environment that 'moulded them in the spirit of Nazism, and prepared them for the kind of war the regime was determined to wage'.[6] While Bartov argues for the significance of Nazi indoctrination in youth organisations, his work's focus is elsewhere, which raises questions about precisely what this process involved, how it related to political schooling in the armed forces and, importantly, whether or not the organisations were actually successful in achieving their aims. Jochen Böhler makes a similar suggestion, citing General von Blomberg's statement in 1934 that the 'majority of young soldiers' had been in the Hitler Youth and Reich Labour Service and were thus 'educated in National Socialist ideology' as evidence.[7] It is, however, problematic to rely upon Blomberg's statements in 1934 to partially account for ideological motivation of soldiers in 1939. While this may have been partially true of the intakes to the military in 1934, as the personnel survey statistics mentioned in chapter three have shown, in 1939 the picture was more complex due to the intake of conscripts, rather than volunteers, who often displayed a distinct lack of knowledge about Nazism upon entering the armed forces, leading military figures to recognise that the recruits 'must be trained by [the military] in order to become convinced by National Socialism'.[8]

This chapter will, therefore, set out what ideological indoctrination in the Hitler Youth and the Reich Labour Service involved, and attempt to analyse the ways in which it may have influenced its members, taking into account the educational material itself, the way in which it was implemented, as well as other factors such as the backgrounds of the youths affected. This means that this study will go beyond simply factoring in the effect of these organisations on the mentalities that existed within the Wehrmacht as a 'given', and instead question whether we actually can simply assume that passing through these organisations would have meant that they provided recruits to the military who were 'trained in the ideology of Nazism'.[9]

The Hitler Youth was an organisation that came to loom large over the lives of young Germans during the Third Reich. It sought to produce racially conscious members of the new German people's community, with a fanatical devotion to Adolf Hitler and the Reich, while also developing martial and physical abilities.[10] One official document issued by the Hitler Youth indicated the aims of the organisation. The 'spiritual schooling' that it imparted, which had a heavy focus upon 'racial teachings', would 'mould the German youth into a group, free of all class and confessional differences, that will carry the future of the Third Reich'.[11]

Early incarnations of a Nazi youth movement existed from the early 1920s onwards, with the organisation that was officially named the Hitler Youth established in 1926. After the Nazis began to dominate the governing coalition formed in 1933, they quickly moved to dissolve almost all other youth organisations, and began to place immense pressure upon young Germans to join the Hitler Youth. At school, teachers bullied young people into joining, even having the ability to prevent students from graduating unless they joined the movement. Such coercion even extended to the realm of sport. The Hitler Youth gained control over sporting facilities, making it impossible for young people to participate in sport without first becoming members of the organisation.[12]

This combination of coercion and, later on, legislation, had its effect. The membership of the Hitler Youth grew rapidly throughout the years of the Third Reich. In 1933, it numbered 2.3 million, which represented 30.5 per cent of those between the ages of ten and eighteen. By 1937, this had more than doubled, rising to 64 per cent. In 1939, once the regime had made membership of the organisation compulsory for 'Aryan' youths, this figure reached 98.1 per cent.[13] This indicates that nearly all recruits who became members of the armed forces during the Second World War, particularly in the latter years, had been members of the Hitler Youth, as were a significant number of recruits who had joined in the years immediately preceding the war.

What exactly did membership of the Hitler Youth involve in terms of ideological schooling? And how did it fit in with the ideological education carried out within the Wehrmacht? The purposes of the Hitler Youth paralleled those of the Wehrmacht in many ways. The Hitler Youth trained young boys in both the physical and 'spiritual' sense, preparing them for their future careers as soldiers. This was built upon the Nazis' assumption that soldiers could not be made in a couple of years. Instead, one had to begin in the formative years of childhood.[14] When they imagined what a 'soldier' would be, the Nazis envisioned not merely a physically conditioned, martially trained combatant, but a member of a movement, a *Kämpfer*, a 'fighter' who was ideologically schooled and committed to their political ideals. A soldier can be physically trained in a relatively short period during adulthood. An ideological soldier takes longer to create, and it is indeed advantageous to begin the process of indoctrination at an earlier age.[15]

The process of creating such soldiers involved more than simply subjecting youths to Nazi propaganda. Instead, the early conditioning of young people to an authoritarian, totalitarian organisation that was infused with Nazi ideology was just as significant. This helped to initiate the process of breaking down the individual and remoulding him in the shape desired by the leadership, a process that is present in any military organisation.[16] The Hitler Youth, through its constant barrage of martial drills, forced marches, physical training and a generally harsh and disciplinarian tone, had the effect of brutalising and dehumanising its subjects. This had the effect, according to Michael H. Kater, of humiliating young boys 'to the point where they lost their self-respect, becoming depersonalised and totally malleable'.[17] The process of depersonalisation is particularly important. It gave youths the sense that they, as individuals, along with their own consciences and morals, were insignificant, and secondary to the aims and ideology of the organisation to which they belonged. H.W. Koch has argued that the Hitler Youth deliberately attempted to

> … eliminate as far as possible the notion of the existence of a private life. Young people, deliberately as well as by force of circumstance, were conditioned to be continuously on duty. Whatever they were doing was in relation to or directly on behalf of the National Socialist state. Childhood ceased at the age of ten.[18]

Within the context of the process of breaking down individuals in order to make them more 'malleable', ideological training took place. Youths passing through the Hitler Youth had to follow a mandatory syllabus of Nazi ideology.[19] The presence of such systematic ideological training in the Hitler Youth meant that young people gained an early knowledge of the themes present in Nazi ideology, particularly that of German racial superiority, and just as importantly, the inferiority of others, particularly Jews, Slavs and the Roma.[20]

Ideological training took numerous forms in the Hitler Youth. It included theoretical lessons on Jews as sub-humans, which were usually taught by older Hitler Youth leaders during camps and meetings, often with the aid of booklets or copies of Julius Streicher's antisemitic newsletter *Der Stürmer*, notorious for its depiction of Jews in the most demeaning and offensive ways.[21] During Hitler Youth camps, a 'political hour' took place each evening. This consisted of question and answer sessions that covered current political events, as well as discussions that were intended to further inculcate the ideological lessons covered in the day's training.[22] It is likely that due to the constant barrage of ideological education in the regimented, closed-off group environment of the Hitler Youth, many boys gradually came to accept ideas that they might have rejected in normal circumstances. While lessons specifically dedicated to political schooling during a youth camp took up only fourteen hours out of more than one hundred and fifty, indoctrination was constantly taking place, as the basic notions of Nazi ideology permeated through the entire curriculum.[23]

One way in which the Hitler Youth organised for indoctrination to go beyond the teaching of lessons on Nazi ideology was in sending members of the Hitler Youth to occupied territories during the war. In what Kater called the 'darkest aspect of [the] entire exercise', Nazi leaders organised for youths to be planted in surroundings chosen specifically for the level of hostility that Germans would encounter there. Members of the Hitler Youth were sent to places like occupied Poland and to the Protectorate of Bohemia and Moravia. Here they encountered open hostility from local populations, making it dangerous for them to venture out without the protection of German soldiers, or at least older members of the Hitler Youth who were carrying weapons. According to Kater, this had the effect of engendering hatred for the Slavic populations of Eastern Europe by confirming all the negative things that the youths had heard during their ideological lessons.[24]

The trips also allowed Hitler Youth leaders to highlight to the youths the difference between the status of their own supposedly superior master race and the apparently inferior peoples of the East. As Germans, the youths visiting these countries arrived as members of the conquering people. Moreover, due to the fact that the areas had recently been conquered, and were currently under the occupation of a ruthless and exploitative regime, many of the areas had been partially or completely destroyed. Perhaps more importantly, they were populated by large numbers of wretched people living in desperate poverty, in terribly overcrowded and unhygienic conditions. This would only have confirmed to the impressionable young Germans the truth of Nazi propaganda that constantly told of the inferiority of the Slavic and Jewish 'races'.[25]

The aim of all of this was to produce the 'youth leader and educator of the future' who would be the 'priest of the national socialist faith and an officer of National Socialism', and who would eventually fill the ranks of the military, or the Waffen SS.[26] Evidence collected by the Army Personnel Office during the war indicated one area in which the Hitler Youth was successful in creating ideal recruits for the armed forces. Former leaders in the Hitler Youth were regarded as the most suitable candidates for the officer corps, and numerous higher-ranking officers confirmed that the training in the Hitler Youth was an essential part of a soldier's 'education'.[27]

The Hitler Youth did not manage to convince everyone of the merits of Nazism. The increasingly militarised and regimented nature of the organisation, as well as its obligatory membership, caused resentment and alienation among some young Germans, many of whom often wanted simply to have their free time to themselves.[28] Moreover, membership of the Hitler Youth did not always mean that boys would regularly attend.[29] Many of the instructors, particularly once military conscription was introduced, were no longer the educated younger people associated with the movement in earlier periods, but instead were older, harsher, anti-intellectual types, which further alienated people and meant that political schooling was less likely to be effective.[30] Furthermore, and somewhat reflective of the broader successes and failures of Nazi propaganda, the Hitler Youth proved relatively unsuccessful in breaking down class and religious loyalties. Many young people from Catholic or working-class areas proved less susceptible to indoctrination, demonstrative of Kershaw's contention that Nazi propaganda often failed to reverse pre-existing beliefs.[31]

It is also important to note that indoctrination in the Hitler Youth took place within the broader context of young people's lives, meaning that outside influences existed. Involvement in the Hitler Youth took place at a time when young people were still living in the family home. Influences in the home varied. Many parents of, for example, Social Democratic or conservative persuasion still exerted influence over their children, although many found this increasingly difficult because the children were away so often, and because they were being formally educated in a school system in which Nazi ideology became an official part of the curriculum.[32]

While conceding the presence of such countervailing influences, along with the variance in responses among different classes and denominational groups, David Welch argues that the organisation's 'assault on the individual', aimed primarily at the youth, was reasonably effective in mobilising young people to the cause of Nazism and the notion of a 'national community'.[33] Bartov concurs, arguing that 'social background seems to have played a far less important role in deciding these youths' position toward the regime than we would expect'.[34] Felix Römer's work on ideology within the Wehrmacht supports the notion of younger soldiers being the most ideologically reliable. Römer emphasises the age of recruits in their likelihood to support the regime, stating that approval rates among those born after 1923 were 74 per cent, compared with 71 per cent born between 1920 and 1923, with 56 per cent of those born before 1916 supportive of Nazism. According to Römer, this constitutes the most compelling evidence we have of the younger generation, socialised in the Hitler Youth, Reich Labour Service and Nazified school system, being the strongest supporters of Nazism.[35] A report by the exiled Social Democrats described how young people were often drawn in by the Hitler Youth: 'The young people follow the instructions of the Hitler Youth and demand from their parents that they become good Nazis, that they give up Marxism … and contact with

Jews. It is the young men who bring home enthusiasm for the Nazis ... the secret of National Socialism is the secret of its youth'.[36]

The Nazis' policy of indoctrinating the young also took place in German schools. The leader of the Hitler Youth, Baldur von Schirach, sought to ensure that the school system would not stand in the way of the aims of the Hitler Youth. The Nazi regime's efforts to bring the school system into line helped to ensure this. The 1933 Law for the Reconstitution of the Civil Service, for example, ensured that politically unreliable teachers were dismissed, forcing out Social Democratic and communist teachers. This was reinforced later in 1933 when the National Socialist Teachers' League purged the teaching profession, forcing out Jewish teachers as well as any teachers who belonged to undesirable democratic parties.[37] By 1936, nearly all teachers were members of the National Socialist Teachers' League. While many teachers joined merely to keep their jobs, it meant that they nonetheless had to conform to the new syllabus, and it was very difficult to dissent from teaching it.[38]

Not only were the teaching ranks purged, but the syllabus itself was to undergo Nazification. In July 1933, the government decreed that history lessons were to be built around the concept of 'German heroism' and 'Hitler as the accomplisher of German unity', with history having the purpose of teaching that life had always essentially been a struggle, with race and blood the central factors. Science teaching also underwent numerous changes, with racial teaching becoming a central feature of the biology curriculum. Geography became imbued with the concepts of *Lebensraum*, 'Blood and Soil' and German superiority. By 1934, it was mandatory for schools to educate students in the 'spirit of National Socialism'.[39]

Exceptions to the uniformity of education did exist. While the teaching profession was generally politically reliable and dissent was almost impossible, many teachers often merely pretended to be Nazis to avoid dismissal.[40] Once again, class distinctions played a part in undermining the Nazis' desired goal of national unity, with working-class children less likely to conform because of the influence of their parents. The clear class distinctions that remained in German society, which were particularly evident during wartime when the effects of rationing and shortages of items were most keenly felt by working-class families, further added to their doubts about the Nazi regime and its claim to stand for a classless racial community.[41]

Due to the volume of political schooling that took place within schools and the Hitler Youth, however, it is hard to imagine that most youths did not at least become familiar with the most basic doctrines of Nazism, particularly in the later years of the regime. While some of the training may well have been superficial or poorly organised, young people would have continually encountered negative images of certain racial groups, even if they had not understood the more complex and abstract reasoning behind them. The result for most young people would have been, at the very least, a basic grounding in Nazi ideology when the time came to join the Reich Labour Service or the military. Importantly, government restrictions on the education curriculum as well as media content, along with the near impossibility of open dissent going unpunished, meant that information that contradicted the teachings of Nazism was limited.

***

The ideological training that began in the Hitler Youth continued in the Reich Labour Service, an organisation that was, for many young Germans, the next progression in their young lives. The Reich Labour Service was originally established by the Nazi regime as a way to get the unemployed back to work and to carry out major infrastructure projects throughout the country. However, it was to become an organisation that, particularly from 1935 onwards, involved a significant amount of Nazi indoctrination.[42]

The Reich Labour Service evolved from a number of voluntary labour organisations that existed in Germany during the Weimar Republic.[43] Most of these organisations came under the umbrella of the Reich Working Group for German Compulsory Labour Service, and were generally formed as a response to rapid rises in unemployment that took place after the onset of the Great Depression in 1929.[44] These organisations were primarily a way for unemployed young people to undertake public works, but they also sought to engage youths in meaningful work that would not only benefit society but improve the workers themselves, both 'physically and intellectually-morally'. The most common areas in which the organisations were involved included forestry, agriculture and work with the aged and the sick. Under the Weimar Republic, labour organisations were to remain strictly non-political and were not to be used for 'anti-state purposes'.[45] Membership of these organisations did, however, remain relatively low. Of the estimated six million unemployed in Germany in late 1932, there were only approximately 285,000 people employed under the Voluntary Labour Service programme.[46]

Soon after Adolf Hitler came to power, he announced that he would establish compulsory labour service as part of his own programme for reducing unemployment and getting young people to contribute to what he regarded as the public good.[47] The Voluntary Labour Service was renamed in August 1933 as the National Socialist Labour Service, and then again in July 1934 as the Reich Labour Service.[48] It was headed by the same man who had led the Voluntary Labour Service, Konstantin Hierl, who was a zealous Nazi.

According to Kiran Klaus Patel, although the Reich Labour Service formed part of one of the most thoroughly researched epochs in history, until relatively recently there has been no complete work on the organisation and its effects on young people.[49] Patel points out that the paucity in scholarship in this area is largely due to the unavailability of source material; most of the Reich Labour Service's documents were destroyed in 1945.[50]

The limited amount of research carried out on the Reich Labour Service contrasts strongly with the way the organisation viewed its own importance, with Konstantin Hierl remarking that it was a 'cornerstone of the reconstruction of our Reich and people'.[51] From the establishment of the Nazi regime onwards, labour service was to serve a number of purposes. Like its predecessors, it was to help deal with unemployment and also to carry out public works. However, it would no longer be apolitical, and soon developed into an organisation that would impart schooling in Nazi ideology and provide preparation for military service.

Six months' membership of the Reich Labour Service became compulsory for young German males between the ages of eighteen and twenty-five in 1935.[52] This further transformed the purpose of the organisation. Konstantin Hierl stated as much in 1935. In a speech that was disseminated throughout the organisation, Hierl marked the occasion by asserting that the Reich Labour Service was 'no longer a temporary measure against unemployment'. Instead, it was a part of the 'state's education of youth'.[53]

Throughout his speech, Hierl indicated the kind of education that the organisation would impart. He stated that the Labour Service would be a 'fighting member of the National Socialist movement', which would come about through political schooling of Reich Labour Service recruits. The organisation's leaders had written a special curriculum that had been in use since early 1934, and this would be taught by specially trained instructors who had all attended three-week courses to train as 'educators'.[54] Hierl went on to urge members of the Reich Labour Service to abandon any working-class notion of class struggle, which was a concept popularised by 'Jewish Marxism'. Instead, they were to turn their attention towards combating 'the Jew', who had spread the notion of international class solidarity as a way to manipulate workers into abandoning their own interests and instead serving the 'only real international solidarity, the international solidarity of Jewry'.[55]

The extent to which Nazi ideology was to be a part of the 'state's education of youth' in the Labour Service is revealed by documents that relate to life in a Labour Service camp. In 1935, the Reich Labour Service distributed a booklet entitled 'The Tasks and Purpose of the Labour Service'. It provides an insight into the goals that the Labour Service hoped to achieve, and outlines the day-to-day life of its members. According to the document, the Labour Service gave Germany the means with which to impose upon youths the 'ground laws' of National Socialist life. It concluded that the Labour Service would not only secure the economic future of Germany, but that it would also be a decisive factor in the 'National Socialist development of Germany in the political, racial, social and cultural realms'. The nature of service in the organisation would assist in achieving these goals:

> Here, German youths are not gathered merely for hours, nor days or weeks. Instead, for a full year they will live in the closest community. From early morning until late at night they will experience order. The impulses of the individual will have finished. In the closed-off world of barrack life, every individual will come to know what it means to live in a community. This is often hard, and it takes self-discipline, obedience and the ability to overcome one's individualism.[56]

In such an environment, the Reich Labour Service also hoped to recreate the conditions that had supposedly forged National Socialist mentality and ideology: 'We live like the soldiers of the World War did at the front!'[57] The Labour Service was organised along militaristic lines, where the foundations would be laid for future military service. Emphasis was placed upon martial virtues like discipline and obedience, as well as by the comparison of the worker in the Labour Service to the *Fronterlebnis*, the 'experience of being at the front' of the soldiers of the First World War.[58]

There also existed a clear emphasis on breaking down the individual.[59] The Reich Labour Service was also taking advantage of the fact that the young men in the organisation were shut off from normal life and the outside world, experiencing the kind of social and physical isolation that are important factors in the process of effective indoctrination.[60]

'The Tasks and Purpose of the Labour Service' provided an outline of a typical day in a Labour Service camp. A worker's day was set out as follows:

06.00: Wake up

06.05–06.20: Physical training/sport

06.20–06.40: Clean barracks, make bed, wash

06.40–06.55: Breakfast

07.00: Flag parade, drill, daily speech from the commander. March off to work site. Six hours' work with half hour pause for morning tea

14.00: Return from work

14.30–15.00: Lunch

15.00–16.00: Rest

16.00–17.00: Physical training/sport

17.00–18.00: State political lessons

18.00–19.00: Instruction

19.00: Dinner

20.00–21.00: Singing, etc.

22.00: Bed.[61]

A day in the Labour Service therefore involved at least one hour of political schooling, with another hour of 'instruction'. The booklets indicate the kind of instruction that was carried out during 'state political lessons'. One such manual, 'Guidelines for State Political Lessons in the Reich Labour Service', was disseminated in Bavaria in 1937.[62] It not only set out the content of ideological lessons, but also included instructions for officers in charge on how to carry out the lessons effectively.

The booklet also contained information on the testing that new members of the organisation had to undergo in order to determine their education levels and capacity for learning. The concept of a recruit's 'education level' was, however, a euphemism for their knowledge of and attitudes towards Nazism. Testing of new recruits included questions like 'Who is the Führer?', 'Where was he born and when did he become Chancellor?' as well as more subjectively phrased questions such as 'What was the name given to the contract of shame that ended the World War and made Germany the slave of its enemies?' and 'What is the Jewish-led enemy of the world, with which National Socialism is engaged in a bitter struggle?'[63] Patel has shown that while systematic records and evaluations of the Labour Service's educational achievements do not exist, two years earlier, in 1935, recruits' ability to answer the above questions were recorded. The responses varied. Around 44 per cent of answers were classed as middling, 30 per cent were good, while 23 per cent were poor.[64]

The booklet also contained thirteen regulations and instructions for teachers. These regulations dictated that instructors were to gain a complete mastery of National Socialist theory included in the Labour Service curriculum, and to become familiar with Hitler's *Mein Kampf*. Instructors were also to make sure that the material was understandable to everyone in the classroom, especially by linking the theoretical material to current political events and questions whenever possible. National Socialist ideology stood foremost in all areas of political instruction. There existed obviously ideological areas of the curriculum, such as 'Ethnic Studies'.[65] Yet other areas of the curriculum were tainted with Nazi ideology. The section 'Labour Service', which outlined the development, work and aims of the organisation, was 'to be explained through the point of view of the national political ideology', with that area of the curriculum to 'stand in the closest relationship with National Socialist ideology'. Instructors were to ensure that 'in all circumstances, politics is to be in the foreground when teaching about the Labour Service', as well as any other topic.[66]

To ensure that the young subjects were taking the syllabus on board, instructors were to carry out question and answer sessions at the end of each lesson. They were to ask questions about the material they had covered, which recruits were to answer 'in full sentences'. Questions that would lead to 'yes' or 'no' answers were not permitted as this would not give enough indication as to whether the recruit had understood the lesson. Anyone who could not answer questions about the subject material was to receive further tuition outside of normal hours.[67]

In 1937, the year in which this document appeared, the Labour Service anticipated that after one year in the organisation, recruits would be able to answer 'at the very least' a list of questions that were set out in the booklet. There were thirty-one questions in total. The list included the following:

- Why do we recognise Adolf Hitler as the saviour of Germany?
- Who recognised the dangers of Jewish Marxism and summoned forces within Germany that would rebuild our country?
- Who bears the guilt for the capitulation of 1918?
- Why is National Socialism the sworn enemy of Bolshevism?
- Why is a treaty with Bolshevist Russia out of the question?[68]

To further assist the recruits in their development of political awareness, the Reich Labour Service issued a type of diary to supplement their ideological schooling. Entitled 'The Camp Comrade', the booklet was issued to workers towards the end of their service. The inside cover implored the workers to remember: 'You are nothing, your *Volk* is everything!' 'The Camp Comrade' served as a way to summarise all that the Reich Labour Service hoped that its members would have learned in their time in the organisation. It warned the workers to be ever vigilant in defence of their people against Jews and Marxist agitators, and reminded them that 'the Reich Labour Service is National Socialist to its bones … It is a child of the National Socialist Party'.[69]

By 1941, the Labour Service had further developed the curriculum that recruits would encounter during their period of service. It issued more booklets that were to be used as training tools in the hours set aside each day for political education. The rhetoric contained in them had radicalised to the point where Labour Service ideological education contained material similar to that found in armed forces and even SS indoctrination material.

One notable document, issued by the Training and Education Office of the Reich Labour Service, began by stating that the Labour Service was, first and foremost, a 'school of German socialism' which, particularly during its early years, had performed the role of turning 'workers with varying opinions into convinced National Socialists'.[70] It claimed that its role had become easier over time, since 'today, the workers arrive already influenced by National Socialism',[71] suggesting that by 1941, compulsory Hitler Youth, as well as eight years of Nazi control over schools and the media, had taken their effect. In turn, the task of the Labour Service now was to strengthen and deepen Nazi attitudes in preparation for military service.[72]

The Labour Service also aimed to build up the 'will' and 'character' of members of the organisation. The notion of fostering the right kind of 'will' was justified by arguing that actions carried out without the impulse of one's own will, or indeed by trying to force people to act against their will, would eventually lead to them becoming fed up with the movement. The key was in explaining the motivations behind the ideology and the actions it was endorsing, in the hope that, having understood them, people would carry them out willingly rather than through coercion. In theory, this would ensure the long-term loyalty of the people, and ultimately the success of the movement.[73] The booklet instructed commanders that fostering this type of 'will' was the highest goal of Labour Service training. It aimed to 'bring people to the point where, *at their own discernment*, they will carry out what needs to be done'.[74]

The Reich Labour Service thus sought to turn out men who would carry out actions that were in line with Nazi ideology without the need for specific orders. These men were to know what was expected of them from superiors, reflecting ideals of the Nazi Party from the earliest stages of the movement, as evident in Kershaw's theory of 'Working towards the Führer'.[75] Importantly for the future service of Reich Labour Service members in the army, this also aligns with the aims of the programme of ideological education that took place in the Wehrmacht, in which soldiers were to act according to the principles of Nazism without specific instruction to do so.[76] It also aligned with the broader command principle of *Auftragstaktik*.

The curriculum itself contained chapters similar to those found in the equivalent military and Waffen SS instruction manuals of the time. The chapter 'The Jewish quest for world dominance' taught members of the Reich Labour Service that 'Jewry must have a central place in one's thinking', while the chapter 'Bolshevik Culture' painted a picture of the Soviet Union. 'Bolshevik Culture' claimed that in each country that German soldiers had invaded up until 1941, they encountered differing opinions about their presence within the local populations. 'Some greeted the troops with jubilation, some with passionate hate.' In the Soviet Union, however, things were different: 'People here have absolutely no individual opinions or ideas. They have been made into collectives, into masses, in which the individual, the personal, has been completely destroyed'.[77] This was a country in which human lives were worth nothing, and people were merely empty shapes, living empty existences between birth and death. Anyone who attempted to break out of the mould and give meaning to their lives would meet with death. This was, allegedly, due to the fact that this 'human herd' was under the control of the Jews. To further indicate the worthlessness of life, the article alleged that cemeteries did not exist in Russian towns and villages. Anybody who died was no longer in the 'material sphere' and was thus immediately forgotten about.[78] Furthermore, the people of the Soviet Union were a Slavic, Asiatic people who had a natural hatred for the Aryan people, which was further encouraged by their Bolshevik leaders. Their racial and ideological status also meant that they were supposedly equipped with a unique capacity to suffer, and to die in their millions during wartime.[79]

The Reich Labour Service also sought to inculcate in its members the 'ideological, racial and territorial foundations' of the war. In keeping with Wehrmacht political schooling, Reich Labour Service ideological education taught of a war that was different to previous conflicts that were fought over disputed borders or territory. This was a 'historically inescapable struggle of the greatest scale'. It was essential for the current generation to understand this, and to summon the strength and the will to engage in this new type of battle, a war in which everything must be viewed within the context of thousands of years of German, and thus European history,[80] and in which they would face an enemy defined along racial lines.[81]

Such sentiments are repeatedly espoused in Reich Labour Service educational material, often taught under the guise of 'historical' or 'cultural' studies lessons, which, as Patel points out, often existed merely to further serve the purpose of indoctrination,[82] and sought to normalise the themes of racial difference, of enemies that were defined by race, of human lives that were worth less than others, and of a bitter, life and death struggle between enemies that could only end in the complete annihilation of one side. Members of the organisation could not possibly have been in any doubt about the racial and ideological dimensions of the war in which they were to take part, and in turn the kind of attitude that was to be expected of them once they became soldiers.

It is difficult to know how effective the training carried out in the Labour Service actually was. Within the relatively scarce records that exist, there are none that systematically document the organisation's successes or failures in the area of political schooling.[83] There are some clues as to its limits, however. It is clear that problems existed in the early years of the organisation. The quality of teaching could be poor, mainly because of poorly trained teachers and a lack of time;[84] this was perhaps reflected by the efforts in 1935 to send all Labour Service officers who would act as instructors on special training courses.[85] There was also, among some recruits, particularly in the early years of the Nazi regime, a lack of knowledge about basic areas of Nazism, making the task of Labour Service officers more difficult.[86]

It is also clear that certain demographics were less responsive to Nazi schooling. According to Patel, results from tests on political knowledge were conspicuously poor in Catholic regions.[87] This is supportive of the statement by one Reich Labour Service official speaking to a conference of Wehrmacht officers, cited in chapter three, who spoke of young men from Catholic areas not knowing who Hitler was, and wondering why there were no pictures of the Pope in the barracks.[88] University students also presented problems. Forced to join up before being allowed to study, a period in the Labour Service was supposed to teach prospective students to respect people who worked in physical jobs and to break down socio-economic barriers between young people. However, the students, mainly drawn from the upper and middle classes, were usually disillusioned by the hard physical work and brutal leaders. Most also left with an increased resentment towards working-class people, who had often picked on them, representing a failure in Nazi social engineering and indoctrination.[89]

In spite of the failures of Reich Labour Service political schooling in its attempts to reverse pre-existing beliefs or break down class barriers and religious loyalties, given the extensive, constant political schooling that took place within this organisation it is difficult to imagine that it did not have some kind of effect on many young men, particularly in areas in which it needed only to build upon already-present prejudices and beliefs, such as antisemitism and fear of Slavs and Bolshevism. These sentiments were the focus of political training, and as demonstrated in chapter one, would not have been entirely new or unfamiliar forms of prejudice for young men who had come of age during the Weimar Republic or Third Reich.[90]

It is also important to note the circumstances under which political schooling took place within the Reich Labour Service. The organisation had many features of an ideal environment in which to condition subjects. The Reich Labour Service itself was confident in the effect that it would have on recruits who were under their complete control for, as one official pointed out, '… a full year … In the closed off world of barrack life'.[91] In this sense, the organisation would play a special role in the National Socialist education structure, because only in the Labour Service could total immersion be achieved for extensive periods. During their time in the Hitler Youth, children were exposed to other educational influences, above all from their parents. The Reich Labour Service, however, alongside the military, could bind a large group together for months at a time without exposure to outside influences, and where they would normally have had contact only with other members of the organisation, which allowed for close control over communication, the 'current upon which all else depends' in indoctrination.[92] This forced young men to become immersed within the organisation, where its norms could be continually espoused and reinforced, without the chance for competing philosophies to gain a platform. In such an environment, people are more likely to 'lose their grip on their individual moral preferences and submit to wider social pressures'.[93]

The group-focused environment of the Reich Labour Service helped to further reinforce this. The crushing of individualism was, after all, one of the stated aims of the organisation.[94] This placed pressure upon people to take on the ideas of the organisation, as 'new recruits to almost any organisation have a strong desire to fit in', with this desire to conform often leading to people becoming 'more willing to adopt the group's prejudicial norms'.[95] Furthermore, for many recruits, particularly during later years of the regime, past experiences in the Hitler Youth, as well as at school, would have meant that the propaganda they encountered in the Reich Labour Service represented the 'normal', official view of the world, and thus did not seem particularly new or radical. Welch has argued that this process, a 'monopoly of organisations', came to 'envelop the individual at every stage of development … by subjecting him to a planned course of indoctrination'.[96] This served the purpose of ensuring the mandatory, and constant, involvement of people in these organisations so completely that 'individuals were no longer left to themselves or ultimately to think for themselves'.[97]

Closely examining the training that took place in the Labour Service and Hitler Youth illustrates that after 1935, when labour service became compulsory, and even more so once the Hitler Youth became mandatory in 1939, recruits to the military would have undertaken political schooling that included rhetoric that was a preparation for the ideological education and propaganda that they would experience in the military itself. Bartov is correct when he argues that an army, particularly a conscript army, is reflective of the society from which it came.[98] The bodies within German society that were active in the socialisation of the young men who would become soldiers are thus crucial factors in attempting to understand the German army. There is strong evidence to suggest that socialisation in these organisations affected many people's attitudes. However, it is nonetheless too simplistic to take as a given that entire generations that were to become soldiers were convinced Nazis due to their socialisation in the Third Reich. Instead, there were different reactions to indoctrination based upon factors such as religion, social milieus, age and religious background, along with the fact that many young people felt alienated by Nazi schooling. As previously shown, and as will be further demonstrated, many members of the Wehrmacht did agree with many aspects of Nazi ideology, particularly those that were radicalised versions of previously existing prejudices and beliefs, or areas in which Nazi ideology produced the only reference point with which to comprehend much of what they would later encounter while deployed in places like Poland and the Soviet Union.[99] But the German military was by no means made up of a politically monolithic body of men. Nor was it successful in convincing all German soldiers of all aspects of Nazi ideology.

The next chapter will further examine differing attitudes towards Nazi ideology within the military by looking closely at one area that produced a particularly large amount of dissent: religion.

Notes

1. Christoph Rass, *Menschenmaterial: deutsche Soldaten an der Ostfront: Innensichten einer Infanteriedivision, 1939–1945* (Paderborn, 2003), 121.
2. Alexander B. Rossino, *Hitler Strikes Poland: Blitzkrieg, Ideology, and Atrocity* (Lawrence, 2003), 217.
3. Omer Bartov, *Hitler's Army: Soldiers, Nazis and War in the Third Reich* (Oxford, 1991), 109–10.
4. Michael H. Kater, *Hitler Youth* (Cambridge, MA, 2004), 28–29.
5. Detlev Peukert, 'Youth in the Third Reich', in Richard Bessel (ed.), *Life in the Third Reich* (Oxford, 1987), 25.
6. Bartov, *Hitler's Army*, 109.
7. Quoted in Jochen Böhler, *Auftakt zum Vernichtungskrieg: Die Wehrmacht in Polen 1939* (Frankfurt, 2006), 34–35.
8. Bundesarchiv/Militärarchiv (hereafter BA/MA) RW6/161, *Erster nationalpolitischer Lehrgang für Lehrer der Kriegsschulen, Akademien usw vom 17.1.37 bis 23.1.37 in Berlin*, 23; BA/MA 6/v.420, *Nationalpolitischer Lehrgang der Wehrmacht vom 12. bis 21. Januar 1938. Nur für den Dienstgebrauch in der Wehrmacht* (Berlin, 1938), 204.
9. Bartov, *Hitler's Army*, 109.
10. Kater, *Hitler Youth*, 37–38, 152; Wolfgang Keim, *Erziehung unter der Nazi-Diktatur* (Darmstadt, 1995), 123–33; Arno Klönne, *Jugend im Dritten Reich: Die Hitler-Jugend und ihre Gegner* (Düsseldorf, 1982), 55–65; Gerhard Rempel, *Hitler's Children: The Hitler Youth and the SS* (Chapel Hill, 1989), 177–78.
11. Institut für Zeitgeschichte, München (hereafter IfZ), DB 44.55, Abteilung P der Reichsjugendführung, *Werden und Wesen der Hitler-Jugend* (Berlin: Lipropa Lichtbildpropaganda).
12. Richard J. Evans, *The Third Reich in Power* (London, 2006), 271–73; Michael Burleigh and Wolfgang Wippermann, *The Racial State: Germany 1933–1945* (Cambridge, 1991), 205.
13. Kater, *Hitler Youth*, 28–29.
14. Rempel, *Hitler's Children*, 177–78.
15. Denise Winn, *The Manipulated Mind: Brainwashing, Conditioning and Indoctrination* (London, 1983), 36–37; Adam Lankford, *Human Killing Machines* (Plymouth, 2009), 52.
16. Lankford, *Human Killing Machines*, 130; Ute Frevert, *A Nation in Barracks: Modern Germany, Military Conscription and Civil Society* (New York, 2004), 182–83; Joanna

Bourke, *An Intimate History of Killing: Face to Face Killing in Twentieth Century Warfare* (London, 1999), 79.
17. Kater, *Hitler Youth*, 31.
18. H.W. Koch, *Hitler Youth: Origins and Development, 1922–45* (London, 1975), 128.
19. Evans, *The Third Reich in Power*, 274.
20. Kater, *Hitler Youth*, 47–48.
21. Ibid., 62.
22. Rempel, *Hitler's Children*, 194–95.
23. Ibid.
24. Kater, *Hitler Youth*, 47–48.
25. Ibid.
26. Ibid., 166; see also Burleigh and Wippermann, *The Racial State*, 206–7.
27. Rempel, *Hitler's Children*, 203.
28. David Welch, *The Third Reich: Politics and Propaganda* (London, 1993), 63; Burleigh and Wippermann, *The Racial State*, 218–25; Evans, *The Third Reich in Power*, 275–76; Kater, *Hitler Youth*; Koch, *Hitler Youth*; Peukert, 'Youth in the Third Reich', 29–31.
29. Jill Stephenson, 'Inclusion: Building the National Community in Propaganda and Practice', in Jane Caplan (ed.), *Nazi Germany* (Oxford, 2008), 110.
30. Evans, *The Third Reich in Power*, 275–76; Peukert, 'Youth in the Third Reich', 26.
31. Tim Mason, 'The Containment of the Working Class in Nazi Germany', in Jane Caplan (ed.), *Nazism, Fascism and the Working Class: Essays by Tim Mason* (Cambridge, 1995), 8, 233; Welch, *The Third Reich*, 58–63; Peukert, 'Youth in the Third Reich', 40; Kater, *Hitler Youth*, 118.
32. Evans, *The Third Reich in Power*, 274–79.
33. Welch, *The Third Reich*, 61, Peukert, 'Youth in the Third Reich', 27–28.
34. Bartov, *Hitler's Army*, 109–10.
35. Felix Römer, *Kameraden: Die Wehrmacht von innen* (Munich, 2012), 79–81.
36. Quoted in Welch, *The Third Reich*, 64.
37. Koch, *Hitler Youth*, 40; Burleigh and Wippermann, *The Racial State*, 208–13.
38. Evans, *The Third Reich in Power*, 266–67.
39. Ibid.; Burleigh and Wippermann, *The Racial State*, 208–13; Keim, *Erziehung unter der Nazi-Diktatur*, 86–117; Kurt-Ingo Flessau, *Schule der Diktatur: Lehrpläne und Schulbücher des Nationalsozialismus* (Munich, 1977), 13–21; Franz-Werner Kersting, 'Wehrmacht und Schule im Dritten Reich', in Rolf-Dieter Müller and Hans-Erich Volkmann (eds), *Die Wehrmacht: Mythos und Realität* (Munich, 1999), 450–55.
40. Welch, *The Third Reich*, 61; Evans, *The Third Reich in Power*, 265–66; Keim, *Erziehung unter der Nazi-Diktatur*, 113–23.
41. Evans, *The Third Reich in Power*, 262; Stephenson, 'Inclusion', 102; Peukert, 'Youth in the Third Reich', 40, Welch, *The Third Reich*, 66.
42. Kiran Klaus Patel, *Soldaten der Arbeit: Arbeitsdienste in Deutschland und den USA* (Göttingen, 2003), 249–71.
43. Hartmut Heyck, 'Labour Services in the Weimar Republic and their Ideological Godparents', *The Journal of Contemporary History* 38(2) (2003), 221; Patel, *Soldaten der Arbeit*, 31–40; Manfred Seifert, *Kulturarbeit im Reichsarbeitsdienst: Theorie und Praxis nationalsozialistischer Kulturpflege im context historisch-politischer, organisatorischer und ideologischer Einflüsse* (Münster, 1996), 27–42.
44. Heyck, 'Labour Services in the Weimar Republic', 232.
45. Ibid., 232–34.
46. Ibid., 235.

47. Ibid., 222; Patel, *Soldaten der Arbeit*, 12–17.
48. Heyck, 'Labour Services in the Weimar Republic', 222.
49. Patel, *Soldaten der Arbeit*, 19–20.
50. Ibid., 20; Seifert, *Kulturarbeit im Reichsarbeitsdienst*, 14.
51. Patel, *Soldaten der Arbeit*, 19.
52. Heyck, 'Labour Services in the Weimar Republic', 221.
53. IfZ, Da 52.05, Reichsarbeitsdienst Pflicht, *Der Reichsarbeitsführer auf dem Parteikongreß*, 26 June 1935.
54. Patel, *Soldaten der Arbeit*, 249–50.
55. Ibid.
56. IfZ, Da 52.05, Oberfeldmeister Dr U. Krüger, *Aufgabe und Sinn des Arbeitsdienstes: Ein Aufruf an die deutsche Jugend* (Berlin, 1935), 39.
57. Ibid.
58. Rass, *Menschenmaterial*, 129.
59. Lankford, *Human Killing Machines*, 4, 128–30. See also Erwin Staub, *The Roots of Evil: The Origins of Genocide and Other Group Violence* (Cambridge, 1989).
60. Lankford, *Human Killing Machines*, 17; Winn, *The Manipulated Mind*, 112–14; Frevert, *A Nation in Barracks*, 182–83; Bourke, *An Intimate History of Killing*, 79.
61. IfZ, Da 52.05, Oberfeldmeister Dr U. Krüger, *Aufgabe und Sinn des Arbeitsdienstes*, 39.
62. IfZ, Da 052.034, *Richtlinien für den Staatspolitischen Unterricht im Reichsarbeitsdienst* (Arbeitsgauleitung Nr. 30 Bayern-Hochland) (Leipzig, 1937).
63. Ibid., 11–12.
64. Patel, *Soldaten der Arbeit*, 249–50.
65. IfZ, Da 052.034, *Richtlinien für den Staatspolitischen Unterricht im Reichsarbeitsdienst*, 73–75.
66. Ibid., 44.
67. Ibid., 25–26.
68. Ibid., 85–102.
69. IfZ, Da 052.055-1935, *Der Lager-Kamerad: Kamaradschaftsblatt für den Arbeitsdienst und den Arbeitsdank e.V.*, 5–7.
70. Da 052.009-1940/41, Erziehungs und ausbildungsamt in der RAD, *RAD Unterrichtsbriefe für Führer 1940-41, 2. Folge 1941*, 5.
71. Ibid.
72. Ibid.
73. Ibid., 2.
74. Ibid, my emphasis.
75. See Ian Kershaw, *Hitler* (London, 2010), 320–23.
76. 'Geheimer Erlass des ObdH über die Erziehung des Offizierkorps, 18.12.1938', quoted in Böhler, *Auftakt zum Vernichtungskrieg*, 29.
77. 'Bolschewistenkultur', in IfZ, Da 052.009-1940/41, Erziehungs und ausbildungsamt in der RAD, 18.
78. Ibid.
79. Ibid.
80. 'Die Weltanschauliche, Rassische und Raumgeschichtliche Grundlagen dieses Krieges', in IfZ, Da 052.009-1940/41, *Erziehungs und ausbildungsamt in der RAD*, 23
81. 'Die Einheit von Rasse und Raum', in IfZ, Da 052.009-1940/41, *Erziehungs und ausbildungsamt in der RAD*, 24–25.
82. See Patel, *Soldaten der Arbeit*, 251–55.
83. Ibid., 251.

84. Ibid., 246–47.
85. IfZ, Da 52.05, Reichsarbeitsdienst Pflicht, *Der Reichsarbeitsführer auf dem Parteikongreß*, 26 June 1935.
86. Quoted in Patel, *Soldaten der Arbeit*, 259.
87. Ibid., 249–50.
88. BA/MA 6/v.420, *Nationalpolitischer Lehrgang der Wehrmacht vom 12. bis 21. Januar 1938*, 204.
89. Stephenson, 'Inclusion', 103; Evans, *The Third Reich in Power*, 300. See also Welch, *The Third Reich*, 58; Peukert, 'Youth in the Third Reich', 40; Mason, 'The Containment of the Working Class', 233.
90. Peter Pulzer, *Jews and the German State: The Political History of a Minority, 1848–1933* (Oxford, 1992), 23; Volker Berghahn, *Imperial Germany 1871–1914: Economy, Science, Culture and Politics* (Providence, 1994), 102–6. See also Peter Pulzer, 'Die Jüdische Beteilung an der Politik', in Werner E. Mosse and Arnold Paucker (eds), *Juden in Wilhelmischen Deutschland 1890–1914* (Tübingen, 1976), 169–72; Vejas Gabriel Liulevicius, *War Land on the Eastern Front: Culture, National Identity and German Occupation in World War I* (Cambridge, 2000), 25; idem, *The German Myth of the East: 1800 to the Present* (Oxford, 2009), 114; Hans-Ulrich Wehler, *The German Empire 1871–1918* (Oxford, 1985), 110.
91. IfZ, Da 52.05, Oberfeldmeister Dr U. Krüger, *Aufgabe und Sinn des Arbeitsdienstes*, 39.
92. Robert Jay Lifton, *Thought Reform and the Psychology of Totalism: A Study of Brainwashing in China* (London, 1961), 420; Patel, *Soldaten der Arbeit*, 201; Seifert, *Kulturarbeit im Reichsarbeitsdienst*, 12.
93. Hugo Slim, *Killing Civilians: Method, Madness and Morality in War* (London, 2007), 221.
94. IfZ, Da 52.05, Oberfeldmeister Dr U. Krüger, *Aufgabe und Sinn des Arbeitsdienstes*, 39.
95. Lankford, *Human Killing Machines*, 17; Bourke, *An Intimate History of Killing*, 98–99.
96. Welch, *The Third Reich*, 65.
97. Ibid., 65.
98. Bartov, *Hitler's Army*, 136.
99. Ibid., 135–44, also 148–55.

Chapter 6

CHRISTIANITY AND THE MILITARY CHAPLAINCY

A Competing Influence in the Wehrmacht?

Years of institutionalised ideological education, along with the beginning of the war itself, had brought with it a number of changes to the military. The training of soldiers and officers had changed, and the behaviour of German soldiers during the Poland campaign demonstrated that the Wehrmacht had become a force driven by ideological considerations alongside military and tactical ones. There was, however, one 'traditional' aspect of the military that remained in place during this time and, if anything, had become strengthened by the onset and experiences of war. This aspect was religion. The early months of the war presented a number of questions about the position of Christianity in a military that trained its men to think and to act according to the tenets of National Socialism.

Religion had long been an important part of the German military.[1] It was officially sanctioned by military authorities, and it was present within the ranks of a body of men that was drawn from a Christian society. The armed forces provided military chaplains and allotted regular hours for religious instruction, and many soldiers attended church parades on Sundays.[2] For those who served in the Prussian army, for instance, the official status of the church was particularly relevant to soldiers since the king was not only the head of state but also the head of the Protestant Church, meaning that patriotic and religious identities were closely related.[3] Officers spoke of it as a means by which loyalty to the state and crown was further strengthened.[4]

During the imperial era, the Prussian war ministry had attempted to promote religious activity by ordering soldiers to attend church at least once a month.[5] However, the war ministry's enthusiasm did not always carry over into high levels of church attendance by the lower ranks. Officers rarely enforced it and regarded religion as a matter for the individual.[6] Nonetheless, its presence as a significant factor in the armed forces was evident in the attitude of Wilhelm I, who was the military's supreme commander. He regarded religion as the 'granite fundament on which soldierly virtues are created and the only support on which they rest securely', with religious education forming a 'part of the soldiers' military education' that would make them 'more reliable, loyal and conscientious' and prevent them from succumbing to the evils of atheism and socialism.[7]

The Weimar Republic saw religion continue to play a role within the military. While individual soldiers were officially granted autonomy in deciding how to practise their own religion and could not be ordered to attend church, the commander of the Reichswehr, Hans von Seeckt, characteristic of his desire to run the military as a 'state within a state', continued the customs of the old Prussian army. He allowed officers to encourage their men to go to church parades, and military chaplains were retained within the military.[8]

Christianity was thus an established part of the military when the Nazis gained power in 1933. Many of those in the senior ranks of the armed forces thought that religion played an important role in the functioning of the military,[9] and this 'solid core of officers firmly attached to traditional ties and values'[10] sought to preserve Christianity's traditional place. Furthermore, the mass influx of civilians into the military that took place once conscription was reintroduced in 1935 did not seem to threaten the position of Christianity within the military; in fact, during the early years of conscription many young recruits, drawn from a society that had been under Nazi rule for a relatively short period, were often ignorant of Nazism and were much more familiar with and attached to Christianity, particularly those from rural areas.[11] This meant that of all the varying belief systems and alternative influences that could possibly stand in the way of Nazi indoctrination in the military, Christianity was the most significant. It cut across ranks, age groups and social classes.

Christianity in the military during this period is an important and fascinating issue to analyse, for two important reasons. Firstly, it caused more dissent (that was recorded) among soldiers within the military than perhaps any other competing ideology or belief system. Secondly, the way in which the military responded to this dissent is also important. As a belief system that stood at odds with many facets of Nazi ideology, Christianity's role was to become a controversial and much debated issue.

Indeed, the role of religion was a contentious issue within the wider context of German society under National Socialism, and the efforts made within the army reflected the wider efforts of the Nazis in forming the German people into a racial group united by Nazi ideology.[12] While the Nazi leadership had some success in suppressing religious activities in civil society, it was not successful in completely breaking down the influence of Christianity in Germany.[13] Since the Wehrmacht was largely a conscripted force by the time the Second World War began, its members reflected wider social trends. In spite of the indoctrination that they would have experienced in a range of Nazi organisations, many soldiers and officers had, to varying degrees, maintained their Christian beliefs.[14]

In turn, the Nazi Party, as well as the supreme command of the armed forces, aspired to curtail the influence of Christianity within the ranks of the military.[15] This proved to be a difficult process. For an organisation that we know was so insistent on imposing Nazi ideology on its members, and one that was under pressure from other elements within the Nazi regime to do so, there existed an unusual degree of tolerance and pragmatism in the approach of the military supreme command to Christianity, as well as a surprising level of compromise by the more radical elements within the regime and the military, particularly once the war began.

While the position of Christianity within the military was still strong during the early years under the Nazis, it soon began to come under attack. Blomberg, in line with his general willingness to Nazify the military, implemented a number of minor changes that sought to erode the influence of religion. He issued instructions in May 1935 that made it illegal for commanders to order their soldiers to attend church. In February 1936 he banned the distribution of religious reading material within the Wehrmacht, and in April 1937 he decreed that soldiers no longer had to attend religious instruction conducted by military chaplains.[16] This caused concern among some senior officers, including General Fritsch, who struggled against the National Socialists' interference in religious matters, as well as Artillery General Friedrich Dollmann, who, in an attempt to avoid a clash between the church, the military and the state, urged chaplains to avoid causing political problems for themselves and soldiers under their care by acknowledging the primacy of Hitler and National Socialism in the military.[17] This was sound advice for those who wanted to keep their job; by 1936, chaplains who were using their position to express disagreement with Nazi ideology were being pushed out of the military.[18]

It was not only senior officers like Generals Fritsch and Dollmann who inhibited the seamless implementation of Nazism at the expense of Christianity. Many recruits presented problems to military authorities due to their religious backgrounds. Many were raised as Christians, and many, particularly those who came of age before the onset of compulsory membership of the Hitler Youth and Reich Labour Service, were also ignorant of Nazism.[19] Officers also posed problems. Shortly before the war, at the previously described training camp in Bad Tölz,[20] numerous officers, while supportive of Nazism, expressed reservations about the constant attacks made on religion and the church. Some of those present later wrote that 'the question over the church led to lively debate',[21] and that 'some officers were indignant at the frequent and repetitive attacks that were made against the church'.[22]

Alongside the difficulties in indoctrinating young men of Christian faith into an ideology that often clashed with their beliefs, the military also had to contend with the continued presence of religion within the structure of the army itself, most notably in the form of Christian pastoral care.[23] Somewhat surprisingly, given the extent to which Nazi ideology became so prominent, as well as the efforts by Blomberg in the early years of the regime to phase it out, Christianity, including pastoral care provided by military chaplains, played an official role in the armed forces even after the outbreak of the Second World War, and it continued to do so throughout the war.

Approximately one thousand Catholic and Protestant chaplains served in the German military during the Second World War. They carried out roles that were similar to those in other armies: they held religious services, administered sacraments, tended to the wounded and the sick, and held mass when the dead were buried. However, Wehrmacht chaplains faced a number of challenges unlike those encountered in previous wars in which Germany had taken part, and unlike those faced by the chaplains serving in other militaries from Western countries at the time. The regime and the military that they served were underpinned by an ideology that stood at odds with, and was often hostile to, Christianity. German military chaplains also had to carry out their job under unusual circumstances, in which they were often witness to atrocities against occupied populations, many of whom were Christians themselves. In such instances, chaplains were placed in a difficult position, regardless of their political leanings. Their presence as representatives of Christianity helped to legitimise such occurrences due to the notion that, since the army was deemed to have the support of a respected religious tradition that served an omniscient deity, God was indeed on their side.[24] As the inscription on the belt buckle of each Wehrmacht soldier stated, *Gott mit uns*, God is with us.

The role of military chaplains was much debated within the military and the party, provoking differing reactions from fervent Nazis and more conservative members of the military. The chaplaincy received support and condemnation, it experienced attempts to maintain its position and to dissolve it, and it played its part in spreading the ideas of both Christianity and, eventually, Nazism. The story of the chaplaincy provides an interesting paradox. While the supreme command of the military sought to ensure the ongoing establishment of Nazism within its ranks, it also made use of an alternative ideology in ensuring that it maintained its fighting effectiveness; it used Christianity to help prop up morale, particularly during the most trying of times. In this sense, while ideological indoctrination was a critical priority, the supreme command was in the end largely unwilling to be dogmatic in its approach when it came to addressing the religious question. Instead, it displayed notable pragmatism based on both wartime experience and the long-standing, and still widespread, presence of Christianity in German society. Examining the chaplaincy, therefore, can provide a further insight into the manner and extent of ideological education in the Wehrmacht – its limits, its reception and the competing influences it faced.

The key to understanding the ambiguous and seemingly paradoxical presence of military chaplains within the Wehrmacht, and in particular during the wartime years, was, in fact, the very occurrence of the Second World War. In the years prior to the outbreak of war, it did not seem as though the military chaplaincy would continue to exist. After Blomberg's attempts to slowly curtail its influence, a much more drastic outcome looked certain in January 1938, when military commanders received a memorandum from the war ministry. It informed officers that, 'According to the will of the Führer, in one year from now there will no longer be pastoral care in the military'.[25] Other senior Nazis, particularly Martin Bormann, regarded the isolation of the Wehrmacht from the church as an urgent goal.[26] There was no room for any competing belief systems within the new, Nazified army. Yet years later, even during the latter stages of the Second World War, military chaplains continued to serve in the Wehrmacht. How did this come about? Why, in spite of the anti-Christian sentiment within the highest ranks of the party, the SS, as well as within the more radically Nazi elements of the army itself, were military chaplains retained in the armed forces? How did their presence square with the Nazi ideological education that was occurring?

A set of directives that the war ministry issued in September 1940, a year into the war, provides an insight into the thinking of the wartime supreme command. It indicated the challenge that religion caused the military, the ways in which the military sought to confront it and the regulation that the armed forces wished to impose upon Christian pastors. It also set out the reasons why the chaplaincy would be retained during wartime.

While Hitler had indicated that he wished to do away with the chaplaincy in 1938, the onset of war complicated matters. Even Hitler himself seemed to have changed his mind. According to the 1940 military directive, 'Thoughts on Military Pastoral Care', Hitler had evidently had a change of heart and authorised the provision of pastoral care within the military.[27] Yet the authorisation of the Führer did not settle the matter. In spite of Hitler's sanction of pastoral care, the Supreme Command of the Wehrmacht (hereafter referred to by its abbreviated German acronym, OKW), led by Wilhelm Keitel, still raised the possibility of doing away with it, due to a perception that religious activity within the armed forces was causing problems because of its incompatibility with Nazism. Doubts were also held within the military itself over its relevance, and 'authoritative figures within the party' viewed the 'involvement of the church in the education and moulding of Germans not only as unnecessary, but also as damaging'.[28] The objections of these party officials were such that the directive went as far as singling out religion as 'the only source of friction' between the armed forces and the party.[29]

These observations brought about the suggestion of removing military pastors from the service, as Hitler had originally ordained in 1938. Yet this proved problematic for a number of reasons. The OKW, as well as many within the lower ranks, held differing views on the matter, and the discussion that ensued revolved around finding a solution that would take these conflicting sentiments into account. In this instance, as well as over the course of the war, the military displayed a pragmatic attitude towards these concerns, deciding to tread the line between ideological purity and the concerns of tradition and practicality. The OKW decided that taking the firm step of immediately doing away with Christian pastoral care completely was not the answer. It voiced concern that such a sweeping cultural transformation would cause resentment, particularly from the older, more conservative officers, many of whom still wished to safeguard traditions that they saw as playing an important role in their profession.[30]

The issue of the Wehrmacht being at war was to prove decisive. In the eyes of Keitel and the OKW, experienced frontline officers who urged the retention of pastoral care provided the most compelling argument. One officer had contended that pastoral care 'during times of war' was 'indispensable', with priests, and religion in general, having a unique effect on soldiers in times of war: 'When constantly face to face with death, as in all situations in which they are not able to cope spiritually, people need something that they can fall back upon'. It was thus important that chaplains were present during these periods: 'Superior officers cannot provide this kind of care, because they do not have time, or are not at all capable of providing it'.[31]

In light of the opinions of these senior officers, the OKW conceded that Christianity, and the military chaplains who would deliver its message, would provide the best of assistance for soldiers during the worst of times. They particularly asserted that the observance of Christian burial ceremonies for fallen soldiers would 'give great strength' to troops. Furthermore, the celebration of mass in the field was regarded as a necessity.[32] According to the directive, people in such traumatic circumstances were drawn towards, and developed a deep yearning for, the 'supernatural'. Interestingly, in order to further justify the thinking behind these decisions, the report cited the wartime experiences of the SS. Reports from the field showed that wounded members of the SS often accepted or even pleaded for the spiritual assistance offered by priests.[33] There were also a number of cases in which field services took place among Waffen SS units at the front,[34] showing that even the most ideologically fanatical of Nazi organisations made concessions to Christianity amidst the chaos and trauma of battle. In turn, the military chose to allow representatives of the Christian churches to continue carrying out such duties, concluding that, 'Beyond doubt, the negative effect of forbidding pastoral care in the field should not be underestimated'.[35]

The military did, however, consider re-addressing the issue once the war was over. The aim was, at the very least, to tactfully downgrade the peacetime role of religion in the military. Yet the OKW, at least in 1940, decided against shutting religion and pastors out of the military completely. This attitude came about due to a number of considerations. In light of the possibility of further conflict in the future, military officials decreed that the Wehrmacht would allow priests to continue to interact with soldiers and officers during peacetime. This would allow them to build rapport, which would enhance their wartime effectiveness as morale boosters. While the notion of pastoral care being an important factor in motivating or comforting the troops may have deviated from the ideal policy, recent experience had forced the military to admit the positive effect that it had on morale, and based its decision on experience rather than purely ideological considerations.

Nonetheless, efforts persisted throughout the war to reduce the influence of Christianity in the armed forces. On numerous occasions, the Wehrmacht leadership issued strict guidelines that regulated the activities of military chaplains. In 1940, a decree was issued by the OKW reminding troops that unlike ideological education, attendance at religious services or counselling from priests was not compulsory. Pastoral care was not forced upon soldiers, who could refuse it, or, the military hoped, simply not actively seek it out. In this sense, the religious question was perhaps unique in the German military, in that it provided soldiers with an unusual degree of individual choice. This concept of individual decision-making extended to officers, who could follow their own religious beliefs and act according to them. This was, however, an area of concern, and conditions were attached to this role. As commanders of numerous young men, officers held potentially influential positions. As a precaution, the military ordained that the more religiously inclined officers were not to attempt to sway their men towards religion. They were not to preach to their men, nor could they order, or even encourage or suggest to their men that they attend church services, signalling a break with earlier traditions during the Weimar and imperial eras.[36]

The military hoped that if these directives were followed, the number of soldiers attending church services would drop off dramatically, reasoning that they would not routinely seek out pastoral care or attend church if they did not have to. Furthermore, military chaplains would no longer have soldiers sent their way for church services by their commanding officers, and instead would be forced to be proactive and convince men to take the time and make the effort to attend services. However, even these activities would not be without regulation from above. Despite being allowed to continue their work, albeit in an obstructed capacity, army chaplains would be under constant surveillance, which the military deemed 'an evil, but the pettiest of evils that in this situation cannot be avoided'.[37]

Anxiety over the role of religion in the military also existed in other organisations. The SS was particularly concerned. Dismayed at the outright existence of any type of religious influence whatsoever, its suspicions were increased by instances of religious elements skirting the strict regulations set down by the armed forces. The SS documented numerous instances of such transgressions in its *Meldungen aus dem Reich*, or Reports from the Reich. The Reports from the Reich were summaries of intelligence reports from regional units of the SD, the SS security service, and were received by Heinrich Himmler, the head of the SS, along with Reinhard Heydrich, the head of the Security Police and the SD. The reports provided candid descriptions and analyses of various aspects of life in Germany and in the occupied territories. They included analyses of public opinion, current events and issues, and were published three times a week until May 1940, and twice weekly thereafter.[38] These reports contained numerous instances of the SS taking an interest in, and expressing apprehension about, the continuing influence of Christianity in the Wehrmacht.

One such report, issued on 14 November 1940, warned that church organisations, both Protestant and Catholic, were sending religious literature to members of the Wehrmacht. This was strictly forbidden. Soldiers were only supposed to receive such literature from military chaplains, not from civilian priests or organisations. According to an order from the OKW on 9 October 1939, all material that soldiers received from chaplains had first to be checked and approved by the Reich Ministry of Public Enlightenment and Propaganda, and then sent to the OKW for potential military censorship.[39] If priests at home were able to contact soldiers in the field, these censorship efforts would be ineffective.[40]

The SS was alarmed at the danger of soldiers being 'overwhelmed by religious literature that would be damaging to the morale and fighting ability of the soldiers', which supposedly was due to the 'political and ideological dubiousness' of many Christian texts.[41] Religious organisations were flouting such laws by attempting to bypass the strictly regulated chaplaincy; they often would appeal to their congregations to send religious literature, using the cover of personal letters, to provide spiritual support to soldiers at the front. The SD reported that in Weimar and Würzburg, for example, priests were handing out free newsletters after mass, which they encouraged people to send along with the next letter they wrote to their son, brother or husband at the front. One report from Augsburg even told of church attendees receiving a ready-made Christian care package of a newsletter inside an envelope, complete with stamp, requiring only the name and postal address of the family member at the front. Editorials in church newsletters also recommended that people should send the latest edition of the newsletter to soldiers at the front when they had finished reading them. Some newsletters, particularly Catholic ones, even offered to reimburse those who could not afford the cost of delivery, since it was 'the duty of every Catholic to send a church magazine to the front … whoever cannot afford the twenty *pfennig* for postage receives the paper for free, courtesy of the diocese'.[42]

Religious organisations also reportedly issued newsletters that sought to avoid detection by having innocuous sounding titles.[43] This issue surfaced repeatedly in the SD reports. In May 1941, the Reports from the Reich reported that despite government warnings, numerous agents from all over the Reich had stated that many church affiliates continued to ignore the law. Priests in the towns of Leignitz, Halle, Bayreuth and Nuremberg, for example, were still sending religious material to soldiers, while trying to remain undetected by mailing the envelopes without return addresses.[44] Again, the SS articulated particular displeasure at officials of the Catholic Church, condemning their attempts to exert influence over Catholic soldiers and their families. One report in October 1939 wrote of increasing instances of church representatives taking steps to involve themselves in the lives of Catholic soldiers' families throughout the Reich. This involved, once again, sending theological literature to men at the front. Priests were also encouraging the Catholic population of Bavaria to inform the church of the names of people whose relations had been killed or wounded at the front so that they could visit them and provide pastoral care.[45]

The SS was also concerned with activities taking place within military hospitals and rehabilitation centres, where priests were often present.

Chaplains' access to the sick and wounded in hospitals was, like other areas within the military, subject to strict regulation. The military forbade chaplains from visiting soldiers in hospitals unless a soldier had specifically requested them by name. To further curtail any possible religious influence, head doctors who worked in confessional hospitals were to ensure that there was no religious influence whatsoever upon the wounded or sick by the owners of the hospital.[46] In spite of these regulations, the SS complained that priests, once again singling out Catholic priests in particular, were cynically attempting to increase their influence over the sick, and were often more concerned with 'rescuing and winning over the souls' of soldiers, rather than 'preserving their lives and health'. The reports also stated that priests took advantage of those 'in moments of physical and spiritual weakness', and that religious services still took place in hospitals. To combat the influence of religion in the military hospitals, the SS made a number of suggestions for further restrictions. It recommended that the religious denomination of hospitalised soldiers be removed from their nametags, and that soldiers should at all times be provided with reading material that was grounded in Nazi ideology. It even recommended that a special Nazi organisation be formed that could serve as an 'ideological guard' in hospitals in order to actively protect wounded soldiers from Christian influence.[47]

While the SS were expressing such concerns, the OKW was, throughout the course of the war, making efforts to reduce the influence that the military chaplaincy may have had. This was evident in a set of guidelines that the OKW issued in 1942. Indicating the importance of this issue, and suggestive of the tension it was still creating with elements of the Nazi Party, Martin Bormann saw fit to circulate it to party officials in order to 'clear up any misunderstandings' over the roles and responsibilities of chaplains. The *Guidelines for Carrying Out Pastoral Care in the Field*, issued by Keitel, set out the role of a chaplaincy that would best serve the interests of the military's wars of conquest. It would provide support for the troops during difficult times. However, it would be strictly forbidden for chaplains to attempt to impose themselves, or the Christian beliefs they represented, in any way that would interfere with, or undermine, the ideologically orientated goals or methods of the army. In effect, all activities of chaplains were to be strictly regulated in a way that ensured that everything they did was subservient to the ideology of Nazism.[48]

The basic thrust of the guidelines was that while pastoral care in the field was an essential institution that provided an important service to Christian soldiers who desired spiritual support, its existence was conditional on a number of important provisos. These conditions sought to ensure that the role of chaplains would be carried out with the following in mind: 'the outcome of the battle for freedom will decide the future of the German people, and therefore the fate of every single German. Pastoral care within the Wehrmacht has to take this fact into reckoning'.[49]

The regulations were detailed and numerous. Continuing, and going beyond those set out two years earlier in 1940, chaplains were not to provide pastoral care to any soldier unless specifically asked to; any involvement on the part of soldiers was strictly voluntary. No soldier was to be disadvantaged in any way if he chose not to take part in religious activity. Keitel not only expressed his concern about church representatives' interaction with living soldiers; he also sought to regulate the involvement that chaplains would have with the dead. He ordered that officers were to take complete control over the burial of soldiers, and that chaplains were only to perform a Christian burial and funeral service for soldiers if they had specifically made it known in their official papers that they desired a religious service. In order to keep the numbers of such men low, chaplains were banned from giving soldiers the necessary forms to fill out to request last rites and a Christian burial. In such cases where no written wish existed for a Christian service, the military decreed that the leaders of fallen soldiers' units were to conduct military funerals. It was even forbidden for chaplains to be the first to inform relatives of the death of a family member at the front. This was also to be the task of a commanding officer or a military doctor.[50] A directive issued by the OKW a few months later in July 1942 went even further, ordering that chaplains were not allowed to write to soldiers' families earlier than ten days after they were informed of his death. Even this was only allowed if the soldier had expressly stated that he wanted this to occur in the case of his death. It was also forbidden for the letter to be 'too religious' and to make use of biblical extracts or other scriptures.[51]

Such directives were indicative of an attempt to slowly reduce the tasks, and therefore the relevance, of military chaplains, and place greater importance on unit commanders as being not only the military leaders, but also the 'spiritual' guides of their men. Officers took on responsibilities outside of their traditional roles, while chaplains had to relinquish many of theirs. Keitel's directive asserted that there was to be a complete separation between the chaplain's role and the officer's role. A pastor was to be an adviser and supporter in matters strictly pertaining to Christianity. Any other discussion whatsoever about motivation, the rights and the wrongs of the war, or any activity undertaken by the military was strictly forbidden. German soldiers were only to discuss such matters with their commanding officers, and chaplains were to steer well clear of such matters:

> Pastoral care is a religious task. The education, moral and intellectual guidance, and political training of soldiers are something for which the troop leaders are responsible. The officer alone is responsible for the thoughts and

behaviour of his troops ... Answering questions that lie outside the area of religion is forbidden as this is not one of the duties involved in providing Christian pastoral care.[52]

The surveillance of chaplains, first decreed in 1940, was to continue, with divisional commanders ordered to supervise chaplains closely to ensure that they adhered to these directives.[53]

Even the narrow religious sphere in which chaplains were able to function was subject to strict control, with military authorities policing the type of reading material that military chaplains could distribute to troops. Chaplains could only hand out reading materials to those who specifically requested it, and they could only give them literature that was officially approved by the OKW.[54] Much of the religious literature that chaplains were permitted to distribute was produced by the German Christian movement, which played a significant role in the military chaplaincy. This meant that much of this supposedly religious literature had a strongly antisemitic and pro-Nazi slant that would only have supported the kind of ideological tracts contained in official Wehrmacht training booklets and newsletters.[55] The OKW also ordered that religious activities such as services in the field were to be kept short. It discouraged separate services for Catholics and Protestants, in order to prevent any sense of denominational division between the men, although multi-confessional services did prove to be popular with soldiers. These services involved, among other things, a prayer for the Führer, the *Volk* and the Fatherland.[56] Priests were not even permitted to announce the occurrence of religious services; this was to be carried out by officers.[57]

Involvement with civilians was also subject to precise regulations. The Wehrmacht forbade military priests from providing any kind of service for the local populations of occupied enemy territories. While chaplains were permitted to make use of church buildings in occupied countries to conduct mass for the troops, it was forbidden for locals to attend, and German soldiers could not attend locally conducted church services.[58] This suggests that military commanders did not want priests to become involved with enemy populations, lest pastors develop a rapport or even sympathy with them that could influence their view of the war, which they could then potentially pass on to the soldiers in their care. The banning of mixed attendance of mass also suggests a desire to prevent the contact of German soldiers with local populations, particularly within a Christian setting. Christianity was, after all, something that German soldiers had in common with many of the people whose countries they occupied. The military's desire to preclude such occurrences suggests that it was anxious to prevent soldiers from developing any kind of bond with or sympathy for enemy civilians through recognition of such common ground; joint attendance of such a familiar ritual as

Christian mass could humanise the people that Wehrmacht propaganda sought to portray as faceless, cruel, treacherous and, importantly in this context, Godless masses.

Somewhat paradoxically, in the midst of such an anti-clerical atmosphere, the military value of chaplains in wartime actually gained increasing recognition as the war went on. Echoing earlier observations that chaplains could provide great comfort to those in the most traumatic of circumstances, in 1942 the Wehrmacht supreme command directed that chaplains were 'to be in a position to use religion to comfort those Christian soldiers who desired it during difficult times, and to give strength to the wounded and the dying'.[59] Chaplains were to make their presence during battle their priority:

> During battle, the chaplain will take his place with those troops who are in the midst of the heaviest fighting and at the main dressing station, unless – and this will be the exception – commanded otherwise to undertake a specific task by their division commander, etc. Besides this, his most important task is to provide pastoral care to those wounded or sick men in hospitals who request it.[60]

Doris L. Bergen has argued that orders along the lines of that quoted above had a dual purpose: to maximise the morale-boosting effects of chaplains, and to maximise the risk to their lives. According to Bergen, chaplains called the measure the 'Uriah Law' after the general in the Bible whom King David sent on a suicide mission so that David could have his widow.[61] The so-called 'Uriah Law', alongside other measures, was to decimate the numbers of chaplains in the Wehrmacht. In the same year as the above instruction was issued, the OKW commanded that no new chaplains would be appointed to replace those who had fallen in battle, been taken prisoner or left due to illness. The numbers of chaplains in the army and the navy were already well below those in the First World War, and the German air force did not have any chaplains at all assigned to its units.[62]

Bergen's assertion requires close attention. Was the high command of the military hoping that the chaplaincy would be decimated in battle? One can view the above order as fitting in with the military's desire to phase out the chaplaincy once the war ended, which was present in earlier directives regarding military chaplains. The military's decision to halt the recruitment of new chaplains adds weight to the notion of the 'Uriah Law' as an attempt to reduce the number of chaplains as quickly as possible. However, the above order also fits in with earlier statements issued by the Wehrmacht that emphasised the important role that pastoral care played in propping up the morale of those men who experienced the worst physical and mental trauma, and stated that phasing out the chaplaincy would be delayed until after the war. It is indeed possible to view the order as a sinister plot by military officials to achieve two goals by exploiting chaplains in situations where they were most needed, and solving the problem of their ongoing presence in the military by maximising the chance that they would be killed. Perhaps the timing of the orders is the most important factor. The so-called 'Uriah Law' was issued in 1942. The Soviet campaign was taking place and the German army was taking part in a 'life and death struggle' with its sworn enemy, 'Jewish Bolshevism'. Nazi ideological education, along with the propaganda and policies of the military, were becoming more radical as the war progressed. Nazi ideology was becoming ever more important in the decision-making processes, and the activities, of the military. But did this extend to the military issuing a command that was intended to decimate a specific section of people within its own ranks?

One can view the order in a different way. The 'Uriah Law', if one returns to the original document, is part of a directive that issues a number of guidelines for the role of the chaplaincy. The point that chaplains referred to as the 'Uriah Law' is point number seven, in a document containing sixteen points. It is true that reading the document in full does indicate that the military was hoping to suppress the activities of chaplains, and to ensure that they would have as insignificant a role as possible. This is particularly relevant in relation to their roles of carrying out religious rituals and acting as personal counsellors to soldiers, particularly concerning subjects that did not strictly constitute religious, theological discussion. However, the repressive nature of the instructions to the chaplains focused mainly upon activities that took place outside of the specific area of battle. In areas relating to the immediate needs of soldiers who were suffering from the physical and mental ordeal of battle, chaplains were, as shown above, required to play an active part. The military had repeatedly described this as their most important role, and, as mentioned earlier, it was the main reason the OKW decided to retain military chaplains.

In this sense, pragmatism is again evident in this order. It is clear that the armed forces wanted chaplains to play a minimal role in the day-to-day existence of soldiers at war, and to have as little involvement as possible with their ideological viewpoints. If peace had been the state of affairs, the evidence suggests that the chaplaincy would most likely have been disbanded, as the war ministry indicated as Hitler's original desire in January 1938.[63] However, the fact that the nation was at war changed things. The supreme command of the military recognised the use of chaplains in raising morale. The very same document that contains the 'Uriah Law' indicates, in its very first point, that chaplains served a role that was the same as any other member of the military: to ensure that Germany would win the war that would 'determine the future of every German'.[64]

Viewing the 'Uriah Law' within this broader context, including not only the wider content of the directive within which it is located, but also the other instructions issued regarding the military chaplaincy, provides us with perhaps the best indication of the intentions of the military high command. What existed was a combination of ideological dedication and pragmatism. Clearly, the military sought to minimise the influence of chaplains, and therefore religion, on the soldiers within its ranks. Christianity was to be pushed aside in favour of National Socialism, which was to influence the actions of the soldiers and officers who had been trained in its tenets. However, in situations where chaplains did have a use, and one that would ultimately serve the National Socialist cause, they were exploited in the strongest sense of the word. While priests were to be kept away from troops while they were engaged in any activity other than battle, they were to be sent to their sides to boost morale when the army saw fit. In terms of the thesis that the army hoped that the deaths of numerous chaplains would be a convenient by-product of their presence in such situations, it is difficult to state conclusively whether or not this was the case. While there is evidence to suggest that it would indeed have served the interests of those pushing for the end of the chaplaincy, other factors suggest that it was not in the immediate interests of the Wehrmacht, while at war at least, to be completely devoid of military chaplains.

There are a number of factors to suggest that while many soldiers sought comfort in the pastoral care provided by chaplains, there were also negative responses from the lower ranks to the presence of Christian pastors in the military. Resistance to the ongoing presence of military chaplains was evidently not restricted to the upper echelons of the Nazi Party and the military. Numerous personal accounts of chaplains tell of derision and open hostility from regular members of the military. As Bergen has demonstrated, chaplains serving in the military, particularly during the latter stages of the war, often had to preach to men who had been socialised in Nazi organisations. This had a number of effects on the reception of Christian pastoral care by the so-called 'Hitler Youth generation'. Many were unfamiliar with Christian teachings, and Nazi indoctrination, both in civilian spheres and in the military itself, had led young men to distrust Christianity due to its Jewish roots.[65]

Numerous accounts of chaplains outlined the suspicion, ridicule and hostility that many of them faced. One pastor, Hans Leonhard, recounted a visit to a military hospital during the war, where he was taunted by a patient, who asked him, 'So, you're a pastor? We don't need one of them. You just want to tell us stories about cattle breeders and pimps', which was how Alfred Rosenberg characterised the Old Testament in *The Myth of the Twentieth Century*.[66] Chaplains sometimes faced real problems in delivering the message of a religion that the Nazi Party had sought to undermine in its indoctrination of young men. Many pastors reported that the youngest men were the most difficult to reach, with many using encounters with chaplains to challenge them and their authority. This could even involve hostile soldiers asking pointed questions about Christianity and its past involvement in events such as witch trials.[67]

Chaplains also faced problems of legitimising themselves and their religion in the hyper-masculine world of the Wehrmacht, in which military values, along with the values of Nazism, contrasted strongly with many of the principles of Christianity. The militaristic Nazi mentality that many soldiers possessed associated manliness with physical strength and courage, ruthlessness, racial superiority and the laws of nature. This outlook scorned Christian virtues like piety, morality and forgiveness, which were viewed as feminine. As one soldier remarked, 'A real man doesn't pray'.[68] Chaplains also complained of not being taken seriously due to their lack of uniform. Another wrote that he faced howls of derisive laughter when he spoke about God and pointed out the immoral behaviour of soldiers.[69]

One must be cautious in relying on such reports, as many are based upon anecdotal evidence or are drawn from priests who wrote about their experience long after the war. Furthermore, such evidence is often tainted by the fact that former chaplains would naturally seek to legitimise their role, and writing of constant hostility from soldiers, officers and party officials helps to distance them from the Nazi regime and its associated criminal activities. However, as Bergen points out, the above encounters with soldiers hostile to religious teaching are consistent with many other accounts located in the contemporary letters, reports and diaries of German chaplains.[70] Such accounts can, therefore, provide some insight into the degree to which ordinary members of the Wehrmacht had taken on the ideological education that they would have received both during and prior to their military service. If chaplains did indeed encounter constant hostility from soldiers, particularly younger ones, one can use this as further evidence of a military that had a significant degree of success in Nazifying its men, particularly those who came of age under the Third Reich. Such an argument is strengthened by chaplains who reported that 'openly Christian characters who know the Bible are rare' and that it was 'almost impossible' to get Christian publications at the front, particularly later in the war, while anti-Christian and anti-religious material was common.[71]

A further reason why the chaplaincy was never really able to gain significant influence in hindering the Nazification of the military, or its ideologically driven actions in the field, was that many of the pastors themselves were supporters of the Nazi cause. As mentioned briefly above, the German Christian movement had a significant presence within the ranks of the military chaplaincy. This movement was a Protestant organisation that sought to bring together the two seemingly disparate belief systems of Nazism and Christianity. They hoped to achieve this by coming up with a specifically 'German' form of Christianity, which identified Christianity with National Socialism. As a result, the movement was racially based, chauvinistic, nationalistic and staunchly antisemitic. It opposed racial mixing, rejected international Christian solidarity, opposed the notion that Jews could become Christians through baptism, and regarded Jesus as an Aryan who sought the destruction of Judaism.

Anti-Jewish sentiment was central to the German Christian movement's ideology. It even established its own research institute, the Institute for Research into and Elimination of Jewish Influence in German Church Life.[72] The organisation's guidelines, published in 1932, included decrees such as: 'We see in race, ethnicity and nation laws of life that God has bequeathed and entrusted to us. It is God's Law that we concern ourselves with their preservation. Mixing of the races, therefore, is to be opposed', and '…as long as Jews possess the right to citizenship … the danger of racial fraud and bastardisation exists … Marriage between Germans and Jews … is forbidden'.[73] Later declarations from the organisation declared that Christianity was the 'irreconcilable religious opposite of Judaism'.[74] The movement also made proclamations during the war that echoed many of the worst sentiments found within the ideological education material of the Wehrmacht. One German Christian newsletter, issued in 1944, declared:

> There is no other solution to the Jewish problem than this: that one day the whole world will rise up and decide either for or against Judaism, and will keep on struggling with each other until the world is totally Judaised or completely purged of Jews. We can say with an honest, pure conscience, that we did not want this war and did not start this war. But we can proudly profess before all the world – the world of today as well as of tomorrow – that we took up the gauntlet with the firm resolve to solve the Jewish question forever.[75]

This statement indicated that the German Christian movement was not only fiercely antisemitic, but that it also saw the world in the same terms as the Nazi movement, and indeed the official line of the Wehrmacht. The Jews presented a 'problem' that needed to be 'solved'.

As part of the German Christian movement's attempt to gain influence over the Protestant Church, it sought to play a major role in pastoral care within the military. Bergen has argued that the German Christian movement was able to infiltrate the military chaplaincy and play a significant role within it, countering earlier studies that regarded the movement as irrelevant to the chaplaincy.[76] German Christians numbered around six hundred thousand. The movement maintained a considerable presence during the National Socialist era, with members holding important positions within the Protestant Church as well as in university theological faculties. The movement had gained significant support in Protestant Church elections in 1933. It won two-thirds of the votes cast and, significantly, was endorsed by Hitler himself.[77]

Numerous members of this movement infiltrated the military chaplaincy. Bergen argues that the militant, nationalistic nature of German Christianity meant that the military chaplaincy provided an ideal fit for the movement, stating that it was 'no coincidence' that the most prominent German Christian, Reich Bishop Ludwig Müller, was himself a chaplain during the First World War.[78] Bergen asserts that during the war, a conservative estimate of the numbers of Protestant pastors who belonged to the German Christian movement would be 30 per cent, with 50 per cent being a real possibility.[79] In fact, Bergen argues that the process by which chaplains were appointed delivered a large German Christian contingency.

Candidates for the chaplaincy underwent a thorough vetting process before being allowed into its ranks. They required clearance from the military and the Gestapo, as well as approval from the regional churches. Regional church involvement often meant that German Christians, who dominated the governing bodies of German regional Protestant churches, had a direct say in the process. Furthermore, membership of the German Christian movement was an indication to the military, as well as the Gestapo, of political reliability.[80] Chaplains were also subject to an Aryan clause and required proof of their own, and their wife's, Aryan blood.[81] This process meant that conditions were favourable for German Christian candidates for the chaplaincy. It also ensured that even the candidates accepted as chaplains who were not German Christians would be unlikely to have caused political problems in the army.

Across the broader context of the chaplaincy, the screening process meant that it was impossible for those with any record of opposition to Nazism to join, resulting in a chaplaincy that was 'dominated by conservative nationalist Christians'.[82] In turn, many of the men who were entrusted by members of the military to provide them with Christian pastoral care were members of a strongly pro-Nazi movement, or were clergymen who had passed a screening process conducted by the military and the Gestapo. This raises important questions over the role of military chaplains, and the likelihood of pastors providing any kind of alternative political influence to soldiers asking for guidance in matters of belief or conscience.

The influence of the German Christians was not restricted to the presence of its members on the ground with the troops. The organisation also produced much of the religious literature distributed to members of the military.[83] The press office of the Protestant Church, together with the military authorities and the military bishop, issued a list of publications for chaplains to distribute. Of approximately one hundred titles, twenty-four were works by German Christian authors or the products of German Christian publishers. A good example of a notable publication was the *Protestant Field Songbook*. Distributed in 1939, shortly before the invasion of Poland, the book received the endorsement of General Walther von Brauchitsch. It contained hymns and songs that were purged of anything that alluded to Christianity's links with Judaism, along with an oath to the flag and a prayer for Führer, *Volk* and military, and was distributed to millions of members of the armed forces.[84] Other pieces of literature issued by the German Christians included the following sermon circulated to soldiers in 1942:

> Judaism has been dashed to pieces on the person of Christ. And the Soviet state too will shatter on Christ: this state that crucified Christ for a second time, that erected a monument to Judas – and has demanded the blood of thousands upon thousands of martyrs ... But the life of our *Volk* too will be decided on the basis of Christ ... So we stand in the midst of the fires of the world ... as protectors and defenders of the German Christian legacy. We stand before God as Germans and as Christians.[85]

Such sentiments echo those found within Wehrmacht political educational material, and it is little wonder that the military approved of such literature. Ever vigilant of controlling the material that soldiers had access to, the OKW strictly regulated the dissemination of religious material during the war, only allowing the distribution of material that it specifically approved. As indicated earlier in reference to SS concerns over churches trying to flout the law, it was illegal for civilian religious organisations to send reading material to soldiers, lest it did not align politically with the official National Socialist line of the military and possibly provide an unwanted basis for dissent.[86] In fact, as the war went on, due to paper shortages, the high command would no longer allot paper for printing religious material. As of 1942, any religious material whatsoever became unavailable, with 'stocks of Christian literature available for distribution almost completely exhausted within months'.[87] This suggests that any distribution of material with Christian content was merely tolerated, provided that it reinforced the Nazi message. When paper supplies ran low, even this material was done away with. If soldiers wanted reading material, the military made sure that they would be supplied with Nazi propaganda that was free of any religious overtones.

The association of the German Christian movement with the military chaplaincy is significant in terms of the influence that chaplains had on soldiers. The traditional role of a military chaplain is to provide spiritual assistance in the Christian sense, and as such, many soldiers of Christian faith would have seen them as figures to be trusted to remain true to their faith and less concerned with Nazi ideological purity than those around them. It is in this sense that the presence of so many German Christian pastors, along with the 'Christian' literature that the chaplaincy disseminated, is so important. The army's strict regulation of the chaplaincy, as evidenced by its careful selection of pastors, its monitoring of them and their activities, as well as its control of the Christian literature that could be distributed, was geared towards ensuring that the chaplaincy would reinforce the fighting strength of the military, in both a tangible and ideological sense. Large numbers of pastors, due to their German Christian membership, would provide ideologically sound advice to soldiers, and it was ensured that others would not provide them with dissenting views, due to the vetting process that kept troublemakers out, and the strict instructions not to discuss anything apart from a narrow definition of what constituted theological conversation.

German Christian pastors thus helped to reinforce Nazi ideological education among the religiously inclined soldiers. The more strictly religious of these soldiers were perhaps more predisposed than others to dissent against Nazism. Yet if they chose to see a pastor to seek spiritual advice, or respite from Nazism, it is likely that they would have only received further propaganda, this time from a trusted figure normally associated with Christianity, and by association tradition and conservatism, rather than with National Socialism. The German Christians' involvement with the chaplaincy therefore had the effect of reinforcing ideological education. The chaplaincy itself comprised elements associated with the message that the German Christian movement preached, of a Christianity that was closely aligned to the beliefs of Nazism and was fervently antisemitic, in both its desire to distance Christianity from its Jewish origins and its willingness to endorse the 'solution' of the 'Jewish problem'. While the German Christian movement may have had a limited impact on German civil society, it had a more pronounced influence within the military.

Such pro-Nazi sentiments were not restricted to Protestant chaplains, however. Catholic chaplains also underwent the same screening process to weed out possible troublemakers, and some chaplains went on to use anti-Bolshevist sentiments as a way to motivate the troops against the 'godless communists'. Furthermore, the most senior Catholic chaplain, Field Bishop Franz Rarkowski, was a fanatical Nazi who often used his sermons to Catholic members of the Wehrmacht to speak of the 'decisive battle in the East'.[88] Rarkowski sought to motivate Catholic soldiers by referring to the war against the Soviet Union as a kind of crusade: 'It is no exaggeration when I say that you soldiers in the East, like the Teutonic Knights of a time that is long behind us, have a task to fulfil that is of unique importance, and whose effects for our people, for Europe and the whole of humanity cannot be overestimated'. Rarkowski spoke of the Bolshevik regime as a 'demonic regime of barbarity', of Bolsheviks who were 'Godless' and who, due to their rejection of religion, were 'primitive' and belonged in 'the realm of the animals'.[89]

***

The authorised presence of Christian pastoral care and spiritual guidance within a military that was so concerned with deriving its principles and driving force from National Socialism seems paradoxical. Yet a closer look at the treatment and the role of the military chaplaincy indicates that the military was able to use it for its own means. Alongside the desire of men at the front to have priests close by in their time of need, it was probably the only reason for its continued existence. While Christianity represented a competing influence, the chaplaincy was so strictly regulated that Christianity was never allowed to significantly undermine the ideological indoctrination of soldiers. Instead, the military harnessed the chaplaincy in order to increase morale, which in the end only served to support the aims of the military and, in effect, the Nazi regime. The strict control over the activities of the chaplains had the same effect. The security clearance required by priests who joined the chaplaincy, the close control over the literature they could disseminate to troops, along with the significant presence of German Christians within the Protestant ranks of the chaplaincy meant that, in many cases, the pastoral care that soldiers received came either directly or indirectly from convinced Nazis, or at least from people who were not suspected of harbouring anti-Nazi sentiments.

As stated in a directive dated 9 February 1942, 'The Nature and Tasks of Pastoral Care':

> The main task of pastoral care in the field is and remains an important means to strengthen the fighting strength of the troops ... Pastoral care must remain a means to an end and must never become an end in itself. It must never become a selfish interest of the church; instead it must help German soldiers maintain their inner strength in order to carry out their difficult tasks. Like every German, the chaplain must carry out his entire work in order to be dedicated to the goal of winning the war. With this in mind, the bearing of the chaplain must be soldierly and ... be dedicated to the love of the Fatherland and have a National Socialist attitude.[90]

Perhaps the strongest way in which the presence of chaplains supported the war aims of the military, along with its attempt to indoctrinate its men, was the very presence of chaplains at the front, particularly during the war of extermination in the Soviet Union. By being present and providing support at the scenes of the vast destruction of human life, and particularly during the perpetration of atrocities, chaplains either consciously or unwittingly helped to legitimise what was occurring from a religious standpoint. This was particularly important for those troops who were genuinely religious. As Bergen points out, the presence of chaplains gave soldiers the illusion that they were part of a virtuous organisation that was fighting the enemy not only of Germany and Nazism, but of God.[91]

Notes

1. Robert O'Neill, *The German Army and the Nazi Party, 1933–1939* (London, 1966), 74; Ute Frevert, *A Nation in Barracks: Modern Germany, Military Conscription and Civil Society* (New York, 2004), 187–88; Karl Demeter, *The German Officer Corps in Society and State 1650–1945* (London, 1965), 220.
2. O'Neill, *The German Army and the Nazi Party*, 73.
3. Frevert, *A Nation in Barracks*, 188; Demeter, *The German Officer Corps*, 220.
4. Manfred Messerschmidt, *Die Wehrmacht im NS-Staat: Zeit der Indoktrination* (Hamburg, 1969), 299.
5. Frevert, *A Nation in Barracks*, 187.
6. Ibid.; Demeter, *The German Officer Corps*, 220.
7. Frevert, *A Nation in Barracks*, 187–88; Messerschmidt, *Die Wehrmacht im NS-Staat*, 300.
8. O'Neill, *The German Army and the Nazi Party*, 73–74; Demeter, *The German Officer Corps*, 221.
9. Institut für Zeitgeschichte, München (hereafter IfZ), MA 261, *Gedanken zur Heeresseelsorge. 23 September 1940*.
10. Demeter, *The German Officer Corps*, 221.
11. Bundesarchiv/Militärarchiv (hereafter BA/MA) RW6/161, *Erster nationalpolitischer Lehrgang für Lehrer der Kriegsschulen, Akademien usw vom 17.1.37 bis 23.1.37 in Berlin*, 23; BA/MA 6/v.420, *Nationalpolitischer Lehrgang der Wehrmacht vom 12. bis 21. Januar 1938. Nur für den Dienstgebrauch in der Wehrmacht* (Berlin, 1938), 204.
12. Richard Bonney, *Confronting the Nazi War on Christianity* (Bern, 2009), 11.
13. See Ian Kershaw, *Popular Opinion and Political Dissent in the Third Reich: Bavaria 1933–1945* (Oxford, 1983), 156–223; Richard J. Evans, *The Third Reich at War* (London, 2009), 238–60.
14. IfZ, MA 261, *Gedanken zur Heeresseelsorge. 23 September 1940*.
15. Messerschmidt, *Die Wehrmacht im NS-Staat*, 276–79.
16. O'Neill, *The German Army and the Nazi Party*, 73–74.
17. Ibid., 74–75.

18. Ibid., 75–76.
19. BA/MA 6/v.420, *Nationalpolitischer Lehrgang der Wehrmacht vom 12. bis 21. Januar 1938*, 204.
20. BA/MA RW 6/V. 166, 'Erfahrungsbericht von Hauptmann Hermann Kraus' in *Sommer-Lehrgang für Offiziere in Bad Tölz*: 'Vortragsreihe über nationalsozialistische Weltanschauung und Zielsetzung vom 11.-17.6.1939 in Bad Tölz'.
21. Hauptmann Hof, 'Zweck und Ziel der "Vortragsreihe"', in BA/MA RW 6/V. 166, *Sommer-Lehrgang für Offiziere in Bad Tölz*, 8.
22. Erfahrungsbericht Hauptmann 7./J.R. 13.', in BA/MA RW 6/V. 166, *Sommer-Lehrgang für Offiziere in Bad Tölz*, 2-4
23. IfZ, MA 261, *Gedanken zur Heeresseelsorge. 23 September 1940*.
24. See Doris L. Bergen, 'Between God and Hitler: German Military Chaplains and the Crimes of the Third Reich', in Omer Bartov and Phyllis Mack (eds), *In God's Name: Genocide and Religion in the Twentieth Century* (Oxford, 2001), 123–38.
25. IfZ, MA33, OKW 863, Der Reichskriegsministerium (Inland), *Besondere Vorkommnisse politischer Art*, Berlin, January 1938.
26. Messerschmidt, *Die Wehrmacht im NS-Staat*, 276.
27. IfZ, MA 261, *Gedanken zur Heeresseelsorge. 23 September 1940*.
28. Ibid.
29. Ibid.
30. Ibid.
31. Ibid.
32. Ibid.
33. Ibid.
34. Messerschmidt, *Die Wehrmacht im NS-Staat*, 292.
35. IfZ, MA 261, *Gedanken zur Heeresseelsorge. 23 September 1940*.
36. Ibid.; Frevert, *A Nation in Barracks*, 187–88; O'Neill, *The German Army and the Nazi Party*, 73–74.
37. IfZ, MA 261, *Gedanken zur Heeresseelsorge. 23 September 1940*.
38. As described in the introduction to the material in the collection of reports in the copies of the National Archives of the USA, microfilm copies of which were examined in the Institut für Zeitgeschichte, Munich.
39. Messerschmidt, *Die Wehrmacht im NS-Staat*, 279.
40. Ibid., 282.
41. IfZ, MA 441/4, *Meldungen aus dem Reich*, Berlin, 5 May 1941, 'Illegale Zusendung von religiösen Schriften an Wehrmachtsangehörige'.
42. Ibid.
43. IfZ, MA 441/3, *Meldungen aus dem Reich*, 14 November 1940, 'Die Zusendung von religiösen Schriften an Wehrmachtsangehörige hält weiterhin an'.
44. IfZ, MA 441/4, 'Illegale Zusendung von religiösen Schriften an Wehrmachtsangehörige'.
45. IfZ, MA 441/1, *Meldungen aus dem Reich. Bericht zur innenpolitische Lage*, Berlin, 30 October 1939.
46. Messerschmidt, *Die Wehrmacht im NS-Staat*, 297–98.
47. IfZ, MA 441/7, *Meldungen aus dem Reich*, Berlin, 4 March 1943.
48. IfZ, MA 127/1, OKW, *Richtlinien für die Durchführung der Feldseelsorge*, Berlin, 24 May 1942.
49. Ibid.
50. Ibid. See also Doris L. Bergen, 'German Military Chaplains in World War II and the Dilemmas of Legitimacy', *German History* 70(2), June 2001, 232–47.

51. Messerschmidt, *Die Wehrmacht im NS-Staat*, 294.
52. IfZ, MA 127/1, OKW, *Richtlinien für die Durchführung der Feldseelsorge*.
53. Ibid.
54. Ibid.
55. Doris L. Bergen, '"Germany Is Our Mission: Christ Is Our Strength!" The Wehrmacht Chaplaincy and the "German Christian" Movement', *Church History* 66(3) (September 1997), 522–36.
56. Messerschmidt, *Die Wehrmacht im NS-Staat*, 287–88.
57. IfZ, MA 127/1, OKW, *Richtlinien für die Durchführung der Feldseelsorge*.
58. Ibid.
59. Ibid.
60. Ibid.
61. Bergen, 'German Military Chaplains in World War II'.
62. Ibid., 241; Messerschmidt, *Die Wehrmacht im NS-Staat*, 283.
63. IfZ, MA33, OKW 863, Der Reichskriegsministerium (Inland), *Besondere Vorkommnisse politischer Art*.
64. See point one of IfZ, MA 127/1, OKW, *Richtlinien für die Durchführung der Feldseelsorge*.
65. Bergen, 'German Military Chaplains in World War II', 242; see also idem, '"Germany Is Our Mission"'.
66. Bergen, 'German Military Chaplains in World War II', 232. See also Alfred Rosenberg, *The Myth of the Twentieth Century* (1930).
67. Bergen, 'German Military Chaplains in World War II', 242.
68. Ibid., 237–39.
69. Ibid.
70. Ibid., 232–33.
71. Ibid., 242.
72. Doris L. Bergen, *Twisted Cross: The German Christian Movement in the Third Reich* (Chapel Hill, 1996), 2–24; Susannah Heschel, 'When Jesus was an Aryan: The Protestant Church and Antisemitic Propaganda', in Bartov and Mack, *In God's Name*, 79–80.
73. Bergen, *Twisted Cross*, 23.
74. Ibid., 24.
75. Quoted in ibid., 26–27.
76. Bergen, '"Germany Is Our Mission"', 523.
77. Bergen, *Twisted Cross*, 6–7.
78. Bergen, '"Germany Is Our Mission"', 524.
79. Ibid., 526.
80. Ibid., 524–26.
81. Ibid., 534.
82. Bergen, 'German Military Chaplains in World War II', 244.
83. Bergen, '"Germany Is Our Mission"', 523.
84. Ibid., 528.
85. Quoted in ibid., 532.
86. See IfZ, MA 127/1, OKW, *Richtlinien für die Durchführung der Feldseelsorge*, point nine: 'The religious reading material handed out to soldiers must only be that approved by the High Command of the Wehrmacht'; see also IfZ, MA 441/4, *Meldungen aus dem Reich*: 'the dissemination of literature to members of the Wehrmacht by civilian religious organisations is forbidden'.
87. Bergen, '"Germany Is Our Mission"', 528.

88. Messerschmidt, *Die Wehrmacht im NS-Staat*, 293–94.
89. Ibid.
90. Quoted in ibid., 301–2.
91. Bergen, 'Between God and Hitler', 124.

Chapter 7

THE SERBIAN CAMPAIGN AND THE EASTERN FRONT

On 22 June 1941, German and Allied forces launched Operation Barbarossa, attacking the Soviet Union on a 2,130-kilometre front with over three million men.[1] The invasion was 'the most savage military campaign in modern history', resulting in the deaths of some twenty-four million Soviet citizens, well over half of whom were civilians.[2] From the outset, the battle against the Soviet Union was defined as a war of extermination. The Nazi leadership, along with the commanders of the armed forces itself, indicated in a series of 'criminal orders' that this conflict would be racial and ideological in nature, with the goals of exterminating the 'Jewish Bolshevist' menace. Historians have often viewed the planning and execution of Barbarossa as a watershed moment in the history of the Wehrmacht, particularly in relation to its participation in war crimes, and the historiography dealing with the crimes of the Wehrmacht is focused heavily on the war in the Soviet Union.[3] Omer Bartov declared that 'on the Eastern Front … the Wehrmacht finally became Hitler's army'.[4] However, the examination of educational material and directives issued to officers and soldiers from 1933 onwards, along with their participation in atrocities in Poland, allows a slightly different interpretation of the activities of the German army in the Soviet Union. While the invasion of the Soviet Union did mark a significant progression in Wehrmacht policy and conduct, the 'criminal orders' issued to soldiers, along with their subsequent activities in the Soviet Union, did not signify a rapid, radical development in the military's policy or conduct. Rather, the barrage of orders and practice constituted a continuation of a trend that had been developing since the mid 1930s.

This chapter will examine the nature of the orders issued before and during the Barbarossa campaign with a view to placing them in context, revealing their status as continuations of the policies evident in the military's training of its soldiers and officers. It will also examine further examples of military political instruction, including ideological lessons and soldiers' newsletters, many of which came to openly approve of and encourage the murder of Soviet citizens. It will also cite incidents that occurred earlier in 1941 during the army's occupation of Serbia, further indicating that the criminal orders of the Barbarossa campaign were not necessary for the German army to carry out the murder of civilians. The examples that are separate from the conflict in the Soviet Union also serve the purpose of highlighting the general nature of the military's activity. The Serbian example gives weight to the notion that the long-term, systematic indoctrination of members of the armed forces was a factor in this organisation's involvement in war crimes. Much of what occurred in Serbia involved a significant level of initiative on the part of those on the ground. Furthermore, the SS did not have the level of involvement in Serbia that they did in Poland or the Soviet Union,[5] illustrating the willingness of members of the army to carry out the ideologically driven role normally only associated with the SS.

As Richard Bessel has pointed out, the invasion of the Soviet Union was the crucial theatre of the Nazi project, as it ostensibly represented the assault on the 'Jewish Bolshevist' system.[6] The campaign was motivated by racism and ideology as well as by purely military concerns. In spring 1941, Hitler had informed senior Wehrmacht commanders that the approaching campaign would be 'very different from the struggle in the west'. It would be a 'purely ideological war', a 'war of extermination'[7] that would, in effect, destroy 'Jewish Bolshevism' and avenge the German defeat of 1918.[8]

The *Kommissarbefehl*, the 'Commissar Decree', laid out the ideological character of the campaign against the Soviet Union. Issued on 6 June 1941 by Hitler, the order dictated that all political commissars of the Red Army should be 'shot at once', since they were the main carriers of 'Bolshevist ideology'.[9] The aim of the measure was to wipe out the political foundation of the Soviet Union, and with it Bolshevism itself.

Other orders issued before the campaign went further than simply citing political opponents as targets. Rather than explicitly designating the Red Army as the main target, the military's aim was to annihilate the entire 'Jewish Bolshevist' system. Shortly before military units began the invasion on 22 June 1941, they received a key order from the Supreme Command of the Wehrmacht, titled 'Guidelines for the Conduct of Troops in Russia'. The directive, which depicted Bolshevism as the 'mortal enemy of the National Socialist German people', asserted that the campaign would require German troops to 'completely eliminate all resistance'.[10] The order also named Jews. As in many such directives and pieces of military educational material, however, the description of the enemy was vague and left much room for interpretation. According to Wolfram Wette, the intended outcome of this directive was that troops would interpret it in a way that meant anyone connected with Bolshevism or Judaism was a legitimate target.[11]

Wehrmacht generals gave orders to troops before and during the initial stages of the campaign that were more explicit. Specific statements attributed to Generals Hoepner, von Manstein and von Reichenau about the nature of the conflict illustrated the behaviour expected of the German soldier. For example, General Hoepner, commander of Panzer Group Four, issued the following order over a month before the invasion:

> The war against Russia is an essential stage in the struggle for the existence of the German people. It is the old struggle against the Slavs ... the warding off of Jewish Bolshevism ... Every military engagement must in its planning and execution be guided by the iron will to achieve the merciless, complete extermination of the enemy.[12]

General Erich von Manstein, commander of the Eleventh Army, issued similar guidelines to his men, urging them that the 'Jewish Bolshevist system must be eliminated once and for all', and that they should remember their task as 'bearers of an ethnic message'.[13] He also instructed troops not to intervene in the actions of the SS task forces, asserting that soldiers 'must show understanding of the necessity of harsh measures against the Jews, who have been the force behind Bolshevist terror. These measures are also necessary to suppress uprisings, which in most cases are instigated by Jews'.[14]

General Walter von Reichenau provided the clearest indication of the kind of campaign that the army planned to carry out. In an order given in October 1941, he dictated:

> The fundamental aim of the campaign against the Jewish Bolshevist system is the complete smashing of the power of and the eradication of the Asiatic influence in the European cultural realm. Duties hereby also arise for the troops which go beyond the customary, one-sided military tradition. The soldier in the East is not just a fighter according to the rules of war, but also the carrier of a ruthless racial ideal ... therefore the soldier must understand the harsh but just expiations against the Jewish sub-human race. It has the further purpose of stopping actions in the rear of the army, which experience has shown us is always instigated by Jews.[15]

The high command had issued orders that, in effect, sanctioned the murder of civilians. What is also notable is that they contained many similarities to the content of the instructions contained within Wehrmacht educational material that troops had been exposed to well before the beginning of the Second World War.

The army's involvement in the mass murder of civilians in Serbia pre-empted both the orders and the conduct of the Barbarossa campaign, and demonstrates a compelling example of the direct, willing and independent involvement of the Wehrmacht in genocide. The invasion of the Balkan states was not planned to be a primarily racially and ideologically motivated war of extermination. Instead, it aimed at providing security for the flank of the German army that was to invade the Soviet Union in the summer, as well as securing the region's natural resources.[16] The operation began in April 1941, before the commencement of the invasion of the Soviet Union and before the orders issued by Generals Hoepner, von Manstein and von Reichenau.

The Serbian example powerfully supports the notion of the war against the Soviet Union merely constituting a continuation of behaviour. The leadership of the armed forces had, in principle, approved the National Socialist policy towards Jews and communists before the invasion of Russia, and officers and soldiers on the ground had taken the initiative to 'solve the Jewish question' by going beyond the letter of their superiors' orders. In effect, the Wehrmacht not only created and implemented a regional model for the extermination of Jews, along with numerous instances of massacres of communists, but it often did so under open-ended orders from above.[17] The Wehrmacht's effort to inculcate the belief that 'the Jew' and 'the communist' represented enemies of the German military should be regarded as one important factor in accounting for the military's murder of such civilians in Serbia.

Walter Manoschek, a leading authority on the military campaign in Serbia, asserts that the process of exterminating Jews began without a comprehensive order, and without Hitler's approval of the liquidation of local Jews.[18] From the onset of the campaign, the military enacted a number of anti-Jewish and anti-communist measures, in close cooperation with representatives of Heinrich Himmler. Within weeks of the occupation, the army commander in Serbia, General Ludwig von Schröder, ordered that all Jews and gypsies be registered, sacked from all forms of employment, forced to carry out labour and to wear yellow arm bands.[19] After these initial steps in the persecution of Jews and gypsies, the so-called 'hostage murders' of Serbian civilians began.[20] These murders came about ostensibly in response to acts of resistance that took place during the occupation. General Franz Böhme, an Austrian who commanded the army in Serbia, received a vague directive from Hitler to 'restore order with the severest measures'.[21] It is here that we see the spirit of the command principle of *Auftragstaktik*, alongside the Nazi regime's style of command, having an effect.[22] The order, which contained Hitler's general intention, left much room for interpretation and individual decision-making by Böhme and other, lower-ranking commanders on how to achieve the objective of 'restoring order'. Böhme subsequently ordered the following response to partisan activity:

> all communists, suspected males, all Jews, and an appointed number of nationalists or democrats will be taken as hostages. The population and the hostages themselves will be informed that, in the event of attacks on German soldiers or ethnic Germans, the hostages will be shot ... for every German killed, 100 hostages will be shot. For every wounded German, 50 will be shot. The executions are to be carried out by the troops, if possible by the unit affected by the attacks.[23]

General Böhme justified such measures by informing his troops that 'a deterring example must be established for all of Serbia, one that will have the established impact on the entire population'.[24] This call for draconian measures led to collective punishment of Serbian civilians when guerrilla activity took place, with Jews and communists in particular singled out for execution. The massacres of Jews, gypsies and other Serbian civilians soon became an everyday feature of the occupation.[25] Böhme later directed that 'all Communists, males suspected of being Communists, all Jews, a certain number of nationalist and democratically-minded residents' were to be shot in response to partisan attacks.[26] The collective, arbitrary targeting of Jews, democrats and communists showed that Böhme had goals in mind that were consistent with National Socialist ideology, rather than purely military practicality.[27]

There is much evidence to suggest that officers lower down the chain of command not only followed Böhme's orders, but some also showed particularly high levels of initiative and exceeded them. Ben Shepherd's study of the German army in the Balkans points out that German officers had freedom in how to implement the 'guidelines' from above. Shepherd claims that of the commanders he had studied, none proceeded with moderation in reacting to partisan activity.[28] Other studies have shown, however, that there were commanders present who at least questioned the brutality displayed by junior officers and soldiers. General Bader, for instance, stated that while it was 'understandable that troops who are ambushed by communist bands should seek retribution',[29] he bemoaned the fact that soldiers often simply caught and executed innocent people uninvolved with the partisans, worrying that this would only encourage locals to support the resistance. But such sentiments were unheeded, and soldiers continued carrying out brutal acts of reprisal.[30] Even the more restrained divisions displayed aspects of National Socialist ideology in dealing with the local population; the 704th Infantry Division, for example, 'treated the civilian population, Jews and Communists aside, with reasonable constraint'.[31]

The 342nd Infantry Division, however, had a particularly brutal record. Commanded by an Austrian officer, Walter Hinghofer, but consisting predominantly of German soldiers, the division shot 1,127 civilians within the first few weeks of deployment, despite reporting hardly any contact with the enemy.[32] These reports often covered the extermination of civilians with vague arguments and justifications.[33] Some lower-ranking members of the army recognised this, with one German soldier writing in a letter home that the purpose of anti-partisan 'hostage taking' was to solve the 'Jewish question', rather than the problem of Serbian resistance: 'the shooting of Jews bore no relation to partisan attacks, which were used only as a pretext for the extermination of the Jews'.[34]

Numerous factors help to explain this conduct. Firstly, the levels of violence against civilians, although high from the very beginning, escalated dramatically whenever instances of insurgency took place.[35] As in the campaign in Poland, this reflected a long-standing German abhorrence of irregular warfare and armed resistance from civilians.[36] In many cases there were direct links between these campaigns and the Serbian occupation: many of the commanders in Serbia had served in Eastern Europe during the First World War and had been involved in brutal counterinsurgency campaigns, which Shepherd regards as 'an incubator of the ideological harshness that Nazism would later come to exploit'.[37] Adding to the fear and frustration felt by many German troops, the harsh, mountainous terrain of the Balkans was highly conducive to partisan warfare, for which the German army was poorly trained and ill equipped.[38]

A crucial point about the various counterinsurgency campaigns of the German military was that the reprisals carried out reflected the prejudices and doctrines that existed within the military. Security needs were amalgamated with ideological ones, making no allowances for the status of civilians and blurring the lines between the military defeat of an enemy and the elimination of certain types of people, as evident, on differing scales, in German South-West Africa in 1904, Belgium in 1914, Poland in 1939 and now Serbia in 1941.[39]

Linked to this abhorrence of irregular warfare was the fact that many of the commanders, including General Böhme, along with many of the regular soldiers who were stationed in Serbia, were Austrian.[40] In motivating his men to act harshly against the local population, Böhme appealed to the anti-Serbian prejudices that had long existed within the Austrian officer corps,[41] along with a particular mistrust of Serbs following the experience of Austrians during the First World War, when it was rumoured that occupying Austro-Hungarian soldiers were regularly killed and mutilated by local insurgents.[42] Böhme made direct reference to this, calling upon his men to take revenge on the Serbs for the 'rivers of German blood' that flowed in 1914 'because of the treachery of the Serbs, men and women'.[43]

Anti-Serbian prejudices, along with a tradition of ferocious reactions to partisan warfare, are not enough, however, to fully account for the kind of behaviour that the Wehrmacht exhibited in the Balkans, particularly its treatment of Jews and communists. Jews and communists were sought out when reacting to insurgency, and also targeted even when certain divisions treated other civilians relatively well.[44] One reason for this may have been the precedents set in previous campaigns, as well as on the home front in the treatment of Jews. According to Evans, the treatment of Jews in the recent campaign in Poland, along with the discrimination that existed in Germany, fostered an assumption that Jews were also the enemy in Serbia.[45] In the case of some of the Austrian-dominated units stationed in Serbia, it is also possible that a particularly strong form of antisemitism existed in Austria,[46] which was reflected in the outbreaks of violence against Jews after its annexation in 1938, and may have played a further role in the particularly harsh attitudes displayed by Austrian troops.[47]

We should also take into account the military's ideological education of its troops. There is a significant gap between antipathies existing within a society and that society's armed forces actually encouraging and building upon them, and training its soldiers to act upon them. The norms established by the armed forces' training of officers and soldiers legitimised and normalised the targeting of certain types of civilians, and their treatment as legitimate enemies. Whether or not all soldiers truly believed that their victims were actually communists, or if the Jews that they were executing had anything to do with the instances of local resistance, relentless training that Jews and communists were the deadliest enemies of Germany and the Wehrmacht meant that the German soldier was not only well within his rights, but in fact duty-bound to treat them as enemies. In the context of the military's wars in Eastern Europe, military training eschewed the concept of limited war, an approach that encourages a 'responsible use of force and compassionate conduct towards the unarmed enemy', which 'sets boundaries to violence' and regards civilians as above the fray.[48] Instead, it implicated certain types of civilians in the war with the military enemy they were fighting, thus portraying them as legitimate targets for elimination. The end product of such an environment was a more radical, ideologically driven version of previous German occupations and counterinsurgency campaigns. German troops were amalgamating security concerns with ideological ones, and, as some soldiers themselves admitted in letters home, often using them as a pretext to kill certain types of people. As in previous campaigns, but to a far greater degree, responses to partisan activity reflected the prevailing doctrines of the German military.[49]

The army's behaviour in Serbia also demonstrates that the Barbarossa campaign did not mark a radical change in its conduct. German soldiers had engaged in large-scale killing of certain racially and ideologically defined groups in a theatre of conflict that was not the major, definitive battlefront against the 'Jewish Bolshevist' enemy, often using partisan activity as a pretext.[50] The occupying army had carried out roles normally carried out by the SS, and to a significant extent the junior officers and soldiers had taken the lead in establishing this type of behaviour. The German army's conduct in Serbia resulted in the extermination of all male Jews in that region within a year, with women and children sent to camps where they were later murdered by the SS.[51]

***

Ideological education in the Wehrmacht continued during the war, with military newsletters one example of this. Issued twice weekly, the newsletters were a combination of propaganda articles and news from the domestic and foreign fronts. Entitled *Announcements for the Troops*, the military distributed the newsletters to its men in all locations: 'in the hospitals, locations where men are on leave, guards in Prisoner of War camps … [and] men at the front'.[52] Officers were to take an active role in the delivery of this form of training, with the bulletins serving as 'basic texts for company discussions', or if time at the front was limited, 'to be read out to the soldiers'.[53] The bulletins were meant not only to motivate the troops, but to reinforce their commitment to the leadership and their ideology. They also sought to prevent a repeat of 1918, when 'the army lacked orientation over the questions of the ideological basis of the conduct of the war'.[54]

Officers received their own separate newsletter, *Announcements for the Officer Corps*. Alongside news and propaganda, officers' newsletters also contained instructions for making the most effective use of the *Announcements for the Troops* to motivate and indoctrinate the men under their command. The newsletters were to 'stand in the closest organisational connection with the *Announcements for the Troops*'.[55] It was compulsory to 'read the entire newsletter' as it gave 'a picture of the thoughts, concerns and goals of the leadership' that could be put into practice in the orders to and inspiration of the men.[56]

These instructions to officers reflected orders that Walther von Brauchitsch set out in October 1940, which decreed that officers in the field were to take an active role in the ideological education of their men.[57] Brauchitsch's orders may have indicated that the military was increasingly confident of the ideological reliability of its officers. The evident success of officers' training camps shortly before the war supports this notion, as do intelligence reports that indicated that the success of the Poland and France campaigns solidified their morale and faith in the political leadership.[58] However, this attitude most likely developed out of necessity. Since the military was at war, and its members were spread over an enormous geographical area, it was forced to rely upon its officers in the field educating those in their units while at the front. Moreover, the military was anxious to keep ideological schooling the prerogative of the army itself, both to keep it out of the hands of Alfred Rosenberg, who had asked Hitler if he could be in charge of 'securing the Nazi world-view' in the military, and also because it thought that it would be more successful that way. Walter von Brauchitsch thought that a commanding officer would have more credibility among his own men than an outsider from the party.[59]

There also existed an anxiety on the part of the Wehrmacht to foster the Nazi ideal of the *Volksgemeinschaft*. The goal of creating a military that embraced the notion of a classless community had existed from the outset of the Nazi era.[60] The armed forces minister at the time, Werner von Blomberg, had ordered in 1934 that the army was to fall in line with the 'new Germany'. Not only did this involve ideological cohesion with the new regime, but it also meant that the army had to abandon the notion of the social superiority of the officer corps. It was no longer to draw all its members from a certain social class, and officers were not to act like a separate entity within the army, but instead to make an effort to mix with the rest of the men.[61]

Yet six years later, despite success in the area of ideological education, the military was less successful in achieving social change within its ranks, reflecting another area in which it did not fully conform to the Nazi ideal. Jürgen Förster provides a telling insight into the problems encountered within the army in achieving the classless model by citing Heinrich Härtl, an army officer and member of the party. In a report to Alfred Rosenberg, Härtl noted that although the Nazi beliefs of most within the army were strong, it was a long way from exemplifying the ideal of the people's community. Härtl lamented the persistence of the 'old Prussian authoritarian system', which he saw as something that stood in direct opposition to the spirit of the Nazi movement.[62] It is impossible to know whether these newsletters helped to break down barriers between officers and other ranks. However, their contents at least provide an insight into the political schooling that officers were imparting.

The issue of *Announcements for the Officer Corps* distributed in June 1942 provides an example of the mixture of propaganda and news that was typical of the newsletters.[63] The bulletin concerns itself mostly with 'Jewry' and

Bolshevism. The battle that the army was fighting in the East had been the culmination of over two decades of the 'exterminatory will of Bolshevism and the destructive will of Jewish democratic world capitalism' that began when the Jewish Bolshevists had supposedly stabbed Germany in the back in 1918.[64] The nature of this battle called upon officers to reinforce their men's awareness of the reasons why they were fighting.[65]

The *Announcements for the Troops* contained similar material to officers' newsletters, with the September 1942 issue representative of the spirit of the bulletins.[66] The lead article, 'Why is the Wehrmacht Fighting in the East?' reminded soldiers of the purpose of the campaign. The German army was 'marching hundreds of kilometres into this barren and unforgiving land ... so that the Jewish Bolshevist world revolution can never again threaten our people's freedom and future!'[67] The 'news' included in the newsletter, however, contained more striking content. Under the headline 'The Jewish question is also being solved in South-East Europe', the lead article referred to events occurring in Serbia, Croatia, Bulgaria and Romania throughout 1941 and 1942. The article openly approved of and encouraged ethnic cleansing, through its glowing tone in describing the decimation of Jewish populations throughout the Balkans:

> Shortly before the war, the Führer warned the Jews that if they once again plunged the world into war it would result in their extermination. World Jewry did not take this warning seriously. The Jews felt so sure of their financial, cultural and political hegemony that they thought it would be impossible to lose. Then they were completely shut out of German life. The cleansing and the solution of the Jewish question in other states have gone ahead according to plan. One never would have thought that so much could be achieved in South-East Europe, where the circumstances are particularly difficult.[68]

The article also gave specific examples of the 'solution of the Jewish question'. The reference to one region stands out, as it only warranted one short sentence: 'Serbia and the Banat are completely free of Jews!'[69]

The reporting of such an event in this manner indicates the importance placed upon informing troops not only of what was occurring, but also of what was acceptable and desired, and in making them aware of the expectations that their superiors had of their behaviour regarding the 'Jewish question'. This way of reporting gave soldiers 'the information they need' in order to 'orientate [them] towards the ideological goals of the war'.[70] This type of propaganda further embedded the ideological nature of the war. While not giving specific orders, it reinforced the weight of expectation that the high command placed upon troops, implying that such conduct was permitted, even encouraged, and would be looked upon positively. Training and indoctrination were informing troops of 'how' to achieve the often open-ended objectives set out by their commanders. In a further indication of the expectations of those commanders, the last line of the report stated that 'the time is not far away when the warning of the Führer will become reality'.[71]

***

The reference to the cooperation of the army with the SS in the Balkans cited within the army newsletter points to an overlapping of the roles of the military and the SS.[72] This merging of roles cannot be put down solely to the incidents that occurred on the battlefront. As briefly mentioned earlier, the military's programme of ideological education bore many similarities to the equivalent programme of political training that existed in the SS, suggesting that the military anticipated that it would have similar responsibilities and functions. This existed in many areas of military ideological education as early as 1935, most notably in the emphasis placed upon portraying Jews as the army's deadliest enemies, as well as the constant focus upon racial hygiene and the duties of soldiers in marrying Aryan women and having children in order to ensure the nation's racial future.[73] However, the material disseminated to members of the armed forces during the Soviet campaign demonstrates most clearly the extent to which military ideological education imparted almost identical themes.

Two examples of such booklets that are representative of political instruction during the Soviet campaign are *The Face of Bolshevism*[74] and *The Jew as World Parasite*.[75] *The Face of Bolshevism* contained articles that addressed the 'Soviet Problem', 'The Soviet Citizen' and 'The Jew in Bolshevism'. The articles sought to inform soldiers about 'not only the military, but also the political and spiritual forces with which Germany finds itself in battle'.[76] Each article addressed the 'Jewish problem' in relation to Bolshevism and the Soviet state. These articles displayed echoes of Hoberg's essay 'The Jew in German History', as they took a similar approach to the Soviet Union, citing the Jew as complicit in its development:

> The Bolshevist movement developed, without a doubt, as a result of the influence of the Jews. And this is not to say that the entire history of the world is a result of a Jewish world conspiracy. Instead, in the sense that when a sickness becomes evident in a people, the Jew is the symbol and manifestation of this sickness, due to its natural instinct to bear down upon a wound, in order to enlarge and deepen it. We can now see this effect in the origins of Bolshevism, since we know how much Lenin depended upon Jewish financiers and Jewish agitators while he was in Switzerland.[77]

As in 'The Jew in German History', which quoted Marx, the article 'The Jew in Bolshevism' referred to another ideological enemy, Lenin, in order to document Jewish involvement in Bolshevism and control of the Soviet system:

> Lenin himself stated: 'We have few intelligent people. We are a predominantly talented people, but lazy when it comes to thinking. The intelligent person among the Russians is almost always a Jew, or a person with a mixture of Jewish blood'. This statement shows how strong the influence of Jewry in Bolshevism was from the beginning ... The Jewish influence in the Soviet Union today works in two ways: the Jews strive for the right to their own independence, while still seeking to exert influence over the non-Jewish population ... The Jews ... financed the revolution and they infiltrated the state. They thus attained the authoritative position of power, and from this safe position in the background they control all areas of public life and politics.[78]

This line of argument attempts to portray the nameless, faceless, dehumanised 'Jew' as the figure lurking behind every act of the Soviet state and its people, implicitly making Jews responsible for the actions of both. 'The Jew in Bolshevism' reinforced and supplemented orders that were issued to troops before the campaign, which effectively gave the German army permission to murder any Jews they came across. This piece of ideological educational material, which is typical of the training manuals issued during the Soviet campaign, encapsulates the military's official policy in training its troops. It supplemented official orders by attempting to inculcate its men with the notion that 'the Jew' was implicated in each act of resistance by the Soviet population, and indeed endorsing and justifying the notion of holding them responsible for partisan activity.

The policy of merging the murder of Jews with the execution of 'partisans' was a common feature of the Soviet campaign,[79] with German generals issuing orders that used the presence of local resistance as a pretext to extend reprisal actions to murder Jews.[80] Once again, security concerns were mixed with ideological ones, with the prevailing doctrine of the army being reflected in its targets for punishment.[81] The commanders of the Sixth Army, for instance, suggested the burning of all Jewish homes and the shooting of their occupants as a possible solution to the problems they were encountering with partisans.[82] Hans Safrian has pointed out that the execution of Jews was often carried out by lower-ranking officers and soldiers, who legitimised executions by claiming that atrocities against German troops, both real and invented, were ordered by 'Jewish commissars'.[83]

These activities went beyond acts of vengeance for instances of opposition. Safrian has also documented the widespread cooperation of the army with the SS in their killing operations, along with the voluntary participation of

German troops in SS mass executions. This became so common that some high-ranking officers, such as Infantry General Karl Von Roques, complained that their men were taking part in the shootings of their own free will and without orders.[84] The Sixth Army responded by forbidding men to take part in SS shootings unless expressly ordered to do so by the SD. Although anti-Jewish measures were allowed in response to sabotage, some higher-ranking officers worried that their men were getting out of control, indicative of the tendency of the lower ranks to take matters into their own hands.[85]

Non-Jewish Soviet citizens were also targets of propaganda in military political schooling. In an article entitled 'The Soviet People', soldiers were informed of the characteristics of the Soviet Union's Slavic population, who were 'primitive when measured against the complex spiritual structure of central Europeans', who acted far less logically 'than we can understand' and were unable to engage in complex, rational thought, instead having to rely upon 'instinct'.[86] Interestingly, despite the disdain towards the supposedly backward Soviets, there existed a clear attempt to explain away the inability of the German army to achieve an easy, quick success:

> How can one explain that wave after wave of futile attacks keep coming, with Soviet troops climbing over the rows and rows of their dead comrades? How can one explain battalions marching into mine fields to sacrifice themselves in order to clear a path for attacks? How can one explain that surrounded units in hopeless situations fight to the last man, although it is senseless and without tactical benefit? Here it is not enough to blame the political commissars … Something else makes the Soviet soldier dangerous in battle.[87]

This 'something else' was the Slavic character. This was supposedly formed by, and reflected in, the seemingly endless steppes of Russia: 'Within this landscape, people are not individual personalities, they are instead simply masses. The individual does not separate from the mass. For them, death is nothing to be feared. What is one among so many?' No summary of the Soviets was complete, however, without a link to the Jews. The Jews saw 'in the population of the Soviet Union a mass of people who would provide ideal cannon fodder for their quest for world domination'.[88]

Military training dehumanised Soviet citizens, and demonised the Jews who supposedly controlled them. In portraying Soviet citizens simply as 'masses', rather than as individual human beings, and by emphasising the ostensible cheapness of human life in the Soviet Union, it attempted to persuade soldiers that the deaths of Soviet citizens were of little consequence, since Soviets themselves saw little value in human life. This document supports Wette's assertion that propaganda during the Soviet campaign served to create a 'psychological distance between German soldiers and enemies through continual denigration and dehumanisation of the latter in order to make killing them easier'.[89]

Military educational material went further than simply demonising the Jews and calling for them to be held accountable for anti-German resistance. A booklet distributed in 1943, *The Jew as World Parasite*,[90] represented the zenith of Wehrmacht antisemitic educational material. It reinforced a number of themes present in earlier lessons, beginning with an endorsement of Hitler's Reichstag speech of January 1939:

> We believe the Führer when he says that the end of this struggle, which was unleashed against us by the Jewish world parasite, will result in the extermination of Jewry in Europe. But until this extermination is complete, we must always remember that the Jew is our absolute enemy and that he has only one goal: our complete extermination.[91]

The Wehrmacht's educational programme therefore exhibited an element that was present in much of Nazi propaganda in the latter years of the war: the notion of a life and death struggle that would end in the extermination of a people, instilling soldiers with an interpretation of the war that went beyond the notion of a 'war of ideologies'. It was now a war for the very existence of the German people: 'Striving for world hegemony is a religious duty for the Jew … The form of Jewish world dominance would be tyranny and slavery … Jewish global hegemony would be the end of the world!'[92]

To counter this 'threat', the German soldier was to become a tool of extermination and, in effect, carry out roles similar to the SS. Comparing the Wehrmacht's educational material with the equivalent documents relating to the ideological education of the SS illustrates this. The SS implemented a systematic programme of education that schooled men in National Socialist racial policy in order to normalise and legitimise the murder of Jews.[93]

Ideological education in the SS was strikingly similar to military political schooling. The SS training manuals *Racial Policy*,[94] *Syllabus for Ideological Education in the SS and Police*,[95] *Syllabus for the Twelve Week Training Block*[96] and *SS Handbook for the Ideological Education of Troops*[97] are representative of SS political training and provide good points of comparison. These manuals contain many of the themes found within military ideological education. The topics within *Racial Policy*, for example, were listed under the headings 'Racial Thought', 'Race and People', 'The Tasks of Racial Policy' and 'The Racial Political Task of the SS'. The booklet goes on to list numerous topics that fall within these categories, all of which drive home the notion of the duties of the SS man, which included ensuring the purity of the German race, combating Jews, crushing Marxism and avoiding racial mixing.[98]

These articles display clear parallels with the educational material the military was implementing as early as 1935. An example illustrative of this is the *Guidelines for Lessons in Political Questions*, distributed in 1936, which stated that the 'protection of the German race' was the 'middle point of National Socialist education and politics', and that 'Jewry' was the most dangerous racial threat.[99] Another piece of military political schooling, 'The Principles of National Socialist Racial Policy', issued in January 1938, outlined the dangers that the Jews presented to the 'purity' of the German *Volk*, and the duty that arose for soldiers in upholding Nazi racial policy.[100] Military and SS training manuals from the latter stages of the war, in this case 1943 and 1944, also demonstrated numerous parallels. The *SS Handbook for the Ideological Education of Troops*, issued in 1944, is almost identical in its tone to *The Jew as World Parasite*, issued one year earlier. Also referring to Hitler's Reichstag speech of January 1939, it describes the life and death struggle against an enemy intent on exterminating the German people, and indicates the role of the SS man:

> The Jew began this war, and he is prolonging it. If the Bolshevists were to break through on the Eastern Front and overrun Europe, it would be the end of the European people ... There is only one goal: fight Bolshevism and the plutocrats. Wipe out the Jews, the arch-enemy of every people![101]

Perhaps the most revealing aspect of a comparison between the military and SS, however, is the intended outcome of the SS programme of ideological instruction. The introduction to the *SS Handbook for the Ideological Education of Troops* contained a key piece of information that explicitly set out the overall aim of the educational programme. It first gave advice to instructors on how best to impart the training, stating that the task of the instructor was to 'awaken political responsibility, political obedience, discipline and readiness to act ... to awaken within the SS man the fanatical desire to fight for the Reich, and to defeat the enemy'.[102] It then stated the most important goal of the training: 'the SS man must learn to instinctively carry out the Führer's political will'.[103] The military's educational programme declared a similar goal. It sought to ensure that soldiers and officers would, 'in every situation, act according to the ideology of the Third Reich, even when such ideology is not explicitly expressed in official regulations and decrees or in orders while on active duty'.[104]

Constant indoctrination in National Socialist policy sought to ensure that the SS or Wehrmacht soldier would interpret instructions from above, which would often be deliberately vague or open-ended, in a particular manner. This fostered the existence of a combination of personal initiative and obedience to orders. Jürgen Matthäus's description of the intention of

SS indoctrination applies well to the corresponding programme within the Wehrmacht: 'the transformation of Himmler's men into perpetrators of the Final Solution demanded ... the manufacturing and constant fostering of an organisational, functional and mental frame of reference, within which the most brutal violence for the struggle against the state's "enemies" made sense and seemed legitimate'.[105] It was about ensuring that soldiers would interpret inexplicit orders or directives in a way that led them to believe that the most extreme violence against racial and ideological enemies was the intended outcome of those orders, and equally that such actions seemed justified and within the bounds of duty.

The similarities of these two curricula allow us to dismantle further the perception of a fundamental separation between the political soldiers of the SS and the so-called 'clean', 'apolitical' Wehrmacht, which has long been debunked by numerous scholars.[106] Furthermore, the examination of the military's education programme and a subsequent comparison with the programme in the SS enables us to go a step further. Not only does examining military ideological education suggest a further factor – alongside the racially tainted orders from above, antipathy towards partisan activity, pre-existing racial prejudices, the 'barbarisation of warfare' in the Soviet Union, and fervent wartime propaganda – to be taken into account in explaining the crimes of the Wehrmacht. It also indicates that the military was training its men to carry out such a role well before the war started, long before the Wehrmacht generals' racist orders during and after the Barbarossa campaign, and long before the experience of the atrocious conditions in the Soviet Union. German soldiers were, from a very early stage, intended to carry out roles that overlapped with those of the SS, and their subsequent involvement in war crimes was not inconsistent with what the high command had encouraged in military training.

This contrasts with the assertion made by Manfred Messerschmidt in his work on political indoctrination in the military, *Die Wehrmacht im NS-Staat: Zeit der Indoktrination*. While Messerschmidt provides, alongside Robert J. O'Neill's *The German Army and the Nazi Party, 1933–1939*, perhaps the most comprehensive study on the politicisation of the German armed forces, his work was carried out long before, and therefore without the benefit of, more recent scholarship that indicated the extensive participation of the Wehrmacht in war crimes.[107] Messerschmidt asserts that while soldiers experienced racist political schooling, which 'cannot be dismissed as side issues in soldiers' education',[108] military indoctrination avoided the sort of training found in the SS that focused on producing an exterminatory mentality. He argues instead that it was, at worst, a form of training that would foster 'understanding' of the tasks that were to be carried out by the SS.[109] It is hard to maintain this argument when one takes into account material like *The Jew as World Parasite* or *The Face of Bolshevism*, as well as the newsletters that soldiers received that condoned and effectively encouraged the mass murder of Jews.

By viewing the ideological education of the armed forces within a broader context that takes into account more recent research that has documented extensive involvement in war crimes, one gains a clearer understanding of the relevance of political schooling. One can view the prewar and wartime indoctrination of the armed forces, and its involvement in war crimes, as part of the same field of study rather than as separate subject areas.

***

A key question within this discussion is the impact that ideological education had upon soldiers, and the extent to which they actually assimilated and implemented what they were taught. This is particularly important when questioning the importance of ideological training alongside other factors, such as obedience to orders, 'brutalisation' through constant exposure to violence, conformity and peer pressure.

Numerous scholars have argued that Nazi ideology infiltrated the German army right down to the lowest levels, notably Bartov, Wette, Stephen G. Fritz, Manoschek and Felix Römer.[110] Sources frequently used to support this contention are the letters penned and sent home by soldiers at the front, while Römer, as well as Sönke Neitzel and Harald Welzer, have examined conversations with and among German prisoners of war recorded by the American army and British intelligence services during the Second World War.[111]

Like any group of men on deployment, German soldiers wrote letters home. Many of these letters survive; they tell of everyday experiences, longing for home and for loved ones. Many of them also contain thoughts about the war and its political dimensions, providing a means by which to investigate the reception of Nazi ideology within the military. Bartov, Wette, Fritz and Manoschek have pointed to numerous examples of these letters that show soldiers articulating their Nazi convictions, along with their support for and, in rare cases, participation in the most radical of the Nazi racial policies.[112]

This form of evidence is not without its limitations, however. The most significant issue is the sheer number of letters that exist, and determining whether one can draw any firm conclusions from the statistically small number that one examines. According to Klaus Latzel, the most reliable estimates of the number of letters sent by soldiers serving at the front during the Second World War range from seven to ten billion. Of these letters, a few hundred thousand are situated in archives and collections, with many more in private homes.[113] Latzel correctly points out that any historian dealing with these letters faces major problems in criticism of sources and method.

The most pressing within the context of this project are determining how representative the letters are, and resisting the temptation of generalisation. One must also consider how genuine the sentiments expressed in the letters are due to the presence of censorship, inhibition and suppression, both from internal and external influences. Soldiers writing to their families and friends were unlikely to mention atrocities. They were even less likely to mention, particularly in written form, their own involvement in atrocities. They may also have been concerned about superiors punishing them for writing freely on such matters.[114]

With these considerations in mind, there is still much that we can draw from these letters, even if the sample size is statistically small. It is a source that cannot be ignored in attempting to learn more about the way in which members of the Wehrmacht viewed the war, as there are few better opportunities to gain a direct insight into the contemporary mind-sets of serving German soldiers. Their contemporary nature is particularly important. Postwar accounts cannot provide the same level of candour and insight into the thinking of German soldiers as can their thoughts when they were part of the events, when Nazism was regarded as the norm and a driving force of the military, rather than a discredited and disgraced political movement that had brought great dishonour to it. The anthropologist Hans Joachim Schröder, for instance, discovered the limitations of such accounts when he interviewed Wehrmacht veterans, finding that veterans were unwilling to speak of many aspects of their war experience.[115]

Censorship is the first problem that one faces when examining letters home from the front. In a sensitive environment such as the front line of a military during wartime, it is only natural that an army attempts to control information in letters travelling between soldiers and people at home. The foremost goal of the military was to prevent sensitive information from falling into enemy hands.[116] This included details about upcoming operations, along with potential propaganda material that accounts of atrocities or mistreatment of civilians or prisoners would have provided. Officially, *Feldpost* 'check points' did exist, where letters were checked not only for compromising information, but also in order to monitor the 'inner structure of the troops'.[117] Yet those who worked at check points were instructed to be reasonably lenient in cases where soldiers wrote anything 'questionable' in a letter home. In such cases, a soldier's personal circumstances were to be taken into account, and if an otherwise reliable soldier wrote something questionable it could be dismissed as 'letting off steam', and dealt with within the unit. Only in cases where a soldier was clearly undermining morale or the unit's mission was it to be reported to higher authorities.[118]

This does not mean, however, that a uniformity of censorship efforts existed. Instead, there is evidence within the letters that suggests that the level of censorship varied, both on the part of the military and from soldiers themselves. The contents of numerous letters that soldiers sent home indicate that in many cases censorship was not enforced, while others contain references to censorship by officers. Some letters reveal that the soldiers themselves were sometimes reluctant to write about certain things, informing those at home that they would be able to tell them more when they returned from the war. Of course, we cannot know whether the absence of political or operational content in other letters was a result of formal army censorship, of self-censorship, or simply because the author was not politically interested enough to make ideological statements.

The forms and degrees of censorship evidently varied from unit to unit. One German corporal experienced close censorship within his unit, writing from an artillery battery shortly after the invasion of the Soviet Union: 'I cannot tell you anything specific about the state of things here … because at the postal check points they are carefully inspecting the letters to make sure that no military information is sent home'.[119] Another corporal, this time a staff member, wrote in early June 1941 that 'none of the letters from home have been opened yet. But letters that are sent from here are often opened, which is why I'm being careful not to write something that I'm not allowed to!'[120] It is important to note that this letter came from a soldier who was working in a staff office, and would most likely have had access to sensitive information.

Other letters indicate that the enforcement of censorship within units could be inconsistent; when it occurred, soldiers deemed it to be out of the ordinary, or as taking place for a particular reason. A non-commissioned officer from the 296th Infantry Division wrote that he, and others in his section, also had to be cautious in what they wrote: 'We all have to lay out our letters on the tables, and they are checked to see if there is anything inappropriate in them'. The letter does, however, suggest that this practice had only been recently introduced, rather than having been a permanent occurrence. 'It's probably because someone among us wrote treacherous things', he wrote.[121] Other letters reveal that soldiers were often cautious due to a less formal method of censorship, this time exerted by their fellow soldiers, which in itself hints at a form of ideological peer pressure within the rank and file of the army: 'Anyway, we will see how things go. Otherwise I don't have anything else to report. One can't really write anything anyway, because everyone else sticks their nose in the letters. They are being checked by other soldiers. It's sad when soldiers don't trust each other anymore'.[122]

Other letters allude to the lack of censorship that existed at the front, in spite of orders from above that decreed that soldiers were not to write about their location or any operational details whatsoever.[123] One private in the infantry remarked that officers rarely enforced this particular order.

He would 'write everything … Our officers have the authority to open and read our letters before they are sent, but they have not bothered to open any of mine'.[124] In other instances, the very content of the correspondence suggests that censorship was not strictly enforced. A number of letters stand out as containing sensitive operational details that, had they been intercepted, would have provided valuable intelligence to the enemy. In one example, two weeks prior to the invasion of the Soviet Union, one soldier, a member of a transport column, wrote that 'rumours are flying around everyone, although I personally do not believe that they have any basis in truth'.[125] Another soldier wrote the following, only days before the invasion: 'Do you know what I heard yesterday? Due to an order from the Führer, all leave for soldiers has been cancelled until at least September. For the entire German armed forces! This must be a sign'.[126] If such potentially compromising correspondence got through, one can further deduce that censorship in many units was inconsistent, and that soldiers felt as though they could write freely, without fear that their letters would undergo systematic checks.

More common, perhaps, was self-censorship, particularly in reference to atrocities. The vast majority of letters do not mention atrocities. Some hinted at them, without specifically admitting to them or providing details. The following example, sent from the Eastern Front in the summer of 1941, is suggestive of such an approach: 'Yesterday I had what was, for me, a very unusual experience, of which I can tell you about later … These things happen in war, and it is not right to write home about it from the field'.[127] Others used euphemisms to allude to their actions. An officer in the East wrote, 'I think that the cleaning up work will be completed soon. The only question remaining after that is the occupation'.[128] The same captain wrote a few weeks later that during such occupations, one only had to 'seek out the active communists and render them harmless'.[129]

While one must be mindful of the existence of censorship, many letters clearly did get through uncensored. This may have been because of the sheer volume of letters being sent every day, and the logistical difficulties in opening and reading them all. Either way, many soldiers felt comfortable writing freely about their thoughts and experiences, and these included political viewpoints as well as knowledge, and often approval, of massacres and other war crimes. Significantly, the presence of letters that spoke, often rather nonchalantly, about the shootings of prisoners of war, communists, partisans, Jews, or the carrying out of the Commissar Decree, suggest that while such incidents may have provoked the outrage of many who disagreed with such acts, many soldiers felt comfortable writing about such matters. In this sense, the issue of censorship need not devalue soldiers' letters as a resource. If anything, awareness of censorship and its nuances can lead to a better understanding of the mentalities of Wehrmacht soldiers; it reveals information about contemporary attitudes towards atrocities, the varying degrees of shame or pride they may have felt about them, as well as their attitude towards their superiors and the military organisation.

The notion of limitations in what soldiers' letters can tell us also raises questions about the notion of language, which is an important factor in analysing *Feldpostbriefe*. Latzel writes that these letters can tell us only 'what the author could express in words. Things that were beyond their ability to articulate are not available to us'.[130] Indeed, limitations of language, or narrowness in language, particularly in describing things in a way that is clearly influenced by ideology, such as specific ethnic groups or the picture of the enemy, are evident in soldiers' accounts of what they saw, and provide insight into their thinking. Many of the letters that make ideological statements contain language that is similar to that found in Wehrmacht propaganda, in the form of oft-repeated clichés, jargon and phrases. Furthermore, soldiers' perceptions and attitudes are often justified with reasoning that aligns with that found in the educational material to which they were exposed. The fact that such language was used, and that such limitations existed in soldiers' abilities to articulate what they witnessed, can in fact tell us much about the level to which men's world-views were shaped by the indoctrination they underwent during their time in the military and in other Nazi organisations.

With this in mind, a close reading of collections of *Feldpostbriefe*, along with numerous other publications that make references to them, reinforces Latzel's assertion that soldiers' letters very rarely mention atrocities, and references to personal involvement in them are even rarer.[131] However, this need not be an impediment. Atrocities are important. Yet the attitudes articulated by German soldiers, whether explicitly or implicitly, are also significant if we are examining ideological education and its effects. When examining this source in a broader sense, and noting any references that soldiers made to the local populations they encountered, or to the reasons why they believed they were fighting, one finds numerous letters that show that many aspects of Nazi ideology had taken some effect. This need not be the regurgitation of the rhetoric present in military indoctrination. While examples of such letters do exist and are important, it is just as useful to look at the less obvious examples of the espousal of Nazi values. These include, but are not restricted to, racist, dehumanising attitudes towards local populations, a tendency to automatically blame certain racial and ideological groups for any hostility or resistance, and the tendency to associate, for example, Jews with communists or Bolsheviks, and vice versa.

Many examples of such sentiments are present. Some soldiers welcomed the decision to invade the Soviet Union and, significantly, viewed the conflict in terms that reflected ideological schooling within the Wehrmacht: 'This morning, thank God, it began against our deadly enemy, Bolshevism.

It was a great relief for me ... if there is going to be war, then we should solve all problems once and for all ... at least then Bolshevism and Jewry will be finished'.[132] One day later, a Luftwaffe airman wrote:

> Who would have thought that it would begin against the Bolsheviks? But when I think about it, the Führer, once again, has done the best thing. Because sooner or later it would have happened ... Now Jewry is facing us everywhere, from one extreme to the other, from the London and New York plutocrats to the Bolsheviks. Everything that is Jewish stands against us. The Marxists are fighting shoulder to shoulder with high finance.[133]

Another wrote that 'the battle against Russia had to begin' for 'political reasons',[134] while another greeted the invasion with particular enthusiasm, writing that 'Adolf and I are marching against our great enemy, Russia. My wish is being fulfilled ... This time we will finish an ungodly enemy'.[135] At the start of July 1941, another soldier wrote that 'I don't find it too bad here, because here you can really unleash your fury upon these red dogs. I don't think it will take very long here, because we are forging ahead like savages'.[136] Another soldier described the war as 'a battle against all the elements that Asiatics, Jewry and Bolshevism etc. can summon. One can thank the Führer and the German soldier that the Fatherland, and Europe, is to be spared'.[137]

During the early phases of the war in the Soviet Union, many soldiers were shocked not only by the primitive living conditions, but also by the different ethnic groups they encountered. This was probably a natural response for young soldiers who, in many cases, were travelling abroad for the first time. Yet the responses to these conditions were suggestive of having been shaped by specific, pre-conceived notions of prejudice as much as by youthful inexperience and naivety. The experience of the Soviet Union in effect confirmed what German soldiers had heard about it and its people. What resulted was, for many soldiers, a view that closely aligned with the Nazi portrayal of Soviet citizens as inhuman masses. A few weeks into the Soviet campaign, one junior officer took the opportunity to write to his family about his experiences:

> I thought I should describe to you the living conditions here in Russia. But they are beyond description. I'll have to tell you about it when I get home. It is absolute bedlam. The people here live like savages. There is no trace of any culture. And this in the 'Soviet Paradise'! It is exactly as harsh as the landscape. Nothing but forest, steppes, lakes and swamps.[138]

Another wrote: 'Nothing that has been written about Russia is exaggerated'.[139] In the eyes of some German soldiers, the primitiveness of the living conditions in Russia was matched by the Russian people themselves. An infantry lieutenant wrote that he was 'disgusted at the primitive way of life of the inhabitants of this country. They are white negroes, nothing more'.[140] Another officer had similar views during the first week in Russia: 'The Russians are beasts. They remind me, with their animalistic faces, of the negroes we encountered in the French campaign'.[141] Another, viewing Soviet prisoners taken early on in the campaign, remarked, 'When you see these faces, you can only shake your head. It's a mixed race ... many are Asiatic'.[142] Another soldier, working behind the front line in a staff office, wrote of the way in which his comrades at the front had described the Soviet prisoners being marched towards captivity: 'My friend saw the columns of Russian prisoners and was appalled by the animal-like faces of these people. One has to do away with humane feelings towards these criminal forms. Everyone here agrees that this war is a war with the beast himself'.[143]

In their disgust at the state of affairs in Russia, some German soldiers were certain of who was responsible. One of the above-mentioned soldiers, after railing at the primitiveness of Russia, wrote: 'Before anything else happens, the Jew has to be wiped out. Hopefully it won't take long until the war takes its course and we can come home'.[144] The reasoning behind this was expressed by other soldiers, with one writing that in the Soviet Union, 'the Jews take up 95% of the leading positions',[145] with another telling his family that 'the locals come and ask us: "Will the Bolsheviks come back? Are you staying? Are you driving the Bolshevik leaders (who are, by the way, mostly Jews) out?"'[146] Some even attributed the lack of hygiene and the presence of diseases to the Jews: 'Yesterday we had a health presentation, given by one of the doctors ... he spoke about typhoid, cholera and the dangerous sexually transmitted diseases, which were brought to this area by Jews'.[147]

Some soldiers believed that while the majority of Russians were desperately poor and living in squalor, there existed a privileged group within society: the Jews, who were supposedly much wealthier and enjoyed favoured status due to their apparent links with, if not outright control of, the regime. One remarked that 'the people here are all very poor, apart from the Jews, who aren't as primitive as the ones in Poland. They are the ones with the money and who are in charge',[148] and another that 'it is only the Jews that have everything, and the workers and the farmers have nothing'.[149] These links to the regime went beyond mere economic advantage, with some soldiers believing that the Jews were responsible for any atrocities that took place in the Soviet Union, either against German soldiers or against local populations. 'It is the Jews who were the leaders in the atrocities in the Ukraine.'[150] The scenes in the Soviet Union were regarded by one soldier as such:

If our enemies here, these beasts, ever come to Germany, there will be massacres unlike the world has ever seen. They have already murdered thousands of the people in this country ... What we have seen ... borders on the unbelievable. The Middle Ages don't compare with what has happened here. And when one reads the *Stürmer* and sees the pictures, one sees only a small indication of what we see here, what is done by the Jews here.[151]

Others simply made certain assumptions about Jews they encountered: 'On encountering two young lads, (Jews!), we determined that they were Soviet officers. On the order of an officer they were then shot'.[152] One infantry corporal described one instance that made the link between the racial and ideological enemies of the German army unambiguous. It undoubtedly had the added intention of giving local civilians the same impression and stirring up any latent antisemitism, or indeed anti-Soviet sentiment that may have existed:

There was an interesting procession here yesterday. All the city's Jews were gathered together and led to a former congregation hall used by the Bolsheviks. There were enormous portraits and busts of Stalin and other leaders, as well as numerous Soviet symbols. The Jews had to carry these symbols and walk through the streets in a long procession through the city to a large field, where they had to throw them all into a pile. The Jews then had to set it alight.[153]

There also existed in some a willingness to blame the Jews first for anything negative that they encountered. This included acts of resistance to the invading army, or any atrocities that had occurred before the Soviet army had pulled out. German soldiers looked to local Jewish populations in finding those responsible and to carry out reprisals. To include a few examples, one soldier, writing of Ukrainian Jews, wrote that 'German soldiers have fallen victim to their treachery'.[154] Another officer based in the Ukraine gave an account of a reprisal carried out against local Jews, who were supposedly to blame for a massacre of Ukrainians during the Soviet occupation: 'On the 2nd of July we took over Luzk ... In the old citadel a thousand Jews were shot. This was a reprisal for the 2,800 Ukrainians who were shot during the Bolsheviks' occupation'.[155] The blame and retaliation for acts of civilian resistance often took a similar course. 'In Jassy, Jews were shooting from the windows at the German soldiers passing through. Well, my comrades certainly did not mess around with them once they caught them.'[156]

The notion of such supposedly underhand tactics aligned with the factor that had German soldiers, from the beginning of the invasion of Poland in 1939 onwards, on edge perhaps more than any other: the dreaded 'hedge shooters'. This term was often applied to anyone who shot at German soldiers from a hidden position, often in hedges, but also in forests, marshes and from buildings in towns and in the countryside. The 'hedge shooters' were singled out for particular hatred: 'Naturally they are all shot immediately, and dead Russians lay around everywhere, but unfortunately many of our comrades have fallen to this disgraceful, underhand tactic'.[157] In many cases, the most feared and hated abstract enemies, and the ones about which soldiers had heard most during their training – the Jew and the Russian political commissar – were conflated with the most feared and hated tangible enemy that soldiers encountered while in the field. This had severe consequences. 'These hedge shooters are dangerous, one shot an SS commander yesterday. The murderer was apparently a Jew. You can imagine that something like this calls for revenge. And it will be carried out.'[158] Another soldier wrote, 'One thing that one has to be careful of are these damned hedge shooters … Believe me, these people will not be handled gently. They will be shot'.[159] Another wrote that 'the Russians fight dirty, hiding treacherously in the forests and in the high corn fields and shooting at single soldiers. We catch plenty of them … among them was a Russian commissar, who was shot straight away'.[160]

In other instances, even when there was no perception of immediate physical danger, the attitudes of some soldiers extended to the endorsement of the most radical activities. 'Yesterday the first Russian prisoners arrived, among them one who was either a captured commissar or a civilian. He was shot immediately. This rule is firm and justified. Also, if we encounter a civilian who is armed, we put him up against the wall straight away.'[161]

What is noteworthy in many letters that openly mention atrocities is the way in which they are described. For those who chose to write about such events, a casual tone often existed, suggesting that the men were not writing about something that was regarded as outrageous, criminal or even particularly out of the ordinary. Take, for example, a letter written by a corporal from the 42nd Infantry Division, writing of the mass shootings of Jews carried out by locals in Romania: 'The Romanians drive all the Jews together and shoot them, regardless of whether they are men, women or children'. The next sentence in the letter reads: 'Hopefully the weather will hold out a bit longer, because if it rains here we might sink, because we have not yet seen any proper roads here'.[162] Another soldier, this time stationed in Serbia, wrote that 'hordes of communists are being shot and hanged daily. But otherwise things are relatively quiet'.[163] Correspondence such as this suggests that in the view of the soldiers in question, such events, and the thinking and justifications behind them, had become normalised.

The most striking feature of all of the letters one encounters are examples of the sentiments of ordinary soldiers that matched those expressed in the indoctrination they would have undergone in the military. Although uncommon, some letters provide almost verbatim regurgitations of the official Nazi line, and many clearly reflect the 'world-view' that ideological indoctrination sought to inculcate. Yet looking beyond the more striking examples of correspondence, which, for example, referenced Jewish control and coordination of organisations as varied as the Communist Party, the US government and Wall Street banks, there are numerous examples of hostile, suspicious or derisive references to Jews. Some wrote with a sense of disgust about encounters in areas of Eastern Europe that had large Jewish populations:

> I walked through the Jewish quarter today … I'm actually not supposed to. I just went that way to take a short cut. I walked as quickly as I could. I will not be going back that way, let me tell you. That place was just typically Jewish. It looked very Jewish and it stank as well.[164]

Another, when encountering Jews in the Soviet Union in July 1941, wrote: 'In the towns here live mainly Jews. Disgusting people; typical Caftan Jews'.[165] Another described the Jews as 'an evil horde, dirty and insulting as cat shit'.[166] Others wrote in a similar vein:

> We gained a good impression of the value and greatness of the 'Chosen People'. One can only describe their homes as 'stinking dens' … Here, among these vermin, a painter would not need long to find models for evil characters from fairy tales! A comrade asked how it could be possible for this race to see themselves as having the right to rule over all other peoples.[167]

Another wrote: 'You only get a really small sign of what we see here of what the Jews have done here, when in Germany one reads the *Stürmer* and sees the pictures. Believe me, even the most sensational news stories are but a fraction of what happens here'.[168]

Other letters further clarified the attitude that distinguished between the 'master race' and the Jews. An army captain writing from the front expressed how he and his men had treated the Jewish population in Kosow, a town in the Ukraine:

> The whole place is crawling with Jews. They are all put to work. Some have to sweep the streets. The girls have to wash and mend our clothes; the boys have to clean our boots. Since the day before yesterday, they all wear a yellow patch. We had to make an example in order to make sure this was carried out, because the oldest Jew said there was no need. When we could not change his mind, we had to shoot him. Since then we have not had any problems. The city, although three quarters of it is burned out, has never been so clean.[169]

Another soldier, based in Romania, wrote: 'Whenever we need something done, we get a few Jews, and they learn how to work. I can tell you, they work like dogs as long as we are standing there, because they are terrified of us Germans'.[170] In another letter, the same soldier wrote home, asking, 'Please don't send me any money, firstly because it is forbidden, and secondly all the money changers here are Jews, and I'm not doing any business with Jews'.[171] A member of the Luftwaffe revealed that he and his comrades held similar views: 'We Germans have no reason to treat these creatures well. They are less than dogs. For us soldiers this is natural'.[172] A soldier based in Hungary wrote a letter that revealed how innate Nazi ideology, and its implementation, had become for many German soldiers, to the extent that anything that did not fit within the National Socialist world-view seemed shocking and unnatural:

> It is all well and good in Hungary, it's just the fact that Jews can walk around freely that is completely unbearable for us Germans. In places where we are fighting, this pack has fled or is living under our rule. The 'garlic people' have to work for us, and have to walk on the road. Here everything is different. They are still in many ways dominant. They have all the money … They actually have a few laws similar to the Nuremberg Laws, but it does not help. Yesterday it was completely alien and disturbing to me when I went to the baths and found Jews there.[173]

In this case, perhaps the best possible indication of the success of Nazi indoctrination, including the military's programme of ideological education, along with the other indoctrination and socialisation encountered during a life lived under the Third Reich, is less the soldiers' endorsement of Nazi ideology and its actions, but more the disgust and bewilderment displayed upon encountering something different.

***

The work of Felix Römer, Harald Welzer and Sönke Neitzel, based upon secret recordings of German prisoners of war, shed further light upon the contemporary attitudes of German soldiers.[174] Römer's work is based upon the use of hidden microphones by US intelligence to record soldiers' conversations while imprisoned in Fort Hunt, Virginia, during the Second World War, while Neitzel and Welzer examined similar types of conversations recorded by British and American intelligence services.

The majority of the conversations that were recorded did not concern the war or politics. Most were about home, drinking and women.[175] Many soldiers remarked that they took no interest in such things, or were 'apolitical'.[176] However, Römer demonstrates why it would be wrong to equate political disinterest with neutrality. Few soldiers were recorded having in-depth discussions about abstract political topics or theories. Yet when politics was discussed, usually in side remarks, or implicitly in comments, it was clear that loyalty to the Nazi regime, and belief in much of its ideology, was implicit in soldiers' statements, with Römer arguing that most soldiers' values were infused with Nazism.[177]

Among the great numbers of supposedly 'apolitical' soldiers, conversations often took place that indicated the depth of racist, antisemitic and anti-Bolshevist sentiments, as well as images of the enemy fostered by Nazism. Many soldiers were convinced that the Jews ran Soviet Russia and were trying to destroy Germany.[178] Racial ideology was deemed by many to justify the exterminatory policy of the war in the East.[179] Loyalty to Hitler and the Nazi regime was a given for the vast majority of soldiers. Of course, the degree of conformity varied, and was often dependent upon soldiers' individual socialisation, with Römer arguing that in general, the younger the soldiers, the more loyal they were to the regime, indicative of a youth spent in Nazi schools and organisations.[180] Römer's findings are supportive of Bartov's claim that German soldiers' views were often coloured by a 'distortion of reality'.[181]

This did not mean that all soldiers held such views. Former Social Democrats, for example, often found each other and spoke of their past experiences as SPD activists and discussed their common beliefs.[182] The US camp authority recognised and sought to emphasise these differences, and in some cases began dividing the prisoners into 'Nazi' and 'anti-Nazi' categories, often separating the two groups within camps, or creating separate camps altogether.[183] The soldiers themselves could even choose between the camps, although Römer points out that the camps that soldiers chose did not always reflect their actual beliefs, and could instead reflect social pressure and opportunism now that their war was over.[184] Nonetheless, more soldiers chose the 'Nazi' camps, with one officer remarking that the only ones who chose to go to the 'anti-Nazi' camps were 'people who did not have a clean slate... Communists... opportunists... Austrians... either way, people who were no good'.[185] The divisions between those classified as 'Nazis' and 'anti-Nazis' were so deep that there were numerous cases of bullying, physical violence and threats made by the 'Nazis', who dominated many of the camps, against the 'anti-Nazis', who were regarded as traitors.[186]

One remarkable discovery made by Römer was that Nazism was so strong among the 'Nazi' prisoners that Nazi ideological education classes were actually held within one of the camps. One German officer stated that 'ideological lessons' were held in classrooms, often led by an SS officer. If an American walked in on the class, the Germans in the room would quickly change over to teaching and discussing literature or history. Furthermore, this was made mandatory among the soldiers, with those who did not show up experiencing bullying in the camp.[187]

Recordings documented by Neitzel and Welzer also indicate that many soldiers' frame of reference had been coloured by Nazism. For example, many saw 'the Jews' as belonging to a 'completely different social universe'. Massacres of Jews were known about by most, but had become normalised.[188] As a response to these events, soldiers tended to 'criticise the way in which mass murder was taking place, but not the fact that it was happening',[189] with one officer recalling an incident in which the SS issued an invitation to shoot Jews, to which 'all the troops went along with rifles and … shot them up'.[190]

Neitzel and Welzer come to the conclusion, however, that 'as a rule German soldiers were not "ideological warriors". Most of them were apolitical'.[191] They also argue that soldiers did not feel they were waging an 'eliminatory' or 'racial' war,[192] writing that

> … the violence practiced by Wehrmacht soldiers was not as a rule more 'National Socialist' than the force used by British or American soldiers. The only cases in which the violence can be seen as National Socialist were those instances where it was directed against people who could under no circumstances be seen as a military threat: the murder of Soviet POWs and above all the extermination of European Jews. War, as is the case with all genocides, created the framework in which the constraints of civilisation were revoked.[193]

Neitzel and Welzer are to a large extent correct in arguing that war created the framework for 'revoking the constraints of civilisation', since the crimes committed by German soldiers involved a number of other factors outlined in this book, including brutalisation and abhorrence of armed civilians, factors directly related to the fact that they were at war. However, one need only compare Germany's war in the West with its war in the East to indicate how National Socialist ideology played a role in much of the violence perpetrated by the German army in the East, where soldiers encountered more of Nazism's ideological enemies. As Römer points out, while some atrocities occurred in the West, the war in the East had a unique character from the beginning, with no limits placed upon the violence carried out by soldiers.[194] It is difficult to imagine that the type of war waged by the Wehrmacht could have happened on the same scale had Nazism not influenced the rank and file of the military. Neitzel and Welzer's phrase, 'the only cases', used in relation to the murders of Soviet prisoners and Jews, is puzzling to say the least, since the numbers of Soviet prisoners and Jews who were murdered were not insignificant, as the use of this phrase seems to suggest.

Perhaps Römer's assessment of 'apolitical' soldiers is useful within this context. While he clearly shows that politics played a secondary role to most soldiers, this did not mean that the influence of Nazism was not present.[195] There is a large grey area that exists between an 'ideological warrior' and someone who is truly 'apolitical'. Yet because most German soldiers were indeed not 'ideological warriors', Neitzel and Welzer argue that we should 'stop overestimating the effects of ideology'.[196] This argument seems to stem from a belief that in order for ideology to have played a role in the mentality and behaviour of a soldier, he had to have been as fanatical a Nazi as the regime wanted him to be. By this measure, they are undoubtedly correct in stating that the majority of soldiers were 'apolitical'. But this is setting the bar too high. It is true that few soldiers became as Nazified as the regime desired. This is clearly illustrated by the ongoing presence of, for instance, Christian beliefs, as well as the failure of many within the Wehrmacht to embrace the notion of the classless *Volksgemeinschaft*. However, this is different to arguing that the vast majority of soldiers were 'apolitical' and that Nazism played little or no role in colouring some of their beliefs, their view of the war, or ultimately their conduct as soldiers.

It is clearly difficult to know the full extent of soldiers' politicisation. Yet there is no need to categorise them as being either 'political warriors' or 'apolitical'. Clearly, many did not fall into either category, instead occupying the large grey area in between. Soldiers did not need to agree with every aspect of the Nazi programme to have been influenced by Nazi ideology, as Römer illustrates. There is ample evidence to suggest that for many soldiers this was the case, since many elements of Nazi ideology were implicit in how they viewed the war.[197] This is particularly significant when it is part of the official training doctrine of a military, in which a soldier's duty is to engage with and kill or capture the enemy. Soldiers need not have been zealous Nazis for Nazism to have influenced their actions as soldiers. They only needed to have regarded certain types of people, by virtue of their racial or political characteristics, as enemies, or even believed that it was part of their duty as soldiers to treat them as such.

This chapter has shown that the Barbarossa campaign was not a watershed moment in terms of the military leadership's instructions to its troops. Instead, it was a continuation of a policy that had begun much earlier. An analysis of the Wehrmacht's educational curriculum allows us to place in context the 'criminal orders' issued by German generals before and during the Barbarossa campaign, as well as the conduct of troops in the field. It has also further dismantled the notion of a clear separation between the functions of the Wehrmacht and the SS by showing the parallels in their political instruction curricula. This indicates that soldiers not only carried out roles normally only associated with the SS, but that the military actively encouraged and trained them to do so. Furthermore, the analysis of *Feldpostbriefe*, along with a discussion of research on recorded conversations of German prisoners of war, shows that while it would be irresponsible to make any sweeping generalisations or categorical conclusions about the effect of this programme, we can say that for a significant number of soldiers, Nazi ideology did have some influence on their view of the war and the people they encountered while waging it. This means that while it is impossible to know the precise extent to which the Wehrmacht's programme of ideological education was responsible for the formation of these attitudes, we cannot ignore the fact that its men underwent extensive schooling in Nazi ideology in the military as part of their training as soldiers.

Notes

1. Richard Bessel, *Nazism and War* (London, 2004), 106–7.
2. Omer Bartov, 'Savage War: German Warfare and Moral Choices in World War II', in Berel Lang and Simone Gigliotti (eds), *The Holocaust: A Reader* (Carlton, VIC, 2005), 220.
3. Jochen Böhler, *Auftakt zum Vernichtungskrieg: Die Wehrmacht in Polen 1939* (Frankfurt, 2006), 21–28, 247; Christian Hartmann, Johannes Hürter and Ulrike Jureit, 'Verbrechen der Wehrmacht: Ergebnisse und Kontroversen der Forschung', in idem (eds), *Verbrechen der Wehrmacht: Bilanz einer Debatte* (Munich, 2005), 21–28. See, as examples, Omer Bartov, *The Eastern Front, 1941–45: German Troops and the Barbarisation of Warfare* (Basingstoke, 1985); idem, *Hitler's Army: Soldiers, Nazis and War in the Third Reich* (Oxford, 1991); idem, 'Operation Barbarossa and the Origins of the Final Solution', in David Cesarani (ed.), *The Final Solution: Origins and Implementation* (London, 1996), 119–36; idem, 'Soldiers, Nazis and War in the Third Reich', *The Journal of Modern History* 63(1) (March 1991), 44–60; Jürgen Förster, 'Operation Barbarossa as a War of Conquest and Annihilation', in Lang and Gigliotti, *The Holocaust: A Reader*, 184–97; Jürgen Förster, 'Der Weltanschauungs- und Vernichtungskrieg im Osten', in *Das deutsche Reich und der Zweite Weltkrieg Band 9/1: Der deutsche Kriegsgesellschaft 1939 bis 1945* (Munich, 2004), 484–505; idem, 'Geistige Kriegführung in der Phase der ersten Siege', in *Das deutsche Reich und der Zweite Weltkrieg Band 9/1*, 506–19; Stephen G. Fritz, '"We Are Trying … to Change the Face of the World" – Ideology and Motivation in the Wehrmacht on the Eastern Front: The View from Below', *The Journal of Military History* 60(4) (1996), 683–710; Ben Shepherd, *War in the Wild East: The German Army and Partisans* (Cambridge, MA, 2004); Walter Manoschek and Hans Safrian, 'Österreicher in der Wehrmacht', in Ernst Hanisch, Wolfgang Neugebauer and Emmerich Talos (eds), *NS-Herrschaft in Österreich* (Vienna, 2000), 123–58; Walter Manoschek (ed.), *Die Wehrmacht im Rassenkrieg: Der Vernichtungskrieg hinter der Front* (Vienna, 1996); Horst Boog et al. (eds), *Der Angriff auf die Sowjetunion* (Frankfurt, 1991); Wolfram Wette, *The Wehrmacht: History, Myth, Reality* (Cambridge, MA, 2006).
4. Bartov, *Hitler's Army*, viii.

5. Wette, *The Wehrmacht*, 104; Ben Shepherd, *Terror in the Balkans: German Armies and Partisan Warfare* (Cambridge, MA, 2012); Manoschek, 'Partisankrieg und Genozid: Die Wehrmacht in Serbien', in *Die Wehrmacht im Rassenkrieg,* 142–167; Manoschek and Safrian, 'Österreicher in der Wehrmacht', 143.
6. Bessel, *Nazism and War*, 106–8.
7. Quoted in ibid., 108.
8. Förster, 'Der Weltanschauungs- und Vernichtungskrieg im Osten', 519.
9. The 'Commissar Decree', 6 June 1941, in Lang and Gigliotti, *The Holocaust: A Reader*, 177–80.
10. High Command of the Wehrmacht, 'Guidelines for the Conduct of the Troops in Russia', quoted in Wette, *The Wehrmacht*, 94.
11. Wette, *The Wehrmacht*, 94.
12. General Erich Hoepner, quoted in Bessel, *Nazism and War*, 108–9.
13. Erich von Manstein, quoted in Wette, *The Wehrmacht*, 96.
14. Ibid.
15. Walter von Reichenau, 'Das Verhalten der Truppe im Ostraum', 12 October 1941, *Dokumente zum Nationalsozialismus*, www.ns-archiv.de/untermenschen/reichenau-befehl.php (accessed 20 October 2010).
16. Manoschek, 'Partisankrieg und Genozid: Die Wehrmacht in Serbien', in *Die Wehrmacht im Rassenkrieg*, 145; Shepherd, *Terror in the Balkans*, 72–73.
17. Wette, *The Wehrmacht*, 103.
18. Walter Manoschek, 'The Extermination of the Jews in Serbia', in Ulrich Hebert (ed.), *National Socialist Extermination Policies: Contemporary German Perspectives and Controversies* (New York, 2000), 182.
19. Manoschek, 'Partisankrieg und Genozid: Die Wehrmacht in Serbien', in *Die Wehrmacht im Rassenkrieg*, 146.
20. Ibid.
21. Manoschek, 'The Extermination of the Jews in Serbia', 171.
22. Shepherd, *Terror in the Balkans*, 10.
23. Manoschek and Safrian, 'Österreicher in der Wehrmacht', 143.
24. General Böhme, quoted in Manoschek, 'The Extermination of the Jews in Serbia', 170.
25. Ibid., 176.
26. Ibid., 173.
27. Manoschek and Safrian, 'Österreicher in der Wehrmacht', 143.
28. Shepherd, *Terror in the Balkans*, 245–46.
29. Manoschek, 'Partisankrieg und Genozid: Die Wehrmacht in Serbien', in *Die Wehrmacht im Rassenkrieg*, 151.
30. Richard J. Evans, *The Third Reich at War* (London, 2009), 236.
31. Shepherd, *Terror in the Balkans*, 117–18.
32. Manoschek, 'Partisankrieg und Genozid: Die Wehrmacht in Serbien', in *Die Wehrmacht im Rassenkrieg*, 160; Shepherd, *Terror in the Balkans*, 141.
33. Manoschek, 'Partisankrieg und Genozid: Die Wehrmacht in Serbien', in *Die Wehrmacht im Rassenkrieg*, 161.
34. Quoted in Manoschek, 'The Extermination of the Jews in Serbia', 177–78.
35. Shepherd, *Terror in the Balkans*, 118.
36. Ibid., 25–31; John Horne and Alan Kramer, *German Atrocities, 1914: A History of Denial* (London, 2001), 1, 90–91; Vejas Gabriel Liulevicius, *War Land on the Eastern Front: Culture, National Identity and German Occupation in World War I* (Cambridge,

2000), 79; Isabel V. Hull, *Absolute Destruction: Military Culture and the Practices of War in Imperial Germany* (Ithaca, 2006), 117–22.
37. Shepherd, *Terror in the Balkans*, 253.
38. Ibid., 4, 68.
39. Ibid., 32–33; Böhler, *Auftakt zum Vernichtungskrieg*, 40–52; idem, *Der Überfall: Deutschlands Krieg gegen Polen* (Frankfurt, 2009), 191; Tilman Dedering, '"A Certain Rigorous Treatment of All Parts of the Nation": The Annihilation of the Herero in German South West Africa, 1904', in Mark Levene and Penny Roberts (eds), *The Massacre in History* (New York, 1999), 209; Horne and Kramer, *German Atrocities, 1914*, 168–69; Benjamin Madley, 'From Africa to Auschwitz: How German South West Africa Incubated Ideas and Methods Adopted and Developed by the Nazis in Eastern Europe', *European History Quarterly* 35(3) (2005), 457–58; Hull, *Absolute Destruction*, 7–69, 117–36.
40. Manoschek and Safrian, 'Österreicher in der Wehrmacht', 141.
41. Shepherd, *Terror in the Balkans*, 255.
42. Ibid., 30.
43. Evans, *The Third Reich at War*, 237.
44. Shepherd, *Terror in the Balkans*, 117–18.
45. Evans, *The Third Reich at War*, 237.
46. Ibid., 239.
47. Hans Safrian, *Eichmann's Men* (Cambridge, 2010), 19–24; Hans Safrian and Hans Witek, *Und Keiner war dabei: Dokumente des alltäglichen Antisemitismus in Wien 1938* (Vienna, 2008).
48. Hugo Slim, *Killing Civilians: Method, Madness and Morality in War* (London, 2007), 6–12.
49. Horne and Kramer, *German Atrocities, 1914*, 174.
50. Shepherd, *Terror in the Balkans*, 101–3.
51. Wette, *The Wehrmacht*, 104; Shepherd, *Terror in the Balkans*, 123.
52. Institut für Zeitgeschichte, München (hereafter IfZ), ED 325/5, Oberkommando der Wehrmacht (ed.), *Mitteilungen für das Offizierkorps*, no. 6, June 1942, 4.
53. 'Die Mitteilungen dienen als Unterlage für Kompanie-Besprechen. Es genügt auch, die Mitteilungen den Soldaten vorzulesen', in IfZ, ED 325/5, Oberkommando der Wehrmacht (ed.), *Mitteilungen für die Truppe*, no. 165, December 1941, 1.
54. IfZ, ED 325/5, *Mitteilungen für das Offizierkorps*, 2–3.
55. Ibid., 4.
56. Ibid.
57. Jürgen Förster, 'Geistige Kriegführung in Deutschland', in *Das Deutsch Reich und der Zweite Weltkrieg*, Vol 9/1 (Munich, 2004), 513.
58. Ibid., 509; Christoph Rass, *Menschenmaterial: deutsche Soldaten an der Ostfront: Innensichten einer Infanteriedivision, 1939–1945* (Paderborn, 2003), 314–28.
59. Förster, 'Geistige Kriegführung in Deutschland', 509–15.
60. IfZ, MA 33, *Der Reichswehrminister*, Berlin, 24 May 1934.
61. Ibid.
62. Förster, 'Geistige Kriegführung in Deutschland', 516.
63. IfZ, ED 325/5, *Mitteilungen für das Offizierkorps*.
64. Ibid., 1–2.
65. Ibid., 4.
66. I examined the (twice weekly) issues that were distributed from mid 1941 until early 1943.

67. IfZ, ED 325/5, Oberkommando der Wehrmacht (ed.), *Mitteilungen für die Truppe*, no. 222, 20 September 1942.
68. 'Auch in Südosteuropa wird die Judenfrage gelöst', in IfZ, ED 325/5, *Mitteilungen für die Truppe*, no. 222, 20 September 1942.
69. IfZ, ED 325/5, *Mitteilungen für die Truppe*, no. 222, 20 September 1942.
70. IfZ, ED 325/5, *Mitteilungen für das Offizierkorps*, 2–3.
71. IfZ, ED 325/5, *Mitteilungen für die Truppe*, no. 222, 20 September 1942.
72. See Bartov, *Hitler's Army*, 48.
73. IfZ Da 33.60, *Richtlinien für den Unterricht über politische Tagesfragen*, 26 March 1936.
74. IfZ, Da 033.177, Alfred Rosenberg (ed.), *Das Gesicht des Bolschewismus. Aus der Schriftenreihe zur weltanschaulichen und politischen Schulung der Wehrmacht* (Berlin, 1943).
75. IfZ, Da 033.062-7, Oberkommando der Wehrmacht (ed.), *Richthefte des Oberkommando der Wehrmacht: Der Jude als Weltparasit* (Offenburg, 1943).
76. 'Das Sowjetproblem', in IfZ, Da 033.177, *Das Gesicht des Bolschewismus*, 3.
77. Ibid., 9.
78. 'Der Jude im Bolschewismus', in IfZ, Da 033.177, *Das Gesicht des Bolschewismus*, 26–30.
79. Antony Beevor, *Stalingrad* (London, 1999), 54.
80. Jürgen Förster, 'The Relation between Operation Barbarossa as an Ideological War of Extermination and the Final Solution', in Cesarani, *The Final Solution*, 95.
81. Shepherd, *Terror in the Balkans*, 32–33; Böhler, *Auftakt zum Vernichtungskrieg*, 40–52; idem, *Der Überfall*, 191; Dedering, '"A Certain Rigorous Treatment of All Parts of the Nation"', 209; Horne and Kramer, *German Atrocities, 1914*, 168–69; Madley, 'From Africa to Auschwitz', 457–58; Hans Safrian, 'Komplizen des Genozids: Zum Anteil der Heeresgruppe Süd an der Verfolgung und Ermordung der Juden in der Ukraine 1941', in Manoschek, *Die Wehrmacht im Rassenkrieg*, 95.
82. Safrian, 'Komplizen des Genozids'.
83. Ibid., 96–97.
84. Ibid., 104.
85. Ibid., 104–8.
86. 'Der Sowjetmensch', in IfZ, Da 033.177, *Das Gesicht des Bolschewismus*, 17.
87. Ibid., 21–23.
88. Ibid., 25.
89. Wette, *The Wehrmacht*, 100.
90. IfZ, Da 033.062-7, *Richthefte des Oberkommando der Wehrmacht: Der Jude als Weltparasit*, 3.
91. Ibid.
92. Ibid., 39–44.
93. Jürgen Matthäus et al. (eds), *Ausbildungsziel Judenmord? Weltanschauliche Erziehung von SS, Polizei und Waffen SS in Rahmen der Endlösung* (Frankfurt, 2003); Evans, *The Third Reich at War*, 177; see also Claudia Koonz, *The Nazi Conscience* (Cambridge, MA, 2003), 221–46.
94. IfZ, Dc 29.11a, Der Reichsführer SS (ed.), *Rassenpolitik* (Berlin, 1940).
95. IfZ, Dc 029.18, SS Hauptamt, *Lehrplan für die weltanschauliche Erziehung in der SS und Polizei* (Berlin).
96. IfZ, Dc 029.047, SS Hauptamt (ed.), *Lehrplan fur Zwölfwochige Schulung* (Berlin, 1941).

97. IfZ, Dc 29.26, Der Reichsführer SS (ed.), *SS Handblätter für die Weltanschauliche Erziehung der Truppe* (Berlin, 1944).
98. IfZ, Dc 29.11a, Der Reichsführer SS (ed.), *Rassenpolitik*.
99. IfZ, Da 33.60, Oberkommando der Wehrmacht (ed.), *Richtlinien für den Unterricht über politische Tagesfragen*, 23 May 1936, 248–49.
100. IfZ, Dc 29.11a, Der Reichsführer SS (ed.), *Rassenpolitik*, 48–49; and Da 033.158-1938.1, Reichshauptamtsleiter Dr Gross, 'Die Leitgedanken der NS Rassenpolitik', in Oberkommando der Wehrmacht (ed.), *Nationalpolitischer Lehrgang der Wehrmacht vom 12–21 januar, 1938*, 39.
101. IfZ, Dc 29.26, 'Thema 18: Der Jude zerstört jede völkische Lebensordnung', in Der Reichsführer SS (ed.), *SS Handblätter für die Weltanschauliche Erziehung der Truppe*.
102. IfZ, Dc 29.26, *SS Handblätter für die Weltanschauliche Erziehung der Truppe*, 7.
103. Ibid.
104. 'Geheimer Erlass des ObdH über die Erziehung des Offizierkorps, 18.12.1938', quoted in Böhler, *Auftakt zum Vernichtungskrieg*, 29.
105. Jürgen Matthäus, 'Die "Judenfrage" als Schulungsthema von SS und Polizei', in Jürgen Matthäus et al., *Ausbildungsziel Judenmord?*, 85.
106. Omer Bartov, *Germany's War and the Holocaust: Disputed Histories* (London, 2003), 7–8; idem, *Hitler's Army*, 7–10; Wette, *The Wehrmacht*, especially chapter five, 'The Legend of the Wehrmacht's "Clean Hands"', 195–250; Ute Frevert, *A Nation in Barracks: Modern Germany, Military Conscription and Civil Society* (New York, 2004), 259–60. For works that propagated the notion of the 'clean Wehrmacht', see, for example, Erich von Manstein, *Lost Victories* (London, 1958); B.H. Liddell Hart, *The Other Side of the Hill: Germany's Generals: Their Rise and Fall, with Their Own Accounts of Military Events, 1939–1945* (London, 1948).
107. Bartov, *The Eastern Front*; idem, *Hitler's Army*; Hamburger Institut für Sozialforschung (ed.), *Ausstellungskatalog 'Verbrechen der Wehrmacht: Dimensionen des Vernichtungsrieges 1941–44'* (Hamburg, 2002).
108. Manfred Messerschmidt, *Die Wehrmacht im NS-Staat: Zeit der Indoktrination* (Hamburg, 1969), 360.
109. Ibid., 360–61.
110. See Bartov, *Hitler's Army*; idem, 'Operation Barbarossa and the Origins of the Final Solution'; Walter Manoschek (ed.), *"Es gibt nur eines für das Judentum: Vernichtung": Das Judenbild in deutschen Soldatenbriefen 1939–1944* (Hamburg, 1995); Stephen G. Fritz, *Frontsoldaten: The German Soldier in World War II* (Lexington, 1995); Wette, *The Wehrmacht*; Felix Römer, *Kameraden: Die Wehrmacht von innen* (Munich, 2012).
111. Römer, *Kameraden*; Sönke Neitzel and Harald Welzer, *Soldaten: On Fighting, Killing and Dying* (London, 2012).
112. See Manoschek, *"Es gibt nur eines für das Judentum: Vernichtung"*; Fritz, *Frontsoldaten*; Bartov, *Hitler's Army*; idem, 'Operation Barbarossa and the Origins of the Final Solution'; Wette, *The Wehrmacht*.
113. Klaus Latzel, 'Feldpostbriefe: Überlegungen zur Aussagekraft einer Quelle', in Hartmann et al., *Verbrechen der Wehrmacht*, 171.
114. Ibid., 171–78.
115. Hans Joachim Schröder, *Die gestohlenen Jahre: Erzählgeschichte und Geschichtserzählung im Interview: Der Zweite Weltkrieg aus der Sicht ehemaliger Mannschaftssoldaten* (Tübingen, 1992), 317.
116. Messerschmidt, *Die Wehrmacht im NS-Staat*, 313.
117. Ibid.

118. Ibid.
119. Baden Württemberg State Library, Feldpostsammlung der württembergischen Landesbibliothek (hereafter WLB), Corporal C, 1st Artillery Battery, 28 June 1941.
120. WLB, Corporal S, 46010, 5th Staff Office, 10 June 1941.
121. WLB, Corporal B, 296th Infantry Division, 8 June 1941.
122. WLB, Corporal B, 296th Infantry Division, 14 June 1941.
123. WLB, Private B, 23rd Infantry Division, 18 June 1941.
124. Ibid.
125. WLB, Private B, 9th Transport Column (Luftwaffe), 8 June 1941.
126. WLB, Lt G, 714th Infantry Division, 18 June 1941.
127. WLB, Colonel B, 9th Luftwaffe, 7 July 1941.
128. WLB, Captain G, 2nd Security Regiment, 8 July 1941.
129. WLB, Captain G, 17 July 1941.
130. Latzel, 'Feldpostbriefe', 172–73.
131. See Manoschek, *"Es gibt nur eines für das Judentum: Vernichtung"*; Fritz, *Frontsoldaten*.
132. WLB, Kurt U, 6th Mountain Division, 22 June 1941.
133. WLB, 2nd Lieutenant N, Fliegerhorst Lyon, 23 June 1941.
134. WLB, 2nd Lieutenant S, 3 July 1941.
135. WLB, Corporal B, 1 July 1941.
136. WLB, Corporal F, 32nd Battalion, 12th Panzer Division, 3 July 1941.
137. WLB, Corporal B, 13th Flak, 16 July 1941.
138. WLB, W.H., 3rd Lichtm. Bttr/Beob. Abt. 14, 15 July 1941.
139. WLB, Lieutenant H, 16 July 1941.
140. WLB, Lieutenant W, 123rd Infantry Division, 6 July 1941.
141. WLB, Major S, 652nd Pioneer Battalion, 26 June 1941.
142. WLB, Corporal M, 167th Infantry Division, 2 July 1941.
143. WLB, Corporal N, Stabs-Kp/Mil. Befh., 31 July 1941.
144. WLB, Corporal F, 256th Infantry Division, 23 July 1941.
145. WLB, Captain G, 2nd Security Regiment.
146. WLB, Lieutenant H, 6th Infantry Division, 17 July 1941.
147. WLB, Corporal B, 198th Infantry Division, 10 June 1941.
148. WLB, Private F, 4.kp/Fla.M.G.Btl, 12 July 1941.
149. WLB, 2nd Lieutenant D, 42nd Battalion, 11 July 1941.
150. WLB, Colonel B, 9th Luftwaffe.
151. WLB, Heinz B, 125th Infantry Division.
152. WLB, Corporal B, 291st Infantry Division, 10 July 1941.
153. Ibid.
154. WLB, Colonel B, 9th Luftwaffe.
155. WLB, Major Hans S, Pioneer Battalion 652, 11 July 1941.
156. WLB, Hans J, German Military Mission in Romania, 26 July 1941.
157. WLB, Corporal B, 269th Infantry Division, 2 July 1941.
158. WLB, Corporal B, 125th Infantry Division.
159. WLB, Heinz H, 6th Infantry Division, 5 July 1941.
160. WLB, 2nd Lieutenant B, 125th Infantry Division.
161. WLB, Heinz H, 6th Infantry Division, 24 June 1941.
162. WLB, Corporal B, 46th Infantry Division, 18 July 1941.
163. WLB, Lieutenant G, 714th Infantry Division.
164. WLB, Corporal H, 46th Battalion Staff, 2 June 1941.
165. WLB, Private V, 32nd Infantry Division, 2 July 1941.

166. WLB, Captain G, 2nd Security Regiment, 15 July 1941.
167. WLB, Corporal H, 4 July 1941.
168. WLB, Lieutenant B, 125th Artillery Regiment, 10 July 1941.
169. WLB, Captain G, 2nd Security Regiment, 17 July 1941.
170. WLB, Engineer J, German Military Mission, Romania, 26 July 1941.
171. WLB, Engineer J, 18 July 1941.
172. WLB, Christoph B, Luftwaffe, 7 July 1941.
173. WLB, Lt G, 714th Infantry Division, 17 July 1941.
174. Römer, *Kameraden*; Neitzel and Welzer, *Soldaten*.
175. Neitzel and Welzer, *Soldaten*, 111; Römer, *Kameraden*, 63.
176. Römer, *Kameraden*, 63–66.
177. Ibid., 64.
178. Ibid., 75.
179. Ibid., 147.
180. Ibid., 81, 110.
181. Bartov, *Hitler's Army*, 106–78.
182. Römer, *Kameraden*, 72.
183. Ibid., 104–10.
184. Ibid., 109.
185. Captain J, quoted in Römer, *Kameraden*, 105.
186. Römer, *Kameraden*, 107–8.
187. Ibid., 108.
188. Neitzel and Welzer, *Soldaten*, 77.
189. Ibid., 120.
190. Ibid., 139.
191. Ibid.
192. Ibid., 237.
193. Ibid., 342.
194. Römer, *Kameraden*, 417–18.
195. Ibid., 64–66.
196. Neitzel and Welzer, *Soldaten*, 319.
197. See Bartov, 'Soldiers, Nazis and War in the Third Reich', 51; Fritz, *Frontsoldaten*, 84–85; Wette, *The Wehrmacht*, 172–82.

Conclusion

Taking a closer look at the ideological education programme that existed within the armed forces can enhance our understanding of the crimes of the Wehrmacht, along with its Nazification prior to and during the war. Intensive ideological training, along with the authoritarian character of the military, contributed to influencing the attitudes and actions of many impressionable young men. The military encouraged its men to regard themselves as political actors who were to fight for a specific Nazi political system and its associated ideology. The idea of race in particular pervaded almost every area of the Wehrmacht's educational programme: conceptions of potential conflicts and enemies, specifically in the East, were characterised in terms of race, and depictions of a soldier's everyday life were tainted by Nazi ideas of racial hygiene and the consequent dangers of any degenerate racial influences. It inculcated the notion that soldiers were, particularly in the East, to take part in an 'unlimited' conflict, defined by and fought along the lines of race and ideology. The line between civilian and military targets was blurred, or done away with completely, with no considerations of placing certain types of 'racially alien' enemy civilian populations above the fray.

This study has also revealed a long-term process of attempting to normalise this kind of conduct. Beginning in the earliest months of the Nazi regime, it progressed until it reached a high point in 1943, when military instruction manuals unambiguously endorsed the genocide of Jews. In fact, the tone and language expressed within the educational booklets and newsletters often reflected the developments of National Socialist policy. Emphasis was placed upon *Lebensraum*, ethnic struggle and 'racial hygiene' in the wake of the reintroduction of conscription and the introduction of the Nuremberg Laws in 1935. In the immediate lead-up to the outbreak of war, the focus shifted towards the 'life and death' struggle between the German *Volk* and its enemies. This process became more radical in tone as events progressed. It culminated in the orders and instructions of the Soviet campaign. In turn, the framework of a progressive evolution in rhetoric reveals much about the components of the broader debate over the development of Wehrmacht policy. Examining ideological education in the Wehrmacht indicates that the notorious orders of 1941 were not sudden radicalisations of military policy. Instead, they were steps in a series of progressions along a path that had begun almost a decade earlier. This approach helps to bring together the fields of the prewar politicisation of the military, the experience of those at the lower levels of this politicisation, and the military's involvement in atrocities during the war as parts of the same area of historical enquiry.

This study has also demonstrated, however, that numerous variations existed in the reception of Nazi political schooling. Responses varied along the lines of (but were not necessarily determined by) rank, political and religious beliefs and awareness, social background, and the amount of time that people had spent in the military or in Nazi organisations. The experience of military service took place within the wider social context of Nazi Germany, with a broad cross-section of society represented in the Wehrmacht. The Nazified press and education system impinged upon the lives of its recruits, as did the political atmosphere in the officer corps prior to the Nazi era. Many recruits would have spent time in the Hitler Youth and Reich Labour Service, and this study has provided a close analysis of the kind of political schooling that took place in those organisations.

These varying experiences and attitudes towards Nazi ideology within the Wehrmacht indicate, therefore, that one cannot make sweeping statements about the effect that this training programme had upon members of the armed forces. However, using examples of personal and official correspondence, this study has gone some way towards explaining how and why the training programme, and the ideology it espoused, had varying degrees of influence upon many members of the armed forces. This adds further weight to Kershaw's contention that Nazi propaganda found more success in building upon established beliefs and prejudices than when it attempted to reverse them. This has been most clearly demonstrated by the successes of ideological education in, for example, reinforcing numerous racial stereotypes, while failing to have a profound impact on reversing the deeply held Christian beliefs of many soldiers and officers. The importance of religion is further emphasised by the somewhat paradoxical existence and role of the military chaplaincy throughout the period of the Third Reich.

In this sense, this study has further advanced the debate over the importance of ideology. It has shown the significance of different aspects of Nazi ideology in affecting the way in which soldiers viewed the war and their enemies. This also fits in with the wider trend of certain aspects of Nazism having a greater impact on the attitudes of certain types of men than others. The participation of many soldiers in atrocities is further suggestive of the influence that ideological education had upon members of the armed forces. It indicates that many had taken on the notion of viewing themselves as soldiers who would pursue certain types of enemies based upon racial and ideological lines, without a clear distinction between military and civilian targets. Omer Bartov's description of the effect of propaganda during the Soviet campaign is fitting:

> ...it did not make them all into committed Nazis; but it provided them with an outlook which profoundly influenced their manner of both physically and mentally coping with and reacting to the realities of the war they were soon to find themselves fighting, whether or not they happened to be enamoured of the regime. In other words, it drastically narrowed their perceived alternatives for action on the battlefield. It equipped them with ... a social Darwinian division of humanity into those who must survive and those who must be exterminated, and a vocabulary that celebrated the abolishment of all previous norms of behaviour, values, morals and beliefs.

Documenting the military's programme of ideological education and arguing that it was an important factor in atrocities adds further complexity to the debate over the crimes of the Wehrmacht. This study has supported the notion of ideology being an important motivator of troops who were involved in war crimes, and it has shown that these crimes were in line with the manner in which the military was training its men from the mid 1930s. This programme definitely should not, however, be viewed in isolation as the primary cause of such criminal behaviour. It was instead one factor among many others that helped shape such behaviour. These other factors included, but were not limited to: the presence of ideologically driven orders from above; the legacy of previous campaigns of the German army that fostered a strong aversion to irregular warfare and a particularly ruthless attitude towards responding to it; the anti-Slavic, antisemitic and anti-communist prejudices that had existed within the German military well before the Nazis came to power; and, finally, the fact that many German soldiers came of age in the Third Reich and were members of organisations like the Hitler Youth and the Reich Labour Service.

I have also emphasised that it is important to pay attention to the somewhat exceptional way in which orders were disseminated and carried out in the German military. The command principle of *Auftragstaktik* was a long-standing feature of the way in which German soldiers and officers operated, and understanding this is crucial in gaining an insight into how orders were translated into action, particularly when considering that the way troops were trained was the crucial factor in allowing this system of command to work, since training was what shaped soldiers' interpretations of the 'tasks' they received from their commanders. This should be considered as another factor that scholars should take into account, particularly when weighing up questions over the relative importance of ideology, orders and training. As Jürgen Förster has pointed out, the complex nature of the crimes of the

Wehrmacht is underlined by the circumstances under which many of these instances occurred. Those on the ground often had to interpret orders that did not give details as to how they should be carried out, or what the precise goals of the orders were. Lower-ranking officers and soldiers thus had the task of interpreting them and carrying them out in a way that they regarded as fulfilling the will of the leadership. Years of systematic ideological education, even if it did not convince troops to adopt the National Socialist world-view, gave an indication of the unspoken expectations that went with their orders. In this sense, the most revealing statement made by the high command in relation to the political schooling of the Wehrmacht, not to mention the way in which it would act when operating under the command principle of *Auftragstaktik*, was issued in 1938 in an attempt to clarify the purpose of educating troops and how the high command hoped it would translate when the military was engaged in battle: 'It is a given that the officer, in every situation, acts according to the ideology of the Third Reich, and furthermore, to do so when such ideologies are not explicitly expressed in official regulations and decrees or in orders while on active duty'. Members of the Wehrmacht often did not receive, nor did they need, explicit, specific instructions to target civilians along ideological and racial lines. Their role as troops who would go beyond the normal function of the military had long been established and reinforced through their training.

Notes

1. Wolfram Wette, *The Wehrmacht: History, Myth, Reality* (Cambridge, MA, 2006), 89.
2. See Omer Bartov, *Germany's War and the Holocaust: Disputed Histories* (London, 2003), 65–72; Jürgen Förster, 'Die politisierung der Reichswehr/Wehrmacht', in *Das deutsche Reich und der Zweite Weltkrieg Band 9/1: Der deutsche Kriegsgesellschaft 1939 bis 1945* (Munich, 2004), 484–505; Robert O'Neill, *The German Army and the Nazi Party, 1933–1939* (London, 1966); Klaus Jürgen Müller (ed.), *Armee und Drittes Reich 1933–1939: Darstellung und Dokumentation* (Paderborn, 1989).
3. Ian Kershaw, 'How Effective Was Nazi Propaganda?', in David Welch (ed.), *Nazi Propaganda: The Power and the Limitations* (London, 1983), 182–83; see also David Welch, *The Third Reich: Politics and Propaganda* (London, 1993), 59.
4. Sönke Neitzel and Harald Welzer, *Soldaten: On Fighting, Killing and Dying* (London, 2011).
5. Bartov, *Germany's War and the Holocaust*, 26–27.
6. Wette, *The Wehrmacht*; Bartov, *Germany's War and the Holocaust*.
7. See Jürgen Förster, *Die Wehrmacht im NS-Staat: Eine Strukturgeschichtliche Analyse* (Munich, 2007), 68; Ulrike Jureit, 'Motive – Mentalitäten – Handlungsräume: Theoretische Anmerkungen zu Handlungsoptionen von Soldaten', in Christian

Hartmann, Johannes Hürter and Ulrike Jureit (eds), *Verbrechen der Wehrmacht: Bilanz einer Debatte.* (Munich, 2005), 163–70.
8. 'Geheimer Erlass des ObdH über die Erziehung des Offizierkorps, 18.12.1938', quoted in Jochen Böhler, *Auftakt zum Vernichtungskrieg: Die Wehrmacht in Polen 1939* (Frankfurt, 2006), 29.

BIBLIOGRAPHY

Archival Sources

Baden Württemberg State Library
Feldpostsammlung der württembergischen Landesbibliothek

Bundesarchiv/Militärarchiv (BA/MA) (Federal/Military Archive, Freiburg)
BA/MA RW 6/V. 159. Wehrmachtsamt/Abt. Inland: (nr. 600/35g.J IVa), *Erziehung in der Wehrmacht*. Berlin, 16 April 1935.
BA/MA RW 6/161. *Erster nationalpolitischer Lehrgang für Lehrer der Kriegsschulen, Akademien usw vom 17.1.37 bis 23.1.37 in Berlin.*
BA/MA 6/v.420. *Nationalpolitischer Lehrgang der Wehrmacht vom 12. bis 21. Januar 1938. Nur für den Dienstgebrauch in der Wehrmacht.* Berlin: Berliner Börsen-Zeitung Druckerei und Verlag GmbH, 1938.
BA/MA RW 6/V. 421, OKW/1619b. *Nationalpolitischer Lehrgang der Wehrmacht vom 29. November bis 2. Dezember. Nur für den Dienstgebrauch in der Wehrmacht.* Berlin: Kameradschaft Verlagsgesellschaft Gersbach & Co, 1938.
BA/MA RW 6/V. 166. *Sommer-Lehrgang für Offiziere in Bad Tölz:* 'Vortragsreihe über nationalsozialistische Weltanschauung und Zielsetzung vom 11.–17.6.1939 in Bad Tölz'.
BA/MA RH37/316. Abschrift – Auszug: Der OBH des Heeres. Berlin, den 20. Juni 1939 – von Brauchitsch. Betrifft: 'Zusammenarbeit des Heeres mit der SS Verfügungstruppe'.

Institut für Zeitgeschichte, München (IfZ) (Archives of the Institute for Contemporary History, Munich)
Da 033.158-1937a. 'Erlaß des Reichskriegministers und Oberbefehlshabers der Wehrmacht vom 30 Januar 1936', in Oberkommando der Wehrmacht (ed.), *Nationalpolitischer Lehrgang der Wehrmacht vom 15 bis 23 Januar 1937* (Berlin: Druck-Börsen-Zeitung Drückerei und Verlag, 1936).
Da 33.17. Oberkommando der Wehrmacht (ed.). *Was uns bewegt 1943 – Heft 1-11: Fragen der Weltanschauung, Politik, Geschichte und Kultur.* Berlin: Wilhelm Limpert Druck und Verlagshaus, 1943.
Da 033.171. Oberkommando der Wehrmacht, in Verbindung mit dem Aufklärungsdienst der SA (eds.), *Der Sieg in Polen. Sonderausgabe für den Braunen Buchring* (Berlin: Zeitgeschichte Verlag Wilhelm Andermann, 1939).
Da 033.176a. Reichswehrministerium (ed.). *Reichswehr*. Berlin, 1932.
Da 33.59. Oberkommando der Wehrmacht (ed.). *Schulungshefte für den Unterricht über nationalsozialistische Weltanschauung und nationalpolitische Zielsetzung. Erster Jahrgang, Heft 5.* Hoberg, C.A., 'Der Jude in der deutschen Geschichte', 3–41.

Da 33.59. Oberkommando der Wehrmacht (ed.). 'Offizer und Politik, Einst und Jetzt', in *Schulungshefte für den Unterricht über nationalsozialistische Weltanschauung und Nationalpolitische Zielsetzung, Erster Jahrgang, 1939.*
Da 33.60. Oberkommando der Wehrmacht (ed.). *Richtlinien für den Unterricht über politische Tagesfragen,* 22 February 1935.
Da 33.60, Heft 6, 'Kinderreichtum – Volksreichtum' and 'Zehn Gebote für Gattenwahl', in *Richtlinien für den Unterricht über politische Tagesfragen,* 26 March 1936.
Da 33.60, *Richtlinien für den Unterricht über politische Tagesfragen,* 26 March 1936.
Da 33.60, *Richtlinien für den Unterricht über politische Tagesfragen. Nur für den Dienstgebrauch der Wehrmacht,* 17 May 1936.
Da 33.60. Oberkommando der Wehrmacht (ed.). *Richtlinien für den Unterricht über politische Tagesfragen,* 23 May 1936.
Da 33.60. 'Die Bolschewistische Weltgefahr', in Reichskriegsministerium (ed.), *Richtlinien für den Unterricht über politische Tagesfragen,* 15 October 1936.
Da 033.062.1. Oberkommando der Wehrmacht. *Der Deutsche Soldat und die Frau aus fremden Volkstum,* 1943.
Da 033.062-7. Oberkommando der Wehrmacht (ed.). *Richthefte des Oberkommando der Wehrmacht: Der Jude als Weltparasit.* Offenburg: Druckerie Franz Burda, 1943.
Da 033.158-1938.1. Reichshauptamtsleiter Dr Gross. 'Die Leitgedanken der NS Rassenpolitik', in Oberkommando der Wehrmacht (ed.), *Nationalpolitischer Lehrgang der Wehrmacht vom 12-21 Januar, 1938,* 21–39.
Da 033.158-197a, 'Dr Gütt, Praktische Maßnahmen der Gesundheits- und Rassenpflege', in *Nationalpolitischer Lehrgang der Wehrmacht vom 15 bis 23 Januar 1937. Nur für den Dienstgebrauch in der Wehrmacht* Berlin, 1937.
Da 033.177. Rosenberg, Alfred (ed.). *Das Gesicht des Bolschewismus. Aus der Schriftenreihe zur weltanschaulichen und politischen Schulung der Wehrmacht.* Berlin: Zentralverlag der N.S.D.A.P, 1943.
Da 034.086. Oberbefehlshaber West Abt. Nationalsozialistische Führung der Truppe. *Die nationalsozialistische Führung der Truppe.*
Da 052.009-1940/41. Erziehungs und ausbildungsamt in der RAD. *RAD Unterrichtsbriefe für Führer 1940-41, 2. Folge 1941.*
Da 052.034. *Richtlinien für den Staatspolitischen Unterricht im Reichsarbeitsdienst* (Arbeitsgauleitung Nr. 30 Bayern-Hochland). Leipzig: Oskar Leiner, 1937.
Da 52.05. Reichsarbeitsdienst Pflicht. *Der Reichsarbeitsführer auf dem Parteikongreß,* 26 June 1935.
Da 52.05. Oberfeldmeister Dr U. Krüger. *Aufgabe und Sinn des Arbeitsdienstes: Ein Aufruf an die deutsche Jugend.* Berlin: Verlag deutscher Arbeitsdienst, 1935.
Da 052.055-1935. *Der Lager-Kamerad: Kamaradschaftsblatt für den Arbeitsdienst und den Arbeitsdank e.V.*
Dc 029.047. SS Hauptamt (ed.). *Lehrplan fur Zwölfwochige Schulung.* Berlin: SS Hauptamt, 1941.
Dc 29.26. Der Reichsführer SS (ed.). *SS Handblätter für die Weltanschauliche Erziehung der Truppe.* Berlin: SS Hauptamt, 1944.
Dc 29.11a. Der Reichsführer SS (ed.). *Rassenpolitik.* Berlin: SS Hauptamt, 1940.
Dc 029.18. SS Hauptamt. *Lehrplan für die weltanschauliche Erziehung in der SS und Polizei.* Berlin: Elsnerdruck.
Diewerge, Wolfgang (ed.). *Deutsche Soldaten sehen die Sowjetunion.* Berlin: Wilhelm Limpert Verlag, 1941.

DB 44.55. Abteilung P der Reichsjugendführung. *Werden und Wesen der Hitler-Jugend.* Berlin: Lipropa Lichtbildpropaganda.
ED 325/5. Oberkommando der Wehrmacht (ed.). *Mitteilungen für das Offizierkorps,* no. 6, June 1942.
ED 325/5. Oberkommando der Wehrmacht (ed.). *Mitteilungen für die Truppe,* no. 165, December 1941.
ED 325/5. Oberkommando der Wehrmacht (ed.). *Mitteilungen für die Truppe,* no. 222, 20 September 1942.
MA 33, *Der Reichswehrminister,* Berlin, 24 May 1934.
MA 33, OKW 861, *Leutnant Karl Hahn, Grevesmühlen.*
MA 34, OKW, *Geheime Kommandosache,* 26 October 1934.
MA 34, OKW 853, *Geheime Kommandosache,* 26 October 1934.
MA 127/1, OKW. *Richtlinien für die Durchführung der Feldseelsorge.* Berlin, 24 May 1942.
MA 241, *Vereinbarung* über *die Eingliederung der Lehrer an Wehrmachtschulen in den NSLB* (Berlin, 12 May 1934).
MA 261. *Die Bölkerung von Lodz und Warschau,* 11 November 1939.
MA 261. *Gedanken zur Heeresseelsorge,* 23 September 1940.
MA 441/1. *Meldungen aus dem Reich. Bericht zur innenpolitische Lage.* Berlin, 30 October 1939.
MA 441/3. *Meldungen aus dem Reich,* 14 November 1940, 'Die Zusendung von religiösen Schriften an Wehrmachtsangehörige hält weiterhin an'.
MA 441/4. *Meldungen aus dem Reich,* Berlin, 5 May 1941, 'Illegale Zusendung von religiösen Schriften an Wehrmachtsangehörige'.
MA 441/7. *Meldungen aus dem Reich,* Berlin, 4 March 1943.
MA 33 OKW 863. Der Reichskriegsministerium (Inland), *Besondere Vorkommnisse politischer Art.* Berlin, January 1938.

Published Primary Sources

The 'Commissar Decree', 6 June 1941, in Simone Gigliotti and Berel Lang (eds), *The Holocaust: A Reader* (Carlton, VIC: Blackwell Publishing, 2005), 177–80.
Deutsch, Harold C., and Helmut Krausnick. *Helmuth Groscurth: Tagebucher eines Abwehroffiziers 1938–1940. Mit weiteren Dokumenten zur Militäropposition gegen Hitler.* Stuttgart: Deutsche Verlags-Anstalt, 1970.
'Geheimer Erlaß des Oberbefehlshabers des Heeres, Generaloberst von Brauchitsch, über Erziehung des Offizierkorps, vom 18. Dezember 1938', in Klaus-Jürgen Müller, *Armee und Drittes Reich 1933–1939* (Paderborn: Ferdinand Schoningh, 1989).
The Hossbach Memorandum, Berlin, 10 November 1937, available at http://avalon.law.yale.edu/imt/hossbach.asp.
'Hitler's Reichstag Speech, 30 January 1939', in Simone Gigliotti and Berel Lang (eds), *The Holocaust: A Reader* (Carlton, VIC: Blackwell Publishing, 2005), 239–42.
Manoschek, Walter (ed.). *'Es gibt nur eines für das Judentum: Vernichtung': Das Judenbild in deutschen Soldatenbriefen 1939–1944.* Hamburg: Hamburger Institut für Sozialforschung, 1995.
Seraphim, Hans Günther (ed.). *Das politische Tagebuch Alfred Rosenbergs aus den Jahren 1934/35 und 1939/40.* Göttingen: Musterschmidt Verlag, 1956.
'Das Verhalten der Truppe im Ostraum', 12 October 1941. *Dokumente zum Nationalsozialismus,* available at www.ns-archiv.de/untermenschen/reichenau-befehl.php.

Secondary Literature

Barth, Boris. *Dolchstoßlegenden und politische Desintegration: Das Trauma der deutschen Niederlage im Ersten Weltkrieg 1914–1933*. Düsseldorf: Droste, 2003.
Bartov, Omer. *The Eastern Front, 1941–45: German Troops and the Barbarisation of Warfare*. Basingstoke: Macmillan, 1985.
Bartov, Omer. *Germany's War and the Holocaust: Disputed Histories*. London: Cornell University Press, 2003.
Bartov, Omer. *Hitler's Army: Soldiers, Nazis and War in the Third Reich*. Oxford: Oxford University Press, 1991.
Bartov, Omer. 'Operation Barbarossa and the Origins of the Final Solution', in David Cesarani (ed.), *The Final Solution: Origins and Implementation* (London: Routledge Press, 1996), 119–36.
Bartov, Omer. 'Savage War: German Warfare and Moral Choices in World War II', in Berel Lang and Simone Gigliotti (eds), *The Holocaust: A Reader* (Carlton, VIC: Blackwell Publishing, 2005), 220–31.
Bartov, Omer. 'Soldiers, Nazis and War in the Third Reich'. *The Journal of Modern History* 63(1) (March 1991), 44–60.
Bartov, Omer, and Phyllis Mack (eds). *In God's Name: Genocide and Religion in the Twentieth Century*. Oxford: Berghahn Books, 2001.
Beevor, Antony. *Stalingrad*. London, Penguin, 1999.
Ben-Ari, Eyal. *Mastering Soldiers: Conflicts, Emotions and the Enemy in an Israeli Military Unit*. London: Berghahn Books, 1998.
Berding, Helmut. 'Der Aufstieg des Antisemitismus im Ersten Weltkrieg', in Wolfgang Benz and Werner Bergmann (eds), *Vorurteil und Völkermord: Entwicklung des Antisemitismus* (Freiburg: Herder, 1997), 286–303.
Bergen, Doris L. 'Between God and Hitler: German Military Chaplains and the Crimes of the Third Reich', in Omer Bartov and Phyllis Mack (eds), *In God's Name: Genocide and Religion in the Twentieth Century* (Oxford: Berghahn Books, 2001), 123–38.
Bergen, Doris L. 'German Military Chaplains in World War II and the Dilemmas of Legitimacy'. *German History* 70(2), June 2001, 232–47.
Bergen, Doris L. '"Germany Is Our Mission: Christ Is Our Strength!" The Wehrmacht Chaplaincy and the "German Christian" Movement'. *Church History* 66(3) (September 1997), 522–36.
Bergen, Doris L. *Twisted Cross: The German Christian Movement in the Third Reich*. Chapel Hill: University of North Carolina Press, 1996.
Berger, Michael. *Eisernes Kreuz und Davidstern: die Geschichte jüdischer Soldaten in deutschen Armeen*. Berlin: Trafo, 2006.
Berghahn, Volker. *Imperial Germany 1871–1914: Economy, Science, Culture and Politics*. Providence: Berghahn Books 1994.
Benz, Wolfgang and Bergmann, Werner (eds). *Vorurteil und Völkermord*. Freiburg: Herder, 1997.
Bessel, Richard. *Nazism and War*. London: Phoenix, 2004.
Beyrau, Dietrich. *Schlachtfeld der Diktatoren: Osteuropa im Schatten von Hitler und Stalin*. Göttingen: Vandenhoeck und Ruprecht, 2000.
Black, Jeremy. *The Age of Total War, 1860–1945*. London: Praeger Security International, 2006.

Blunden, Andy and Grant, Matthew (eds), *Karl Marx, On the Jewish Question*. London, 2010. Available at: https://www.marxists.org/archive/marx/works/download/pdf/On%20The%20Jewish%20Question.pdf
Bonney, Richard. *Confronting the Nazi War on Christianity*. Bern: Peter Lang, 2009.
Böhler, Jochen. *Auftakt zum Vernichtungskrieg: Die Wehrmacht in Polen 1939*. Frankfurt: Fischer Taschenbuch Verlag, 2006.
Böhler, Jochen. *"Grösste Härte ...": Verbrechen der Wehrmacht in Polen, September, Oktober 1939*. Warsaw: Deutsches Historisches Institut Warschau, 2005.
Böhler, Jochen. *Der Überfall: Deutschlands Krieg gegen Polen*. Frankfurt: Eichborn, 2009.
Bourke, Joanne. *An Intimate History of Killing: Face to Face Killing in Twentieth Century Warfare*. London: Granta, 1999.
Boog, Horst, Jürgen Förster, Joachim Hoffman, Ernst Klink, Rolf-Dieter Müller, and Gerd R. Ueberschär. *Der Angriff auf die Sowjetunion*. Frankfurt: Geschichte Fischer, 1991.
Browning, Christopher. 'From "Ethnic Cleansing" to Genocide to the "Final Solution": The Evolution of Jewish Policy, 1939–1941', in Berel Lang and Simone Gigliotti (eds), *The Holocaust: A Reader* (Carlton, VIC: Blackwell Publishing, 2005), 143–66.
Browning, Christopher R. *Ordinary Men: Police Battalion 101 and the Final Solution in Poland*. London: Penguin, 2001.
Burleigh, Michael, and Wolfgang Wippermann. *The Racial State: Germany 1933–1945*. Cambridge: Cambridge University Press, 1991.
Carsten, F.L. *The Reichswehr and Politics, 1918–1933*. Oxford: Oxford University Press, 1966.
Caspar, Gustav-Adolf, and Herbert Schottelius. 'Die Organisation des Heeres 1933–1939', in Hans Meier-Welcker (ed.), *Handbuch zur deutschen Militärgeschichte 1648–1939* (Frankfurt: Bernard und Graefe, 1978), 581–621.
Cesarani, David. *The Final Solution: Origins and Implementation*. London: Routledge, 1996.
Chickering, Roger. *Imperial Germany and the Great War, 1914–1918*. Cambridge: Cambridge University Press, 2004.
Citino, Robert M. *The Path to Blitzkrieg: Doctrine and Training in the German Army, 1920–1939*. London: Lynne Rienner Publishers, 1999.
Condell, Bruce, and David T. Zabecki (eds.). *On the German Art of War: Truppenführung*. London: Lynne Rienner Publishers, 2001.
Craig, Gordon A. *The Politics of the Prussian Army 1640–1945*. Oxford: Oxford University Press, 1955.
Davis, Colonel R.R. 'Helmuth von Moltke and the German-Prussian Development of a Decentralised Style of Command: Metz and Sedan 1870'. *Defence Studies* 5(1) (2005), 83–95.
Dedering, Tilman. '"A Certain Rigorous Treatment of All Parts of the Nation." The Annihilation of the Herero in German South West Africa, 1904', in Mark Levene and Penny Roberts (eds), *The Massacre in History* (New York: Berghahn Books, 1999), 204–222.
Deist, Wilhelm. 'The *Gleichschaltung* of the Armed Forces', in Militärgeschichtliches Forschungsamt (ed.), *The Build-Up of German Aggression* (Oxford: Oxford University Press, 1990).
Demeter, Karl. *The German Officer Corps in Society and State 1650–1945*. London: Weidenfeld and Nicolson, 1965.
Deutsch, Harold C. *Hitler and His Generals: The Hidden Crisis, January–June 1938* Minneapolis: University of Minnesota Press, 1974.

De Mildt, Dick. *In the Name of the People: Perpetrators of Genocide in the Reflection of Their Post-War Prosecution in West Germany: The 'Euthanasia' and 'Aktion Reinhard' Trial Cases.* London: Martinus Nijhoff Publishers, 1996.

Dimjian, Gregory G. 'Warfare, Genocide, and Ethnic Conflict: A Darwinian Approach'. *Baylor University Medical Center Proceedings* 23(3) (July 2010), 292–300.

Dower, John W. *War without Mercy: Race and Power in the Pacific War.* New York: Pantheon Books, 1993.

Evans, Richard J. *The Coming of the Third Reich.* London: Penguin, 2004.

Evans, Richard J. *The Third Reich in Power.* London: Penguin, 2006.

Evans, Richard J. *The Third Reich at War.* London: Penguin, 2008.

Feuchtwanger, Edgar. *Imperial Germany 1850–1918.* London: Routledge, 2001.

Flessau, Kurt-Ingo. *Schule der Diktatur: Lehrpläne und Schulbücher des Nationalsozialismus.* Munich: Ehrenwirth, 1977.

Förster, Jürgen. '"Aber für die Juden wird auch noch die Stunde schlagen, und dann wehe ihnen!".. Reichswehr und Antisemitismus', in Jürgen Matthäus and Klaus-Michael Mallman (eds), *Deutsche, Juden, Völkermord. Der Holocaust als Geschichte und Gegenwart* (Darmstadt: WBG, 2006), 21–37.

Förster, Jürgen. 'Complicity of Entanglement? Wehrmacht, War and Holocaust', in Michael Berenbaum and Abraham Peck (eds), *The Holocaust and History: The Known, the Unknown, the Disputed and the Reexamined* (Bloomington: Indiana University Press, 1998), 266–283.

Förster, Jürgen. 'Geistige Kriegführung in der Phase der ersten Siege', in Militärgeschichtliches Forschungsamt (ed.), *Das deutsche Reich und der Zweite Weltkrieg Band 9/1: Der deutsche Kriegsgesellschaft 1939 bis 1945* (Munich: Deutsche Verlags Anstalt, 2004), 506–19.

Förster, Jürgen. 'Operation Barbarossa as a War of Conquest and Annihilation', in Berel Lang and Simone Gigliotti (eds), *The Holocaust: A Reader* (Carlton, VIC: Blackwell Publishing, 2005), 184–97.

Förster, Jürgen. 'Die Politisierung der Reichswehr/Wehrmacht', in Militärgeschichtliches Forschungsamt (ed.), *Das deutsche Reich und der Zweite Weltkrieg Band 9/1: Der deutsche Kriegsgesellschaft 1939 bis 1945* (Munich: Deutsche Verlags Anstalt, 2004), 484–505.

Förster, Jürgen. 'The Relation between Operation Barbarossa as an Ideological War of Extermination and the Final Solution', in David Cesarani (ed.), *The Final Solution: Origins and Implementation* (London: Routledge, 1996), 85–102.

Förster, Jürgen. 'Das Verhaltnis von Wehrmacht und Nationalsozialismus im Entscheidungsjahr 1933'. *German Studies Review* 18(3) (October 1995), 471–80.

Förster, Jürgen. *Die Wehrmacht im NS-Staat: Eine Strukturgeschichtliche Analyse.* Munich: R. Oldenbourg Verlag, 2007.

Förster, Jürgen. 'Der Weltanschauungs- und Vernichtungskrieg im Osten', in Militärgeschichtliches Forschungsamt (ed.), *Das deutsche Reich und der Zweite Weltkrieg Band 9/1: Der deutsche Kriegsgesellschaft 1939 bis 1945* (Munich: Deutsche Verlags Anstalt, 2004), 519–38.

Förster, Jürgen. 'Weltanschauliche Erziehung in der Waffen SS', in *Ausbildungsziel Judenmord? Weltanschauliche Erziehung von SS, Polizei und Waffen SS im Rahmen der Endlösung.* (Frankfurt: Fischer, 2003), 87–113.

Frevert, Ute. *A Nation in Barracks: Modern Germany, Military Conscription and Civil Society.* New York: Berg, 2004.

Frevert, Ute. *Die Kasinierte Nation: Militärdienst und Zivilgesellschaft in Deutschland.* Munich: C.H. Beck, 2001.

Fritz, Stephen G. *Frontsoldaten: The German Soldier in World War II*. Lexington: University of Kentucky Press, 1995.
Fritz, Stephen G. *Ostkrieg: Hitler's War of Extermination in the East*. Lexington: University of Kentucky Press, 2011.
Fritz, Stephen G. '"We Are Trying … to Change the Face of the World" – Ideology and Motivation in the Wehrmacht on the Eastern Front: The View from Below'. *The Journal of Military History* 60(4) (1996), 683–710.
Goldhagen, Daniel *Hitler's Willing Executioners*. New York: Alfred A. Knopf, 1996.
Green, Thomas F. 'Indoctrination and Belief', in I.A. Snook. (ed.). *Concepts of Indoctrination: Philosophical Essays* (London: Routledge, 1972), 20–36.
Habeck, Mary R. 'The Modern and the Primitive: Barbarity and Warfare on the Eastern Front', in George Kassimeris (ed.), *The Barbarisation of Warfare* London: Hurst Publishers, 2006, 83–100
Hamburg Institute for Social Research (ed.). *Crimes of the Wehrmacht: Dimensions of a War of Annihilation 1941–1944*. Hamburg: Hamburger Edition, 2002.
Hamburger Institut für Sozialforschung (ed.), *Ausstellungskatalog 'Verbrechen der Wehrmacht: Dimensionen des Vernichtungsrieges 1941–44'* Hamburg: Hamburger Edition, 2002.
Hartmann, Christian, Johannes Hürter, and Ulrike Jureit. *Verbrechen der Wehrmacht: Bilanz einer Debatte*. Munich: Verlag C.H. Beck, 2005.
Hartmann, Christian. *Wehrmacht im Ostkrieg: Front und militärisches Hinterland 1941–1942*. Munich: Oldenbourg, 2009.
Heer, Hannes, and Klaus Neumann (eds). *War of Extermination: The German Military in World War II 1941–1944*. Oxford: Berghahn Books, 2000.
Herf, Jeffrey. *The Jewish Enemy: Nazi Propaganda during World War II and the Holocaust*. London: Harvard University Press, 2006.
Heschel, Susannah. 'When Jesus Was an Aryan: The Protestant Church and Antisemitic Propaganda', in Omer Bartov and Phyllis Mack (eds), *In God's Name: Genocide and Religion in the Twentieth Century* (Oxford: Berghahn Books, 2001), 79–105.
Heyck, Hartmut. 'Labour Services in the Weimar Republic and Their Ideological Godparents'. *The Journal of Contemporary History* 38(2) (2003), 221–36.
Horne, John, and Alan Kramer. *German Atrocities, 1914: A History of Denial*. London: Yale University Press, 2001.
Hughes, Daniel J. 'Schlichting, Schlieffen, and the Prussian Theory of War in 1914'. *The Journal of Military History* 59(2) (April 1995), 257–277.
Hull, Isabel. *Absolute Destruction: Military Culture and the Practices of War in Imperial Germany* Ithaca, NY: Cornell University Press, 2006.
Isenberg, Noah. *Between Redemption and Doom: The Strains of German-Jewish Modernism*. Lincoln: University of Nebraska Press, 1999.
Janssen, Karl-Heinz, and Fritz Tobias. *Der Sturz der Generäle: Hitler und die Blomberg-Fritsch-Krise 1938*. Munich: Beck, 1994.
Jochmann, Werner. 'Struktur und Funktion des deutschen Antisemitismus 1878–1914' in Wolfgang Benz and Werner Bergmann (eds), *Vorurteil und Völkermord*. (Freiburg: Herder, 1997), 177–218.
Kater, Michael H. *Hitler Youth*. Cambridge, MA: Harvard University Press, 2004.
Jureit, Ulrike. 'Motive – Mentalitäten – Handlungsräume: Theoretische Anmerkungen zu Handlungsoptionen von Soldaten', in Christian Hartmann, Johannes Hürter and Ulrike Jureit (eds), *Verbrechen der Wehrmacht: Bilanz einer Debatte* (Munich: Verlag C.H. Beck, 2005), 163–70.

Keim, Wolfgang. *Erziehung unter der Nazi-Diktatur*. Darmstadt: Wissenschaftliche Buchgesellschaft, 1995.
Kershaw, Ian. 'How Effective Was Nazi Propaganda?' in David Welch (ed.), *Nazi Propaganda: The Power and the Limitations* (London: Croon Helm, 1983), 180–205.
Kershaw, Ian. *Hitler*. London: Penguin, 2010.
Kershaw, Ian. *Popular Opinion and Political Dissent in the Third Reich: Bavaria 1933–1945*. Oxford: Oxford University Press, 1983.
Kersting, Franz-Werner. 'Wehrmacht und Schule im Dritten Reich', in Rolf-Dieter Müller and Hans-Erich Volkmann (eds), *Die Wehrmacht: Mythos und Realität* (Munich: R. Oldenbourg, 1999), 436–455.
Kitchen, Martin. *The German Officer Corps, 1890–1914*. Oxford: Clarendon, 1968.
Klönne, Arno. *Jugend im Dritten Reich: Die Hitler-Jugend und ihre Gegner*. Düsseldorf: Diederichs, 1982.
Koch, H.W. *Hitler Youth: Origins and Development, 1922–45*. London: Macdonald and Jane's, 1975.
Koonz, Claudia. *The Nazi Conscience*. Cambridge, MA: Harvard University Press, 2003.
Krausnick, Helmut, Hans Buchheim, Martin Broszat, and Hans-Adolf Jacobsen (eds). *Anatomy of the SS State*. London: Collins, 1968.
Lankford, Adam. *Human Killing Machines*. Plymouth: Rowman and Littlefield Publishers, 2009.
Latzel, Klaus. 'Feldpostbriefe: Überlegungen zur Aussagekraft einer Quelle' in Christian Hartmann, Johannes Hürter, and Ulrike Jureit. *Verbrechen der Wehrmacht: Bilanz einer Debatte* (Munich: Verlag C.H. Beck, 2005), 171–181.
Legro, Jeffrey W. 'Military Culture and Inadvertent Escalation in World War II'. *International Security* 18(4) (Spring 1994).
Levin, Judith, and Daniel Uziel. 'Ordinary Men, Extraordinary Photos', *Yad Vashem Studies* 26, http://www.yadvashem.org/odot_pdf/Microsoft%20Word%20-%202290.pdf.
Liddell Hart, B.H. *The Other Side of the Hill: Germany's Generals: Their Rise and Fall, with Their Own Accounts of Military Events, 1939–1945*. London: Cassell, 1948.
Lifton, Robert Jay. *Thought Reform and the Psychology of Totalism: A Study of 'Brainwashing' in China*. London: Victor Gollancz, 1961.
Liulevicius, Vejas Gabriel. *The German Myth of the East: 1800 to the Present*. Oxford: Oxford University Press, 2009.
Liulevicius, Vejas Gabriel. *War Land on the Eastern Front: Culture, National Identity and German Occupation in World War I*. Cambridge: Cambridge University Press, 2000.
Longerich, Peter. 'From Mass Murder to the "Final Solution": The Shooting of Jewish Civilians during the First Months of the Eastern Campaign within the Context of the Nazi Jewish Genocide', in Berel Lang and Simone Gigliotti (eds), *The Holocaust: A Reader* (Carlton, VIC: Blackwell Publishing, 2005), 198–219.
Longerich, Peter. *The Holocaust: The Nazi Persecution of the Jews*. Oxford: Oxford University Press, 2010.
Madley, Benjamin. 'From Africa to Auschwitz: How German South West Africa Incubated Ideas and Methods Adopted and Developed by the Nazis in Eastern Europe'. *European History Quarterly* 35(3) (2005), 429–464.
Manoschek, Walter (ed.). *Die Wehrmacht im Rassenkrieg: Der Vernichtungskrieg hinter der Front*. Vienna: Picus Verlag, 1996.
Manoschek, Walter. *'Serbien ist judenfrei': Militärische Besatzungspolitik und Judenvernichtung in Serbien 1941/42*. Munich: Oldebourg, 1993.

Manoschek, Walter. 'The Extermination of the Jews in Serbia', in Ulrich Hebert (ed.), *National Socialist Extermination Policies: Contemporary German Perspectives and Controversies* (New York: Berghahn Books, 2000), 163–85.
Manoschek, Walter and Hans Safrian. 'Österreicher in der Wehrmacht', in Ernst Hanisch, Wolfgang Neugebauer and Emmerich Talos (eds), *NS-Herrschaft in Österreich* Vienna: ÖBVHT, 2000, 123–58.
Mason, Tim. 'The Containment of the Working Class in Nazi Germany', in Jane Caplan (ed.), *Nazism, Fascism and the Working Class: Essays by Tim Mason*. Cambridge: Cambridge University Press, 1995, 231–273.
Matthäus, Jürgen. 'Die "Judenfrage" als Schulungsthema von SS und Polizei', in Jürgen Matthäus, Konrad Kwiet, Jürgen Förster, and Richard Breitman (eds), *Ausbildungsziel Judenmord? Weltanschauliche Erziehung von SS, Polizei und Waffen SS in Rahmen der Endlösung* (Frankfurt: Fischer Taschenbuch Verlag, 2003), 35–86.
Matthäus, Jürgen, Konrad Kwiet, Jürgen Förster, and Richard Breitman (eds). *Ausbildungsziel Judenmord? Weltanschauliche Erziehung von SS, Polizei und Waffen SS in Rahmen der Endlösung*. Frankfurt: Fischer Taschenbuch Verlag, 2003.
Messerschmidt, Manfred. *Die Wehrmacht im NS-Staat: Zeit der Indoktrination*. Hamburg: R. v. Decker, 1969.
Messerschmidt, Manfred. 'Die Wehrmacht als tragende Säule des NS-Staates (1933–1939)', in Walter Manoschek (ed.), *Die Wehrmacht im Rassenkrieg: Der Vernichtungskrieg hinter der Front*. Vienna: Picus Verlag, 1996, 39–54.
Messerschmidt, Manfred. 'The Wehrmacht and the Volksgemeinschaft'. *The Journal of Contemporary History* 18(4) (October 1983), 719–44.
Mühlhäuser, Regina. *Eroberung, Sexuelle Gewalttaten und intime Beziehungen deutscher Soldaten in der Sowjetunion 1941–1945*. Hamburg: Hamburger Edition, 2010.
Müller, Klaus Jürgen (ed.). *Armee und Drittes Reich 1933–1939: Darstellung und Dokumentation*. Paderborn: Ferdinand Schöning, 1989.
Müller, Klaus Jürgen. *The Army, Politics and Society in Germany, 1933–45: Studies in the Army's Relation to Nazism*. Manchester: Manchester University Press, 1987.
Müller, Klaus Jürgen. 'The Army and the Third Reich', in Neil Gregor (ed.), *Nazism* (Oxford: Oxford University Press, 2000), 168–170.
Müller, Rolf Dieter and Volkmann, Hans-Erich, (eds) *Die Wehrmacht: Mythos und Realität*. Munich: Oldenbourg Wissenschaftsverlag, 1999.
Muth, Jörg. *Command Culture: Officer Education in the US Army and the German Armed Forces, 1901–1940, and the Consequences for World War II*. Denton: University of North Texas Press, 2011.
Neitzel, Sönke, and Harald Welzer. *Soldaten: On Fighting, Killing and Dying*. London: Simon & Schuster, 2012.
O'Neill, Robert. *The German Army and the Nazi Party, 1933–1939*. London: Cassell, 1966.
Patel, Kiran Klaus. *Soldaten der Arbeit: Arbeitsdienste in Deutschland und den USA*. Göttingen: Vandenhoeck & Ruprecht, 2003.
Peukert, Detlev. 'Youth in the Third Reich', in Richard Bessel (ed.), *Life in the Third Reich* (Oxford: Oxford University Press, 1987), 25–40.
Pohl, Dieter. *Die Herrschaft der Wehrmacht: deutsche Militärbesatzung und einheimische Bevölkerung in der Sowjetunion 1941–1944*. Munich: Oldenbourg, 2008.
Pulzer, Peter. *Jews and the German State: The Political History of a Minority, 1848–1933*. Oxford: Blackwell, 1992.
Pulzer, Peter. 'Die Jüdische Beteilung an der Politik', in Werner E. Mosse and Arnold Paucker (eds), *Juden in Wilhelmischen Deutschland 1890–1914* (Tübingen: Mohr, 1976), 143–239.

Pulzer, Peter. *The Rise of Political Anti-Semitism in Germany and Austria*. Cambridge: Harvard University Press, 1968.
Rass, Christoph. *Menschenmaterial. deutsche Soldaten an der Ostfront: Innensichten einer Infanteriedivision, 1939–1945*. Paderborn: Schöningh, 2003.
Rempel, Gerhard. *Hitler's Children: The Hitler Youth and the SS*. Chapel Hill: University of North Carolina Press, 1989.
Rigg, Brian. *Hitler's Jewish Soldiers*. Lawrence: University Press of Kansas, 2002.
Römer, Felix. 'Das Geheimnis von P.O. Box 1142', *Der Spiegel*, online edition, 4 January 2010, http://einestages.spiegel.de/static/topicalbumbackground/5681/das_geheimnis_von_p_o_box_1142.html.
Römer, Felix. *Kameraden: Die Wehrmacht von innen*. Munich: Piper, 2012.
Rosenberg, Alfred. *The Myth of the Twentieth Century*. 1930.
Rossino, Alexander B. *Hitler Strikes Poland: Blitzkrieg, Ideology, and Atrocity*. Lawrence: University Press of Kansas, 2003.
Safrian, Hans. *Eichmann und seine Gehilfen*. Frankfurt: Fischer Taschenbuch Verlag, 1995.
Safrian, Hans. *Eichmann's Men*. Cambridge: Cambridge University Press, 2010.
Safrian, Hans. 'Komplizen des Genozids: Zum Anteil der Heeresgruppe Süd an der Verfolgung und Ermordung der Juden in der Ukraine 1941', in Walter Manoschek (ed.), *Die Wehrmacht im Rassenkrieg: Der Vernichtungskrieg Hinter der Front* (Vienna, Picus Verlag, 1996), 90–115.
Safrian, Hans, and Hans Witek. *Und Keiner war dabei: Dokumente des alltäglichen Antisemitismus in Wien 1938*. Vienna: Picus, 2008.
Salewski, Michael. 'Wehrmacht und Nationalsozialismus 1933–1939', in Militärgeschichtliches Forschungsamt (ed.), *Handbuch zur Deutschen Militärgeschichte 1648–1939* (Munich: Bernard & Graefe, 1978).
Samuels, Martin. *Command or Control? Command, Training and Tactics in the British and German Armies, 1888–1918*. London: Frank Cass, 1995.
Schäfer, Kirstin A. *Werner von Blomberg: Hitlers erster Feldmarschall*. Paderborn: F. Schöningh, 2006.
Scheck, Raffael. *Hitler's African Victims: The German Army Massacres of Black French Soldiers in 1940*. Cambridge: Cambridge University Press, 2008.
Scheck, Raffael. '"They Are Just Savages": German Massacres of Black Soldiers from the French Army in 1940'. *The Journal of Modern History* 77(2) (June 2005), 325–44.
Schröder, Hans Joachim. *Die gestohlenen Jahre: Erzählgeschichte und Geschichtserzählung im Interview: Der Zweite Weltkrieg aus der Sicht ehemaliger Mannschaftssoldaten*. Tübingen: Max Niemeyer, 1992.
Seifert, Manfred. *Kulturarbeit im Reichsarbeitsdienst: Theorie und Praxis nationalsozialistischer Kulturpflege im Context historisch-politischer, organisatorischer und ideologischer Einflüsse*. Münster: Waxmann, 1996.
Shalit, Ben. *The Psychology of Conflict and Combat*. New York: Praeger, 1988.
Shepherd, Ben. *Hitler's Soldiers: The German Army in the Third Reich*. New Haven: Yale University Press, 2016.
Shepherd, Ben. *Terror in the Balkans: German Armies and Partisan Warfare*. Cambridge, MA: Harvard University Press, 2012.
Shepherd, Ben. *War in the Wild East: The German Army and Partisans*. Cambridge, MA: Harvard University Press, 2004.
Showalter, Dennis E. '"No Officer Rather than a Bad Officer": Officer Selection and Education in the Prussian/German Army, 1715–1945', in Gregory C. Kennedy and

Keith Neilson (eds), *Military Education Past, Present and Future* (London: Praeger, 2002), 35–61.
Slim, Hugo. *Killing Civilians: Method, Madness and Morality in War*. London: Hurst and Company, 2007.
Snook, I.A. (ed.). *Concepts of Indoctrination: Philosophical Essays*. London: Routledge, 1972.
Staub, Erwin. *The Roots of Evil: The Origins of Genocide and Other Group Violence*. Cambridge: Cambridge University Press, 1989.
Stephenson, Jill. 'Inclusion: Building the National Community in Propaganda and Practice', in Jane Caplan (ed.), *Nazi Germany* (Oxford: Oxford University Press, 2008), 99–121.
Taylor, Kathleen. *Brainwashing: The Science of Thought Control*. Oxford: Oxford University Press.
Uziel, Daniel. *Propaganda Warriors: The Wehrmacht and the Consolidation of the German Home Front*. Oxford: Peter Lang, 2008.
Volkmann, Hans-Erich. 'Von Blomberg zu Keitel: Die Wehrmachtführung und die Demontage des Rechtsstaates', in Rolf-Dieter Müller and Hans-Erich Volkmann (eds), *Die Wehrmacht: Mythos und Realität* (Munich, 1999), 52–53.
Von Manstein, Erich. *Lost Victories*. London: Methuen, 1958.
Wehler, Hans-Ulrich. *The German Empire 1871–1918*. Oxford: Berg, 1985.
Welch, David. *The Third Reich: Politics and Propaganda*. London: Routledge, 1993.
Wette, Wolfram (ed.). *Der Krieg des kleinen Mannes: Eine Militärgeschichte von Unten*. Munich: Piper Verlag, 1995.
Wette, Wolfram. *The Wehrmacht: History, Myth, Reality*. Cambridge, MA: Harvard University Press, 2006.
Williams, E.S. (ed.). *The Soviet Military: Political Education, Training and Morale*. Basingstoke: Macmillan, 1987.
Winn, Denise. *The Manipulated Mind: Brainwashing, Conditioning and Indoctrination*. London: The Octagon Press, 1983.

INDEX

A
Allied troops, 33–34
Announcements for the Officer Corps (newsletter), 149, 150–51
Announcements for the Troops (newsletter), 149, 151–52
anti-Bolshevism. *See* Bolshevism
anti-Slavism
  in Nazi racial policy, 37, 53, 100–101, 110, 154–55
  pre-Nazi, 4, 24, 86–87, 181
  See also Lebensraum
antisemitism
  atrocities in Poland, 59–60, 80–85
  Austrian, 148
  and Christianity, 128, 131–33, 136
  dismissal of Jews from the military, 18–19, 54–55
  and the Eastern Front, 21–22, 143–49, 162–68, 170
  in the Hitler Youth and schools, 100–101, 103
  in military education, 37, 44, 53–55, 69–74, 151–58
  motivation, 2–3, 169
  pre-Nazi, 4, 19–21, 181
  and the Reich Labour Service, 105, 109–10
  and the Weimar Republic, 23–24
  See also Bolshevism; Final Solution; racial policy
atrocities. *See* war crimes
Auftragstaktik, 74–80, 84–85, 90, 109, 145–46, 181–82

Austrian troops, 147–48
Austro-Prussian War (1866), 75

B
Bad Tölz summer course, 64–69, 120
Bader, General Paul, 146
Balkans, 3, 145–49, 151. *See also* Eastern Front
Bartov, Omer
  army as reflection of society, 112
  The Eastern Front, 1941-45, 2
  indoctrination of Hitler Youth, 38, 98, 102
  Nazi ideology in the Wehrmacht, 158, 169
  Wehrmacht atrocities, 3–4, 142, 181
Beck, General Ludwig, 17, 19, 63
Bergen, Doris L., 129, 132, 133–34, 138
Bessel, Richard, 143
Blaskowitz, General Johannes, 89
Blomberg, General Werner von, 18–19, 41–45, 47, 61–62, 97–98, 119, 150
Böhler, Jochen, 3–4, 60, 80, 88, 89–90, 98
Böhme, General Franz, 145–46, 147–48
Bolshevism
  and antisemitism, 23–24, 55, 143–45, 151–55, 162–66
  'The Bolshevist World Threat', 1
  and Catholicism, 136–37
  in Nazi political education, 109–10, 111
  prewar anti-Bolshevism, 4, 22, 181
  See also Soviet Union
Bormann, Martin, 121, 126
Bourke, Joanna, 32, 34

198 • Index

Brauchitsch, General Walther von, 62, 73–74, 80–81, 135, 149–150
Brown, James A.C., 36
Browning, Christopher, 3
brutalisation of soldiers, 3, 56, 60, 89, 158

C

Catholicism, 86, 102, 111, 124–26, 136–37. *See also* chaplaincy; Christianity
censorship, 31, 124–25, 159–162
chaplaincy
    acceptance of Nazi ideology, 119, 132–33, 136–37
    German Christian movement, 132–36
    Guidelines for Carrying Out Pastoral Care in the Field, 126–27, 129
    interaction with civilians, 128–29
    religious literature, 124–25, 128, 134–35
    retention during Second World War, 121–24
    role, 120–21, 126–28, 137–38, 180
    soldiers' hostility to, 131–32
    'Uriah Law', 129–131
children and young people
    indoctrination, 5–6, 37–38, 45–47, 98, 169
    parental influence, 102, 111
    school syllabus, 103–4
    See also Hitler Youth; Reich Labour Service
Christianity
    as cause for dissent, 8, 23, 51, 67–68, 180
    as established part of the military, 117–120
    German Christian movement, 128, 132–36
    and the Hitler Youth, 102
    and the Reich Labour Service, 111
    religious literature, 124–25, 135
    See also chaplaincy
Civil Service Law (1933), 18, 54–55, 103
civilians
    dehumanisation, 34, 167–68
    Francs-Tireurs, 86, 87
    German South West Africa, 87
    as military enemy, 35, 148–49, 179, 180–82
    and military priests, 128–29
    Polish, 3, 56, 59–60, 80–85, 88–89
    Serbian, 145–48
    Soviet, 2, 142, 144–45, 163–66
class
    Catholic working class, 86, 102
    officers, 16, 17
    and the Reich Labour Service, 105, 111
    and the Social Democrats, 20, 23
    and support for Nazism, 102–3
    Volksgemeinschaft, 150, 171
    See also officer corps
Clausewitz, Carl von, 63
'Co-operation of the Army with the Armed SS' (OKW), 73
collaboration, SS and armed forces, 1–2, 45, 48, 54, 73–74, 89, 152–54
command structure
    antisemitism, 21, 72
    Auftragstaktik, 35, 74–80, 84–85, 109, 146, 181–82
    Blomberg-Fritsch crisis, 60–63
    and Christianity, 118–124, 126–131, 135
    Nazi ideology, 49–52, 70, 72–74, 89–90, 181
    war crimes, 142, 144–48, 151–52, 157
    See also officer corps; training, military
'Commissar Decree', 2, 143, 161
communism, 70, 103, 145–46, 148, 166
    See also Bolshevism; Soviet Union
conscription, 5, 16, 45–50, 97–98, 105, 112, 118–19
correspondence
    Bad Tölz summer course, 66–69
    Feldpostbriefe, 7, 158–168
    Polish campaign, 81–83
    Serbian campaign, 147, 149
criminality. *See* violence; war crimes

D

dehumanisation
    and antisemitism, 70–72, 81–83, 152–53, 155, 167–68
    bilateral nature, 30, 32–34
    educational materials, 44
    Herero people, 87
    Soviet citizens, 154–55, 163–64

young people, 100–101
  See also theories of indoctrination
Der Stürmer (newspaper), 100, 165
Die Wehrmacht im NS-Staat (Messerschmidt), 157
discipline. *See* obedience and peer pressure
dissent
  Blomberg, 61
  and Christianity, 8, 118–120, 135–36
  open expression by officers, 67–69
  POWs, 169
  in schools, 103–4
  suppression, 18, 31–32
Dollmann, General Friedrich, 119
Dower, John W., 33–34

E
Eastern Front
  antisemitism, 21–22, 164–65, 167–68
  atrocities, 55–56, 86–89
  criminal orders, 2–3, 142, 143, 145–47, 167–68, 171
  dehumanisation of the enemy, 33, 154–55, 163–64
  effect on military ideology, 22–23, 147–48
  and the Hitler Youth, 101
  letters, 158–168
  See also Poland; Serbia; Soviet Union
Educational Booklet for Lessons on the National Socialist World-View and Orientation Towards Political Goals, 63–64
educational materials, 7, 43–44, 53–55, 70–72, 107–10, 149–158, 179.
  See also Bad Tölz summer course; propaganda; training, military
Eglfing-Haar Insane Asylum, 65, 66–67
emigration, forced, 71–72
enemy
  dehumanisation, 33–34, 44, 80–83, 87, 154–55, 163–65
  'hedge shooters', 165–66
  vagueness of identity, 24, 35, 55
  See also civilians; racial policy
The Eternal Jew (film), 54
Evans, Richard J., 148

F
The Face of Bolshevism (ed. Rosenberg), 152, 153, 154
Feldpostbriefe. See correspondence
Final Solution, 71–72, 149, 151, 156–58, 170, 179–180. *See also* antisemitism
First World War, 21–24, 76, 86–87, 147–48. *See also* Weimar Republic
Förster, Jürgen, 73, 150, 181–82
France, 20–21, 61, 86, 88
Franco-Prussian War (1870–71), 75, 86
Francs-Tireurs, 86, 87
Frevert, Ute, 32
Fritsch, General Werner von, 17, 23, 61, 62, 119
Fritz, Stephen G., 81, 158
Fuller, General John F.C., 76

G
German Christian movement, 128, 132–36
German South West Africa, 87, 147
Goebbels, Joseph, 52
Goethe, Johann Wolfgang von, 70
Goldhagen, Daniel, 2, 3
Göring, Hermann, 45, 48, 61, 62
Green, Thomas F., 37
Gross, Dr Walter, 53, 67
group consensus, 31–34, 36, 100, 112. *See also* obedience and peer pressure
Guercke, Major, 51–52
Guidelines for Carrying Out Pastoral Care in the Field (OKW), 126–27, 129
Guidelines for Lessons in Everyday Political Questions (OKW), 45, 54
Guidelines for Lessons in Political Questions (OKW), 156
'Guidelines for the Conduct of Troops in Russia' (OKW), 2, 143–44

H
Hahn, Lieutenant Karl, 51, 52
Hammerstein, General Kurt von, 17
Härtl, Heinrich, 150
Hermann, Major Wolf, 68–69
Hess, Rudolf, 52
Heydrich, Reinhard, 62, 88, 89. *See also* SD (*Sicherheitsdienst*)
Hierl, Konstantin, 104, 105

Himmler, Heinrich, 52, 62, 73
Hinghofer, Walter, 147
Hitler, Adolf
  compulsory labour service, 104
  invasion of Poland, 80
  invasion of Serbia, 145–46
  invasion of the Soviet Union, 143
  military chaplaincy, 121–22
  Reichstag speech 30 January 1939, 72, 155, 156
  relationship with the military, 15, 16–19, 61–63
Hitler Youth
  aims, 98–99
  compulsory service, 47, 99
  deindividualisation and dehumanisation, 38, 100
  political schooling, 7, 8, 89–90, 100–104, 112, 180
  resistance to, 101–2
  and the Wehrmacht, 3–6, 45, 48, 65, 97–98, 181
Hitler Youth (Koch), 100
Hitler's Soldiers (Shepherd), 4
Hoberg, C.A., 70–72, 81–82, 152–53
Hoepner, General Erich, 144
Hof, Captain, 65–66, 67
Horne, John, 87–88
Hungary, 168

I
ideology
  and atrocities, 2–5, 59–60, 86–90, 143–49, 179–181
  and Christianity, 117–123, 126, 130–33, 136
  control over communication, 30–31, 34–35
  of the German military, 18–24, 52, 97–98, 112–13, 158–59, 162–172
  and orders, 8–9, 77–80, 83–85, 181–82
  SS and Wehrmacht, 1–2, 73–74, 143, 152–57
  training of Hitler Youth, 5–6, 37–38, 47, 99–104
  training of the Reich Labour Service, 5–6, 37–38, 47, 105–12

  See also SS (*Schutzstaffel*); training, military
individuality, nullification of, 32–33, 36, 38, 100, 106, 112
indoctrination. *See* theories of indoctrination
information
  ambiguity, 35, 77
  control of access, 30–31, 37, 50, 104
Institute for Research into and Elimination of Jewish Influence in German Church Life, 133
insurgency. *See* partisans
intermarriage. *See* racial policy
An Intimate History of Killing (Bourke), 32, 34

J
The Jew as World Parasite (OKW), 152, 155, 156
'The Jew in German History' (Hoberg), 70–82, 81–82, 152–53
Jew Süss (film), 54
Jewish Question. *See* antisemitism; Final Solution

K
Kater, Michael H., 100, 101
Keitel, General Wilhelm, 52, 62, 63, 122, 126–27
Kershaw, Ian, 24, 30, 55, 62, 102, 109, 180
Koch, H.W., 100
Koonz, Claudia, 6, 33, 37
Kramer, Alan, 87–88
Kraus, Captain Hermann, 64

L
language
  limitations, 162
  as tool of indoctrination, 34–35
Lankford, Adam, 31, 32
Latzel, Klaus, 158, 162
'Law for the Restoration of the Civil Service' (1933), 18, 54–55, 103
'Leadership of Troops' (training manual), 77
'Leaflet for the Conduct of German Soldiers in the Occupied Territory of Poland' (OKW), 80–81

League of German Girls, 51
Lebensraum, 37, 44, 65, 69, 80, 87, 179. *See also* Eastern Front
Lenin, Vladimir, 152–53
Leonhard, Hans, 131
letters. *See* correspondence
Lifton, Robert Jay, 30–31, 34
Ludendorff, General Erich, 23, 76

M
Manoschek, Walter, 3, 81, 145, 158
Manstein, General Erich von, 18–19, 144
Marx, Julius, 21
Marx, Karl, 70–71
Matthäus, Jürgen, 156–57
media, 31, 43, 100, 109, 125, 149–151. *See also* propaganda
Mein Kampf (Hitler), 43, 65, 107
Meldungen aus dem Reich (SS reports), 124, 125
Messerschmidt, Manfred, 20, 157
Moltke, Field Marshal Helmut von, 75–76
Müller, Bishop Ludwig, 134
Müller, Klaus Jürgen, 19, 60
Muth, Jörg, 42–43, 75
The Myth of the Twentieth Century (Rosenberg), 131

N
A Nation in Barracks (Frevert), 32
National Socialist Teachers' League, 44, 103
'The Nature and Tasks of Pastoral Care' (OKW), 137
Nazism
 and Christianity, 118–123, 131–38
 ignorance of, 46–47, 98
 opposition in the military, 17, 51–52, 169
 pervasiveness in the military, 48–50, 90, 158, 162–63, 168, 171–72
 style of command, 79–80, 146
 Volksgemeinschaft, 150
 and war, 15
 See also antisemitism; ideology; *Lebensraum*
Neitzel, Sönke, 6, 158, 168, 170, 171

newsletters, 125, 149–152, 179. *See also* propaganda
Nuremberg Racial Laws (1935), 54–55, 179

O
obedience and peer pressure
 and criminality, 83–85, 88–89
 and ideology, 8–9, 50, 156, 158
 in the Reich Labour Service, 106, 112
 studies of indoctrination, 32–33, 37–38
 in the Wehrmacht, 2–3, 18–19, 160
officer corps
 anti-Nazi views, 17, 51–52, 67
 Auftragstaktik, 74–80, 84–85, 90, 181–82
 Bad Tölz summer course, 64–69, 120
 Blomberg-Fritsch crisis, 60–63
 brutality, 146–49
 and Christianity, 117–120, 122–24, 127–28
 collaboration with the SS, 73–74, 89, 154
 and the Hitler Youth, 101
 ideology and security, 86–87
 political training, 42–44, 50–51, 52–54, 149–150
 right-wing ideology, 16, 18–21, 23
 Volksgemeinschaft, 150
 See also command structure
OKW (Supreme Command of the Wehrmacht). *See* command structure
'On the Jewish Question' (Marx), 70–71
Operation Barbarossa. *See* Soviet Union
orders. *See Auftragstaktik*
Oster, General Hans, 17

P
partisans, 82, 86–87, 146–49, 153, 164–66, 181
pastoral care. *See* chaplaincy
Patel, Kiran Klaus, 104–5, 107, 111
peer pressure. *See* obedience and peer pressure
Petzel, Walter, 89
Pfannmüller, Dr Hermann, 65, 66
Poland
 atrocities, 3–4, 59–60, 80–85, 87–89

Hitler Youth, 101
 and Nazi racial policy, 53, 55–56, 81–85, 89–90
 SS and armed forces collaboration, 73–74, 89
 See also Eastern Front
police, German, 83–84, 88–89
politics
 'apolitical' soldiers, 1–2, 6, 143–44, 157–58, 168–171
 Blomberg-Fritsch crisis, 60–63
 military as instrument of, 63–69, 179, 182
 military newsletters and booklets, 149–156
 prewar politicisation of military, 4, 5–6, 15–20, 25, 41–55
 schooling of the Hitler Youth, 99–104
 schooling of the Reich Labour Service, 105–12
 See also ideology; training, military
'The Principles of National Socialist Racial Policy' (OKW), 156
prisoners of war, 6, 30, 34, 161, 164, 168–170
propaganda
 Allied, 33–34
 in a controlled environment, 31, 112, 135–36, 162
 identity of enemy, 35
 military newsletters, 149–152
 and pre-existing beliefs, 4–5, 24, 102, 180
 during the Soviet campaign, 152–55, 181
 susceptibility of children, 37–38, 99–101
 use of theatre and film, 54
 See also theories of indoctrination
Propaganda Warriors (Uziel), 4
Protestant Field Songbook, 135
Protestantism, 117, 124, 133–35. *See also* chaplaincy; Christianity; German Christian movement
Prussia, 19–21, 63–64, 75–76, 117–18, 150. *See also* Franco-Prussian War (1870–71)

R
racial policy
 adoption by military, 18, 23–24, 70–74, 90, 168–170
 Bad Tölz summer course, 64–69
 Berlin conference 1937, 52–53
 and the Eastern Front, 22–23, 84–88, 145–49, 163–68
 German Christian movement, 133
 and German youth, 100–104
 racial hygiene, 37, 54–55, 66–69, 152, 179–180
 and the Reich Labour Service, 109–10
 role of Wehrmacht, 1–3, 9, 59–60, 182
 war of extermination, 79–82, 87, 88–89, 142–45, 155–58, 170
 See also anti-Slavism; antisemitism
Racial Policy (SS training manual), 155–56
Rarkowski, Bishop Franz, 136–37
recruitment. *See* conscription
Reich Labour Service
 'The Camp Comrade', 108
 deindividualisation and dehumanisation, 38, 106, 111–12
 origin and purposes, 104–5
 political schooling, 3–8, 45–47, 97–98, 108–11, 180
 'The Tasks and Purpose of the Labour Service', 105–8
 and the Wehrmacht, 47–49, 90, 181
Reichenau, General Walther von, 18, 144
Reichswehr, 15–18, 76–77, 118
Röhm, Ernst, 19
Romania, 151, 166, 168
Römer, Felix, 102, 158, 168–69, 170–71
Roques, General Karl Von, 154
Rosenberg, Alfred, 52, 131, 150
Rossino, Alexander B., 3–4, 89
Russia, 53, 144, 154, 163–64, 166. *See also* Soviet Union

S
SA (Sturmabteilung), 17, 19, 45, 48, 90
Safrian, Hans, 3, 153–54
Schirach, Baldur von, 103
Schlichting, General Sigismund von, 75–76
Schröder, General Ludwig von, 145
Schröder, Hans Joachim, 159

Schwarz, Franz Xaver, 64
Schwiegersöhne (play), 54
SD (*Sicherheitsdienst*), 124, 125, 154. *See also* Heydrich, Reinhard
Seeckt, Hans von, 16, 76–77, 118
Serbia, 4, 143, 145–49, 151, 166
Shepherd, Ben, 3, 4, 79, 86, 87, 146, 147
Showalter, Dennis E., 76
Slav countries. *See* anti-Slavism
Slim, Hugo, 32
Social Democrats, 20, 23, 102–3, 169
Soldaten (Neitzel and Welzer), 6, 170
'The Soviet People' (OKW), 154
Soviet Union
   Feldpostbriefe, 162–67
   invasion as crusade, 135, 137
   Nazi propaganda, 152–55, 181
   racial and ideological grounds for invasion, 1, 37, 55, 59–60, 109–10, 169
   war of extermination, 2–3, 142–45, 157, 170, 179
   See also Eastern Front; Russia
SS Handbook for the Ideological Education of Troops (SS training manual), 155–56
SS (*Schutzstaffel*)
   and army recruits, 48
   and Christianity, 123, 124–26
   collaboration with Wehrmacht, 1–2, 45, 73–74, 89, 144, 152–54, 171–72
   Einsatzgruppen, 59, 74
   ideological teaching, 37, 43, 54, 69, 155–58, 169
   in Poland, 80, 84, 88–89
   and the Reich Labour Service, 108, 109
   in Serbia, 143, 149
   Waffen SS, 101, 123
'Stab in the Back' myth, 22–23
Supreme Command. *See* command structure
Syllabus for Ideological Education in the SS and Police (SS training manual), 155–56
Syllabus for the Twelve Week Training Block (SS training manual), 155–56

T
teaching and indoctrination, 36–37, 43–47, 50–55, 89–90, 103–4, 169. *See also* Hitler Youth; Reich Labour Service; training, military
Terror in the Balkans (Shepherd), 79, 146
'The Tasks and Purpose of the Labour Service' (booklet), 105–8
theories of indoctrination
   children and young people, 37–38, 99–101
   controlled environment, 30–32, 111–12
   dehumanisation, 33–34, 44, 70, 154–55
   manipulation of language, 34–35, 162
   methods, 36–37
   nullification of individuality, 32–33, 100, 106, 112
Thought Reform and the Psychology of Totalism (Lifton), 30–31, 34
'Thoughts on Military Pastoral Care' (OKW), 122
training, military
   Auftragstaktik, 74–80, 85, 181–82
   educational materials, 7, 149–158, 179–180
   politicisation, 41–47, 50–55, 63–69, 169–172
   racism and antisemitism, 70–72, 81–83, 90, 152–57, 162, 166–68
   role of SS, 73–74, 157–58
   theories of indoctrination, 32–37
   violence against civilians, 60, 84, 88, 148–49
   See also Bad Tölz summer course; Hitler Youth; Reich Labour Service; theories of indoctrination
Treaty of Versailles, 15, 17, 23, 42, 80. *See also* Weimar Republic
Trotha, General Lothar von, 87

U
Ukraine, 53, 164, 165, 167
Uziel, Daniel, 4

V
Vietnam War, 34
violence

and dehumanisation, 33–34, 70–72, 153–55
Eastern and Western Fronts compared, 170
existence of boundaries, 78, 84–85, 88, 156–58
motivation, 2–3, 5, 9, 59–60, 86–87, 147–48
See also antisemitism; war crimes
Volksgemeinschaft, 150, 171

W

war crimes
  Allied and US, 34
  censorship, 159–162
  First World War, 86
  in France, 88
  in German South West Africa, 87
  ideological motivation, 89–90, 153–54, 157–58, 162–68, 170–72, 179–182
  obedience to orders, 9, 79
  in Poland, 3–4, 55–56, 59–60, 74, 80–85, 87–89
  presence of military chaplains, 120, 138
  in Romania, 166
  in Serbia, 145–49, 166
  in the Soviet Union, 2–3, 142–44, 164–66
War of Extermination: Crimes of the Wehrmacht' (exhibition), 2
Wedemeyer, Captain Albert C., 77
The Wehrmacht (Wette), 4
Weimar Republic, 15–20, 23–24, 42–43, 76–77, 104, 118
Welch, David, 102, 112
Welzer, Harald, 6, 158, 168, 170, 171
Wette, Wolfram, 4, 144, 154–55, 158
Wilhelm I, Emperor of Germany, 118
Winn, Denise, 31, 32
Wizotski, Major, 66